M000102269

CLEARED OUT

Long before the whitefellas, the Martu had their own law. The old people, the first lot of people, used to teach the young people about the law. They taught the boys and girls how to behave themselves.

They lived on the land and they were the owners of the land. There was no humbug about the land and everyone had the same voice. They used to look after one another. They had respect for everyone. All the people had country. On the Martu side they used to have one voice. One voice for a grandmother and a grandfather and a grandson. They used to have respect for other people's country. They used to run the land. The people learned the Martu law for everything.

When Captain Cook came to this land he had a look and said it was an empty land. He took the land through the white law. But the land was there with the Martu law. Captain Cook split the people up. But all the people were still here. Captain Cook made the country a different story.

Billy Gibbs (deceased)
Chairperson, Western Desert Puntukurnuparna,

in Sue Davenport (ed), *Yintakaja-lampajuya: these are our waterholes*, Western Desert Puntukurnuparna and Pilbara Aboriginal Language Centre, South Hedland, 1988.

CLEARED OUT

FIRST CONTACT IN THE WESTERN DESERT

Sue Davenport, Peter Johnson & Yuwali

First published in 2005 by
Aboriginal Studies Press
for the Australian Institute of Aboriginal
and Torres Strait Islander Studies
GPO Box 553, Canberra, ACT 2601

Reprinted 2007, 2008, 2010, 2011, 2014

© Sue Davenport, Peter Johnson and Yuwali 2005

All author royalties from this book go to the surviving Martu people from this story.

Apart from any fair dealing for the purpose of private study, research and criticism or review, as permitted under the *Copyright Act 1968*, no part of this publication may be produced by any process whatsoever without the written permission of the publisher.

National Library of Australia Cataloguing-In-Publication data:

Davenport, Sue.
Cleared out: first contact in the Western Desert.

Bibliography.
Includes index.
ISBN 0 85575 457 5.

1. Woomera Rocket Range—History. 2. Aboriginal Australians—South Australia—Woomera. 3. Aboriginal Australians—South Australia—Woomera—Government relations. 4. Guided missiles—South Australia—Woomera—Testing. 5. Woomera (S. Aust.)—History. I. Johnson, Peter, 1957– . II. Yuwali. III. Woomera Rocket Range. IV. Title.

994.2380049915

Edited and designed by Bruderlin MacLean Publishing Services
Front cover photograph of Yuwali by Vic Surman (1964), background photograph (film still) by Walter MacDougall; back cover photograph by Bob Verburgt (date unknown)
Maps on pages xiv, xv, 8 and 37 by Brenda Thornley; all other maps by Christine Bruderlin
Printed by Ligare Book Printer, Sydney

This project has been assisted by the Australian Government through the Australia Council, its arts funding and advisory body.

Foreword

Most people view the ultra-remote Western Desert from the air. It lies seemingly inert: a corrugated, arid landscape of concentric rises, sand, scrub, salt pans and red dirt intermingling in a mosaic which spreads as far as the eye can see.

For the Martu, the subject of *Cleared out: first contact in the Western Desert*, and other peoples of the inland desert regions of Australia, this vast, austere country — replete with sandhills and desert oaks — has always been home.

In this place of three seasons, as it's known by its inhabitants, the terrain over which people have come and gone over centuries of occupation is a central part of their belief system, a sophisticated and integrated framework that has given meaning to lives lived in one of the harshest environments on earth.

Cleared out is an intimate and scrupulously thorough account of what happened when whitefella society and Aboriginal society, living deep in the desert, came face to face. Local elder the late Billy Gibbs is quoted as saying, 'Captain Cook made the country a different story'. This compelling account bears these words out in spades.

By charting the initial undertaking to locate and bring in those Martu who remained hitherto out of reach, Sue Davenport, Peter Johnson and Martu woman Yuwali have provided a unique insight to this remarkably recent event. The fact that Yuwali — then a young woman living with one of the last remaining groups still outside the reach of modernity — provides a first person record of this encounter, gives this book real weight.

The recovery mission was necessitated by the decision of the Australian and British governments in the late 1950s to include the Martu's country as part of a testing range for rockets and nuclear weapons.

The various responses of government bureaucracies, concerned politicians, supporters of Indigenous interests, anthropologists and finally the patrol officers whose task it became to shepherd the remaining groups of people still out, are all closely examined here.

Whatever role the Europeans played, and wherever their sympathies lay, it is the coalescing of their eventual conclusions about the prospects of Indigenous culture to withstand the traumatic passage from first contact to European intervention that is one of the most challenging aspects of *Cleared out*.

Safeguarding those people who remained on the 'fringes of civilisation', as the phrase went, was a core goal for the federal and state governments and the bureaucrats charged with this task. The fact that it was accompanied by the absorption of Indigenous lands and an ongoing assumption on the part of all concerned that 'detribalisation' was inevitable — rather than a temporary phenomenon — is emblematic of the history of European interactions with extant Aboriginal society.

The fatal gaps of perception and understanding of Indigenous culture feature in this history, but so too does the role played by other Aboriginal people — in this case the guides brought in to facilitate the exquisitely difficult first encounter that eventually happened on the shores of Lake Percival in 1964.

Yuwali's account of first seeing a car, and then a white man, and the marathon cat-and-mouse chase that ensued is riveting history. It is made all the more poignant by the fact that it is ultimately a fellow countryman who persuades the party to travel back to the outpost settlement of Jigalong, and so physically sever the bond between Yuwali and her country, a bond which was the foundation of her existence up to that time.

This book highlights one of the immense challenges in Indigenous affairs, namely that the dominant culture cannot — until it engages in a genuine and equal dialogue — expect to do anything more than overlay its current perceptions and political philosophies over Indigenous culture. Yet, amazingly, Indigenous culture — while suffering residual trauma — is still resilient. It engages and adapts with the new circumstances it finds itself in, but at its heart remain different values and understandings.

This poignant retelling of a momentous occasion, when a small band of women and children foraging around soaks and sandhills sight for the very first time a white man, is a cautionary tale for anyone who makes glib pronouncements about the way forward for Australia's Indigenous peoples.

We will need much perseverance to successfully help address the mountain of challenges facing Aboriginal and Torres Straight Islander people. Just as importantly we need to listen carefully and recognise that while substantial aspects of Indigenous ways may have been emasculated by the stronger material culture, the very contemporary story Yuwali tells in *Cleared out* is an affirmation that Indigenous identity and culture can and will survive.

Peter Garrett

Contents

Preface

The first time I heard Yuwali's story, in 1987, it was one of a collection of women's stories from the Jigalong, Punmu and Parnngurr communities of Western Australia. Yuwali had been asked to tell not *a* story but *her* story. That story forms the core of this book. Even at the time it attracted an audience of unusually quiet and attentive Martu listeners. It stayed with me for over a decade.

It fascinated me on many levels, and continues to fascinate me. Eventually, this led me to carry out research into the events surrounding Yuwali's story, working with Peter Johnson and Yuwali herself.

Thankfully, almost all of the players were still alive at the time of my research, despite the fact that the events occurred in 1964. Only one of the key participants had died: Walter MacDougall, one of the most extraordinary characters in the history of white exploration of the Western Desert, had passed away in 1976. All of the other participants were extremely ready to help, generously offering their memories and primary material.

The following are some notes about our sources and the manner in which the primary material was collated and used.

Methodology

Oral versions of this story were collected from Yuwali in 1987 and again in 1999. On each occasion, Yuwali gave a detailed chronological account of the events, an approach which was both unusual and striking. The versions differed in small matters of detail, but were marked by their similarity.

Extracts from these two oral histories have been combined into the diary-style narrative. The basis for selection of extracts was the expressiveness or clarity of the story. There were no significant discrepancies in fact between the accounts.

Similarly, Junju (a relative of Yuwali's, and a key participant) gave two much shorter oral accounts of the events, also in 1987 and 1999. The selection of extracts from her accounts was made on the same basis. (Wherever material has been used from a subsequent, directed interview, it has been credited separately.)

The translation of the oral accounts was carried out by Martu first-language speakers Dawn Oates, Nola Taylor and Desmond Taylor. The translations were functional rather than literal. On occasion we have slightly modified them, for the following reasons. Yuwali and Junju were mature and doubtless fluent, articulate and correct speakers of their languages. The translations to English were made by people whose first language is not English, and contained some grammatical errors. We have corrected these minor errors to afford appropriate dignity to the original Martu speaker. We have not done this where there was any ambiguity as to the intended meaning.

The diary accounts from the patrol officers (Walter MacDougall, Robert Macaulay and Terry Long) are from the reports they wrote in 1964. Additional material from later interviews is indicated in the heading. The officers' reports were written quickly and contain errors of spelling and grammar. We have made some minor corrections to spelling for consistency, but have not identified other errors (with notes such as [sic]) unless these corrections were essential to avoid confusion.

The officers' accounts were based on day-by-day entries in their reports. Despite the fact that, on one patrol, Walter MacDougall was clearly one day out in his diary, the accounts of MacDougall, Macaulay and Long are easily aligned. The oral accounts of the women have been aligned with those of the patrol officers through identifying coinciding events and places, and through Yuwali's very detailed (and, when aligned, remarkably reliable) day-by-day chronology.

Where other archival material has been quoted, we have once again made some minor corrections to spelling for consistency and have only inserted acknowledgement of errors (such as [sic]) sparingly. Errors are common in some of the source material and acknowledgement of them disrupts the flow of the story.

The majority of the photographs used in the text are those taken by participants in the patrol: Vic Surman, Robert Macaulay, Bob Tonkinson and Terry Long; and digitised frames from film taken by Walter MacDougall. These have been supplemented with photographs that I took on a trip to the Percival Lakes in 1999 with several of the participants in the story, and some general topical photos.

The Martu

Yuwali and her group are part of a larger community now known as the Martu [1], a collective term whose use as a group-identity marker dates from about the early 1980s. Martu is a Manyjilyjarra word that translates as 'man' or 'one of us (Aboriginal person)'.[2] It's now used to describe people who have appropriate connections to one or more of eight dialect-named groups and their corresponding territories, which cover much of the Gibson, Little Sandy and Great Sandy deserts in Western Australia.[3] The ancestors of the Martu are believed to have lived in this area for at least 5000 years.[4]

Throughout this book, we refer to Yuwali's people as the Martu. This is because they now self-identify and hold native title as this community. However, it also recognises that Yuwali's country is important to all of the Martu, containing a key site, the resting place of a major Dreaming figure.

Naming

There has been some standardisation of the naming and spelling of the Martu names of people and places in order to assist the reader.

For example, the waterhole Yulpu was referred to by MacDougall as Yuldu, and Yimiri as Inari. Similarly, the spelling of people's names varied in the archival reports; in different accounts Nyani was referred to as Njani and Nyanji. We have followed the accepted orthography of Martu Wangka (Martu language) for all names.

These changes to the names of people and places were made only when the identity of the subject was quite clear to us and the use of the different names could have been confusing to readers.

In the diary section, the Martu names of Yuwali's group have been used consistently, despite the fact that in Yuwali's and Junju's original accounts they sometimes used the anglicised names of some of the children. Once again, this change to consistent usage has been made to avoid confusion for readers.

Similarly, different versions of a Martu name may have been used in the original oral accounts — for example, Pinkirri or Pinkirrini — but a consistent version has been used in the text.

Ages

The age of each person in Yuwali's group was estimated by one or several of the white people with whom they came in contact: Terry Long, Robert Macaulay or Bob Tonkinson. We have used these approximate ages to give some accurate sense of each character.

Geography, maps and directions

Throughout this book the term 'Western Desert' is used to describe the country in which the Martu live and in which these events took place. The Western Desert actually occupies a much larger area, stretching from the Nullarbor in the south to the Kimberley in the north, and from the Percival Lakes in the west through to the Pintupi lands in the Northern Territory. However, for the sake of brevity and consistency, we describe the portions of the Gibson, Great Sandy and Little Sandy deserts that form the relevant area as 'the Western Desert'.

The maps in the diary section are functional representations of the Percival Lakes area rather than being geographically accurate. They have been designed to complement the narrative — providing a sense of where sites are in relation to one another, and the relative distances between them — but they are not to scale and site location is not exact. This is for two reasons. The first, and most important, is to protect the location of significant sites. The second is the difficulty of precisely locating all sites without visiting each of them and securing exact coordinates.

Readers may find it difficult to reconcile the Martu accounts of the direction in which they travelled with the directions shown on the diary maps. Martu will often say, 'We went north, then we went east'. This will always be accurate, in so far as it goes. However, they may omit to say that this was for a short distance in each direction, and was followed by a much longer walk south. We have retained Yuwali's and Junju's references to the directions in which they travelled, because they are integral to the way in which the accounts are structured and recollected.

One place name created particular problems. All parties in the 1950s and 1960s referred to Ninety Mile Beach, which is now officially known as Eighty Mile Beach. We have been unable to trace the lost ten-mile stretch of beach.

Non-Martu characters

There is no simple yet elegant way to consistently and clearly refer to non-Martu participants and society. On different occasions through this book we have used the terms 'European' (where we, the authors, are making the distinction) and 'whitefella' (where there is a notional Martu distinction). These terms may not always be strictly correct and on occasions some people may even find these terms offensive. We can only plead the difficulty of the task.

Imperial measures and distances

In the original patrol officers' entries distances and measures are made in imperial measure. These have been left in the original, with a corresponding metric value in square brackets.

Warning

Aboriginal and Torres Strait Islander people are respectfully advised that this book contains names and images of deceased persons, and culturally sensitive material.

Sue Davenport
Newman, WA, 2005

Acknowledgements

We are grateful to all of the participants in this story who gave us their assistance and to all the other people who helped us to research and prepare this book.

In particular, we would like to thank the Martu men and women who contributed to the stories, field trips, translation and the preparation of the book: Yuwali, Junju Judson, Thelma Judson, Douglas Judson, Dawn Oates, Nola Taylor, Desmond Taylor, Muuki Taylor, Dulcie Gibbs, Roley Williams, Rosie Williams and Elizabeth Sailor.

All of the non-Martu people involved in the patrols were unstinting in their help and support and generous in the provision of their wonderful photographs: Terry Long (and family), Frank Gare, Bob Verburgt (and family), Vic Surman (and family), Alec Oliver (and family), Bob Tonkinson, Robert Macaulay (and family), Jim and Ivy Plumb and Trevor Levien.

For their advice and generous access to time and resources, we are grateful to Fr Kevin McKelson, John and Dianne Walsh, Fiona Walsh, Jeremy Long, Nicolas Peterson, Bill Edwards and John Dallwitz. Peter and Lyn Connell generously made a quiet writing room available to us when we had none. We also thank Katherine and Judy Johnson for their special insights and help.

We are grateful to Chris Muller and Peter Kendrick from the Western Australian Department of Conservation and Land Management for their great support on the field trip back to the Percival Lakes.

In the research, preparation and editing of the book, we must thank Helen Skeat, Robert Macaulay and Melinda Smith. We are particularly grateful to Bob Tonkinson for his time and patience in reviewing the draft and for his generous advice, and to Myrna Tonkinson for her advice and hospitality.

This book grew from a research report that was funded by the Australian Institute of Aboriginal and Torres Strait Islander Studies. The book would not have been possible without the continuing support of AIATSIS.

Finally, we thank the Parnngurr and Punmu communities and the Jigalong Community Council for their generous support.

Sue Davenport and Peter Johnson

Annotated list of people and organisations

Parts of this story are complex. Many different government departments — state, territory and federal — were involved, and some had changes of name during the course of the events described. Some people retired or resigned. The following list is not exhaustive, but provides a quick reference to the key players in the story and commonly used abbreviations.

Berndt, Ronald	Professor who founded the departments of Sociology and Anthropology at The University of Western Australia
Boswell, RW	Director of the WRE after 1958 (succeeding HJ Brown, with a title change)
Brown, HJ	Controller of the WRE until 1958
Butement, WAB (Alan)	Chief scientist, Commonwealth Department of Supply
Cook, Eric	Secretary of the Board of Management, Research and Development (Department of Supply)
Dedman, John	Commonwealth Minister for Defence
DNW	The Western Australian Department of Native Welfare, formerly (until 1954) the Department of Native Affairs
Duguid, Charles	Adelaide doctor and advocate for Indigenous people
Elkin, AP	Professor of Anthropology at The University of Sydney
Evetts, JF	Chief executive officer of the LRWO
Gare, Frank	Western Australian Commissioner of Native Welfare from 1962
LRWO	The Long Range Weapons Organisation, the joint British–Australian organisation established in 1946, which became the WRE in 1955
Long, Jeremy	Investigation officer (Social Welfare), Welfare Branch, Northern Territory Administration, in 1963–64
Long, Terry	Acting superintendent, North-West Division, DNW, in 1964
Macaulay, Robert	The second native patrol officer appointed by the WRE
MacDougall, Walter	The first native patrol officer appointed by the WRE
Middleton, Stanley	Western Australian Commissioner of Native Welfare, 1948–62
Newman, Jack	Range superintendent for Woomera
NPO	Native patrol officer with WRE
O'Grady, Frank	Chief engineer at WRE
WRE	Weapons Research Establishment, formerly the Long Range Weapons Organisation

Maps

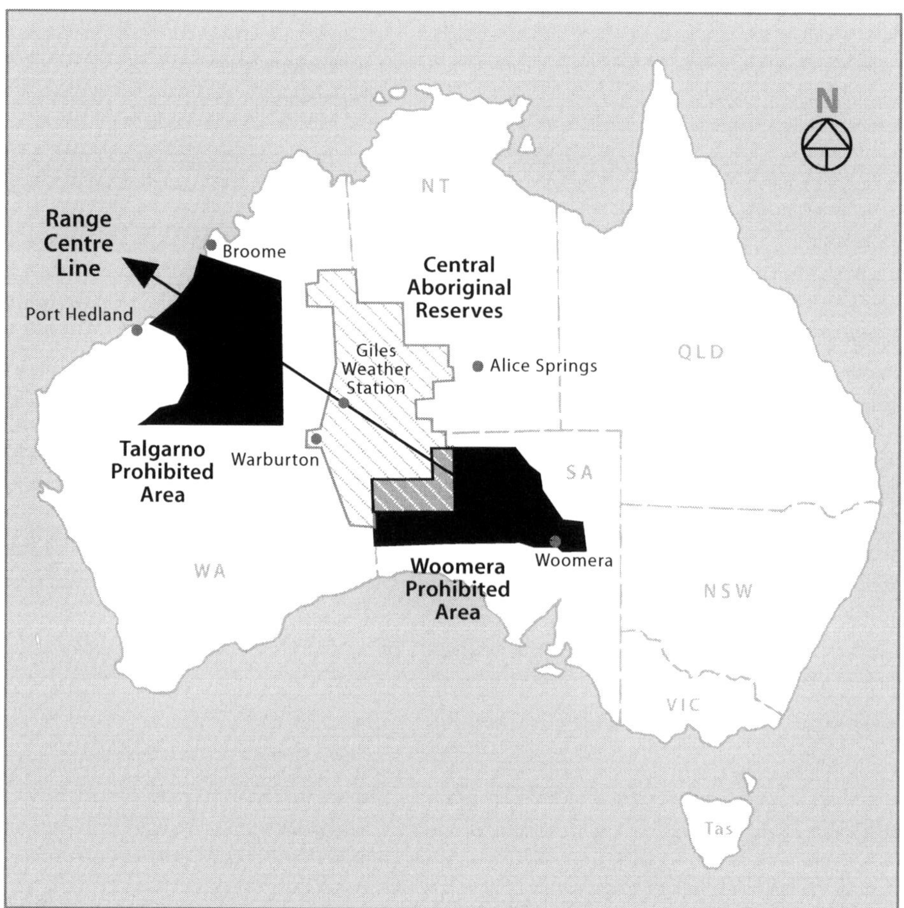

Australia, 1964, showing the rocket firing line, and the Woomera and Talgarno prohibited areas. The term 'Central Aboriginal Reserves' was used extensively at the time to refer to the group of reserves administered separately by the Commonwealth (in relation to the Northern Territory), South Australia and Western Australia.

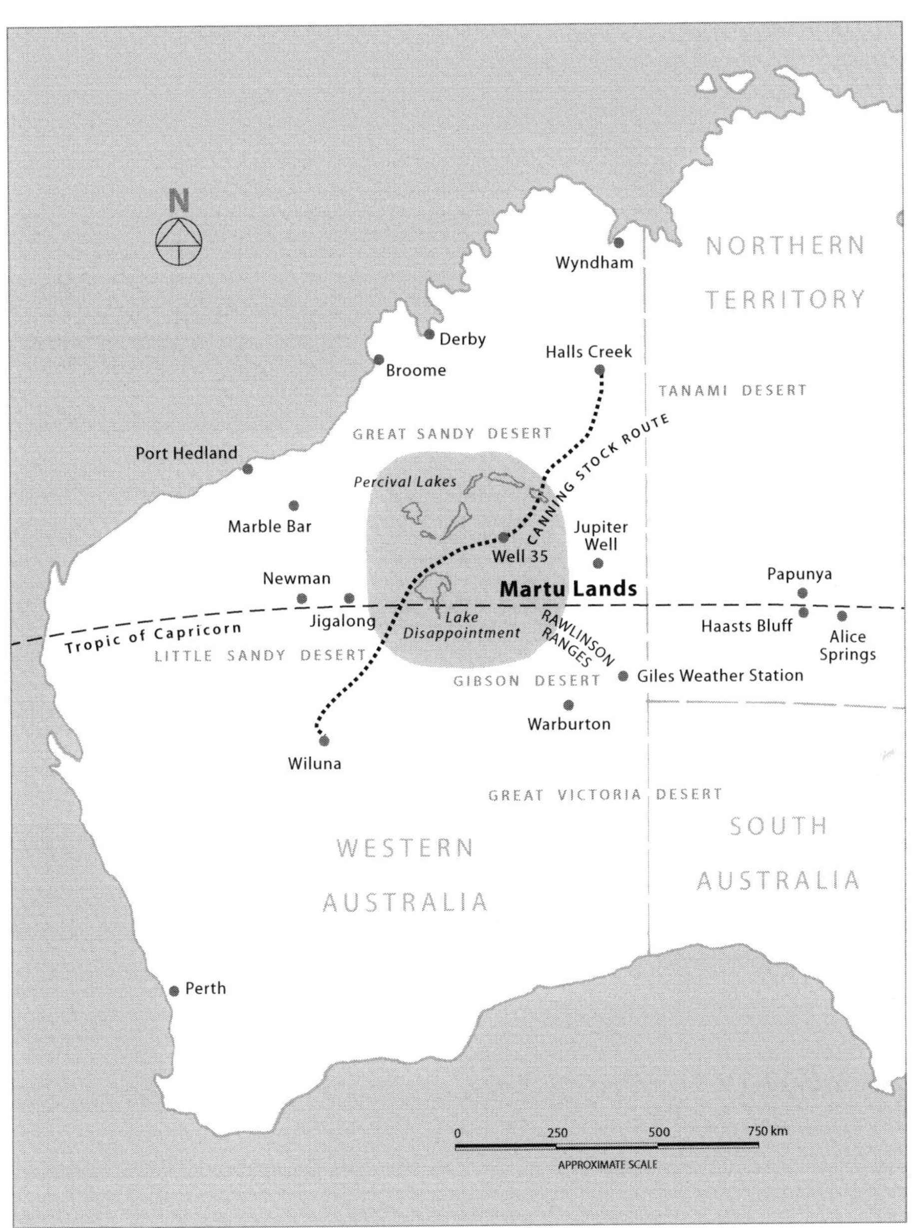

Western Australia, showing the overlapping desert area referred to in this book as the 'Western Desert'.

PART ONE

THE BEGINNING

Genesis of the story

The heart of this book is a first-contact encounter which took place in 1964 between Indigenous and European Australians in the Western Desert. However, the story really begins almost two decades earlier. Between 1946 and 1948 a series of events took place, events whose consequences were to converge on a dry salt lake in a remote corner of Western Australia.

The first of these events took shape in Canberra and London. In November 1946, the Australian Government announced the development of a rocket-testing range to be located in South Australia. The range was a joint initiative of the Australian and British governments, and was intended to assure the safety of both nations as they emerged from the shadows of the Second World War.

Australia had been chosen by Britain as a test site largely because its vast, sparsely inhabited interior appeared to be 'the only place within the British Commonwealth'[1] suitable to launch, track and target rockets. However, among the many technical challenges there was one inconvenient human problem: the area in which the rockets were planned to land was not uninhabited. It was, in fact, home to an unknown number of nomadic Indigenous people.

This 'human problem' triggered the second event of importance to the story: the emergence of a small but vocal body of opposition to the rocket range. The Australian Government's response was the appointment, in November 1947, of a native patrol officer, Walter MacDougall. Over the next twenty-five years MacDougall (and, later, one other officer) was entrusted with ensuring the safety and welfare of any Indigenous people in an area covering roughly one quarter of Australia.

The third significant event took place in Western Australia. A new broom swept through the state government's Native Affairs portfolio. A 1948 report highly critical of the department's past administration recommended a new 'welfare-based' approach to Indigenous people.[2] Stanley Middleton was appointed to oversee this change. Middleton completely revamped the Department of Native Affairs, shaping its character and policies through the 1950s and into the 1960s.

Elsewhere in Western Australia, on the edge of the Western Desert, the fourth seemingly unrelated event took place. A maintenance depot at Jigalong, on the Rabbit-Proof Fence, was handed over to the Apostolic Church of Australia for the creation of a mission. Jigalong had for many years incorporated a camel-breeding centre that had also come to function as a depot providing basic rations to Indigenous people who had 'come in', or left the desert for a settlement. At the time of the first missionaries' arrival in 1947, however, Jigalong was a desolate outpost.

Meanwhile, in the heart of this desert country, the final event took place. At a small waterhole called Yulpu, near the home of the great rain-making serpents

Wirnpa and Karrparti, Yuwali was born. She spent the next seventeen years of her life among the salt lake and sandhill country around Yulpu. This was her world, a world that relied on an intricate knowledge of country, a knowledge richly described and given meaning by the Dreaming and the Law.

From 1947 until 1964, the stories that developed from these beginnings gradually converged. Through those years, Yuwali remained oblivious to them, living in Wirnpa country.

Wirnpa: The rainmaker

Wirnpa the snake-man lived and hunted in the Percival Lakes area with a mob of rainmakers like himself. One day he left his home at Wirnpa waterhole and set off south. He stopped at a spring east of Mount Newman, where he met a mob of other ancestral beings. He hunted, and then they cooked seedcakes and ate a feast. There, Wirnpa left some rainmaking paraphernalia.

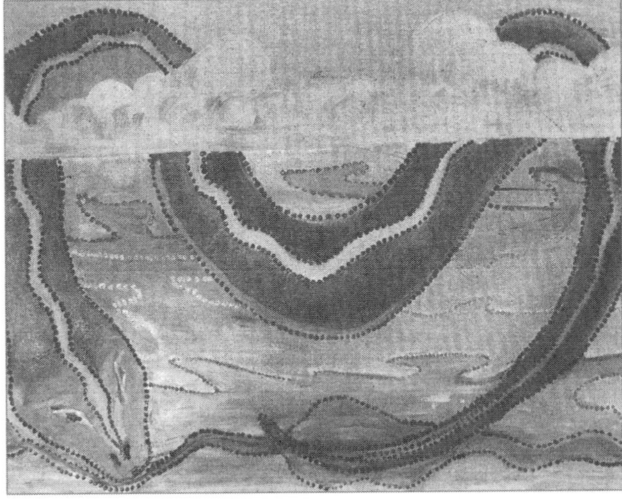

Wirnpa, the rain-making snake.
PAINTING: VICTOR BURTON, PUNMU, 1999

Wirnpa went on south towards the Kalgoorlie area. At a rockhole he met the Two Men ancestral beings, Wati Kujarra, and they hunted and ate a feast. The Two Men tried to make Wirnpa go and hunt, but he convinced them of his greater age and seniority so they gave up and went hunting instead. Wirnpa went east and camped at a number of places. He went on to a seed-making place and ate a feast of seeds with the mob of grass-seed people who were there. Then he went on to Manyjilyjarra country, where he left a snake and ate a seed-cake feast by himself, before going to a number of other places. At Yinaru he found an ailing rainmaker called Japula who had collapsed under the weight of all the sacred rainmaking objects he was carrying, so Wirnpa carried Japula on to his home and left him there. After Wirnpa had gone, Japula tried to leave but had to return because he was old and tired and had too much water in his stomach.

Wirnpa went on northwards and met the Kangaroo ancestral being, Marlu, who was now heading back towards the south. Marlu asked Wirnpa for some rainmaking things, which Wirnpa gave him. In exchange, Marlu gave Wirnpa some ceremonial objects, then they went their respective ways.

Wirnpa saw the tracks of a mob of Minyipurru, the Seven Sisters ancestral beings, and followed them. When he found them he asked them where they were going, and they told him east. Wirnpa went on and came across Karlaya, the Emu, who was lying alone near a waterhole after having been bitten by dingoes. Wirnpa could see the dingoes nearby.

Wirnpa travelled on, becoming wet with sweat, and he could smell himself. He went on northwards and saw that a lot of the old rainmakers had turned into water snakes and were living in waterholes. While Wirnpa was away on his travels, the other rainmakers who had been left behind got into a big spear fight, and all of them injured one another in the thighs. Unable to walk, they had all crawled off in different directions until they could go on no further. The spots where they lay became waterholes, and they turned into snakes and went to live inside the waterholes.

He went on to Karrparti, who had not yet turned into a snake. Wirnpa went hunting and caught a marsupial. Karrparti cooked it, plus a seedcake damper, and they ate a feast, which they fed to each other. They got up and left, but both complained of tiredness, so Karrparti made himself a windbreak then lay down at Karrparti waterhole, where he still lives, as a snake. Wirnpa went onwards and saw sheet lightning to the north, and rain falling. He was looking for his father, but he was too late because all were already turned into snakes. He wept for them.

Wirnpa went east until he became tired and lay down at Wirnpa, where he went inside the water as a big snake, and big clouds rose up from the waterhole. Wirnpa was the last man, the last one to lie down and die. Physically they all died, but spiritually they are all there and living on for ever in the ground, in the sky, in all things, all over the place. Wirnpa travelled widely and met other ancestors and instituted the feasting — a very important part of the rainmaking ceremony — and did things that then became part of what people must do.[3]

The people of Wirnpa

> My father had too many wives. He went away with three wives. He left two wives: my mother and her sister. We were walking around there for a long time without any men. For a long time; a long, long time. Two hot times [summers] — three times, yes, three. I never thought of men. We were minding our business, but we never thought of anyone coming to look for us.[4]

In April 1964, Yuwali was about seventeen. She and her grandmothers, her mother, her father's sister and a large number of children were moving around Wirnpa country. They were walking the country that they had always walked, their various camps clustered around the salt lakes. However, they were travelling without men — an unusual situation — and were no longer coming across any of their relatives.[5]

Yuwali in 1964.
PHOTO: TERRY LONG

This country had been travelled and formed by the great rain-making snakes, Wirnpa and Karrparti, and other Dreaming beings like Marlu (the kangaroo), Kirrki (the banded plover) and Kaarnka (the crow).[6] These ancient travellers had journeyed over the country, hunting, feasting, meeting up, instituting ceremonies and having adventures. As they travelled, the beautifully decorated beings left their marks in every place: the shapes of hills and rocks, the winding of creeks and the creation of rockholes.[7]

> After their activities on earth came to an end, the Dreaming beings, worn down by their superhuman efforts and by the weight of the sacred paraphernalia they carried, ended their earthly pursuits. Their bodies disappeared or metamorphosed into stones or other natural features or celestial bodies, never to be seen on earth again; nonetheless, their spiritual essence remained as powerful as ever.[8]

Even after they disappeared from the earth, the beings from the Dreaming continued to control the reproduction of plants and animals. Martu believe that the continuity of life relies on and emanates from them. Every human is created when a spirit child from the Dreaming enters its mother.[9] Wirnpa is a major rain-making snake, and men with the appropriate rights may conduct ceremonies in *yalijarra*, the hot time, calling on Wirnpa and other rainmakers to ensure that the rain comes.[10]

The Dreaming beings give life its form. While they no longer appear on earth, they left *yulupirti* ('everlasting') — the Law. The Law provides guidance on how life should be conducted: birth, initiation, marriage, death, knowledge of where people can travel freely and where only initiated men can go, the structure of the kinship system, how an animal should be butchered and distributed, what is to be done when a camp is left. The Law explains the world and how things have always been: the country, each person's source and role, and all of the many obligations that are owed to people throughout society. Everything finds its place within the Law, as it is continuously revealed to people.[11]

Yuwali and her family travelled through the country just as the Dreaming beings had travelled. They hunted and ate as the Dreaming beings had hunted and eaten. They knew their country, and it provided for them.

Yuwali was born at Yulpu rockhole, in the heart of Wirnpa country. This area is now known in English as the Percival Lakes. Bare salt for most of the year, the lakes run east–west for about 200 kilometres. They are surrounded by permanent sandhills, also running roughly east–west.

> We used to go and run up the sandhills, jump down and roll in the sand. We used to play hide and seek and climb the trees.[12]

Much of the Western Desert is red, sandhill country. Unlike the image many hold of deserts, these sandhills are permanent and are usually covered in spinifex, gums

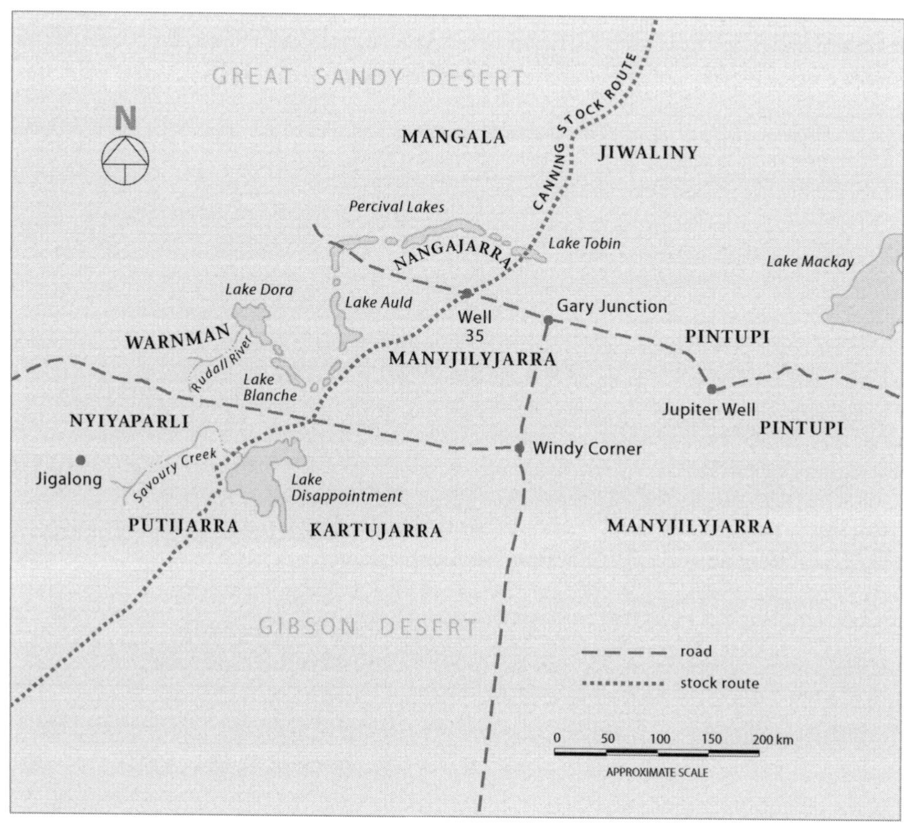

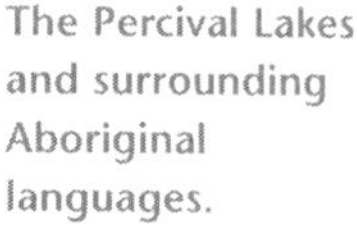
The Percival Lakes and surrounding Aboriginal languages.

and other trees and shrubs, with mulga and beautiful desert oaks growing in the corridors between them. In many areas, large anthills are dotted throughout these corridors. But this country also contains other very distinctive landforms: rocky hills dotted with caves, and broad plains of sand, spinifex and gibber.

Different languages belong to different parts of the desert and surrounding country. Yuwali's father was a Mangala man and her mother Nangajarra. Yuwali, coming from the Wirnpa area, identified herself as a Nangajarra speaker.[13] But she also spoke the neighbouring languages of her father and those of other women in the group: Manyjilyjarra and Jiwaliny.

Wirnpa, the key rain-making site, was an important place for many people throughout the desert, including Mangala and Jiwaliny people from the north, Manyjilyjarra from the east and Warnman from the west.[14] It was a place where people travelled and met and shared ceremony. It was a place from which wives were coveted, because of its importance.[15]

To European eyes, the Western Desert is 'the harshest physical environment on earth ever inhabited by man before the Industrial Revolution'.[16] The Martu, like all those in the desert, long ago perfected the means of prospering there.

As a child, Yuwali walked with her family and learned her country, taught by her grandparents. She learned all of the water sources, when they would have water, the routes between them and the country around them. Each water source has a name and a story, each line of waterholes is part of a larger Dreaming story.

Yimiri, a permanent source of water near Yuwali's birthplace. PHOTO: TERRY LONG, 1964

There are many different types of waterhole in the desert: soaks and wells, claypans that hold water during the rains, large semi-permanent rockhole lagoons, and a very small number of permanent springs.[17] Yuwali's country included three of the few permanent sources of water in the desert: Wirnpa (the name used by the Martu to denote both a specific water source and a broader area), Yimiri and Kurtararra. These were their *yinta*, main camps to which they returned in the driest times.[18]

Yuwali's people needed to know the location, nature and condition of all water sources in their country at all times. The locations of wells and soaks were known precisely, as they frequently required digging out — to a depth of several metres — before the water was found.[19] When such a well was not being used, branches were stuffed down the hole to protect it from animals and debris and to retard evaporation.[20]

From her infancy Yuwali had learned to read the country, to know the plants, to know the habits and tracks of animals, to know what to eat and what not to.[21]

Bob Tonkinson, an anthropologist who worked with the Martu over several decades, said:

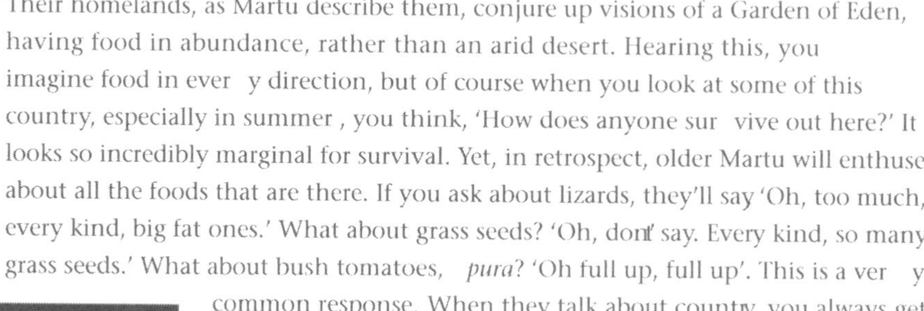

Their homelands, as Martu describe them, conjure up visions of a Garden of Eden, having food in abundance, rather than an arid desert. Hearing this, you imagine food in every direction, but of course when you look at some of this country, especially in summer, you think, 'How does anyone survive out here?' It looks so incredibly marginal for survival. Yet, in retrospect, older Martu will enthuse about all the foods that are there. If you ask about lizards, they'll say 'Oh, too much, every kind, big fat ones.' What about grass seeds? 'Oh, don't say. Every kind, so many grass seeds.' What about bush tomatoes, *pura*? 'Oh full up, full up'. This is a very common response. When they talk about country, you always get a very positive view of the resources that were there and how much of everything there was.[22]

Food staples included seeds, *kanyjamarra* (bush yam, *Vigna lanceolata*), goannas and feral cats. PHOTOS: SUE DAVENPORT, 2003

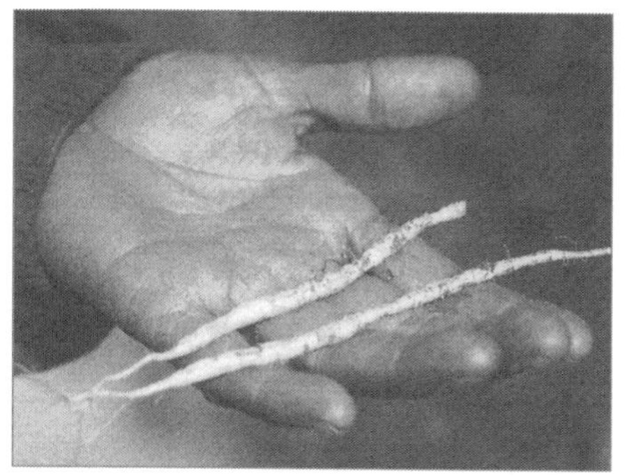

In fact, the traditional food collected by the Martu depended on the season and the luck of the hunt. Men hunted large game, such as kangaroos or emus, but were not always successful. They also dug out lizards, snakes and small marsupials such as bilbies. Most of the food obtained was collected by women[23], who sought vegetable foods, goannas, lizards, frogs, cats, rabbits and other small game.

We used to get meat like pussycat, fox, dingo, lizard, goanna and the blue-tongue lizard. Mummy used to go camping out to get some seed and some meat and she would come back the next day when she got some things. We used to grind [the seed] in the rock. We used to place a dish underneath and grind all the seed into a dish. Daddy used to go out and hunt for meat.[24]

Most meat was cooked in the same way. The animal was first gutted and thrown briefly on the fire to singe the hair or scales. These were then scraped off and the whole animal cooked in hot ash and sand. Seed cakes and some other vegetable foods were also cooked in this 'oven'.

The availability of food and water depended on where and when the rain fell. Reading the weather and knowing the effect of different types of rain was knowledge that people acquired:

People remembered the layout of their country and the times and extent of rainfall. With all this knowledge, people could decide on the direction of their movement to the most suitable camping grounds which would provide the necessary food supply. The

> availability of water and cultural demands, such as the following of dreaming tracks, also influenced the time and direction of walking and the choice of camps.[25]

Sandals made from woven strips of bark from the green birdflower bush (*Crotalaria cunninghamii*). PHOTO: TERRY LONG, 1964

There were also seasonal patterns to people's travel, reflecting changes in the availability of water and foods. The Martu recognise three distinct seasons.[26] *Yalijarra* runs from December to March. It starts hot and dry, with water found only in permanent springs and wells. During this season, people would gravitate towards known, safe, permanent water sources (such as Wirnpa, Yimiri and Kurtararra). Where there was also an abundance of one or more food sources nearby, larger groups would gather at these safe locations, providing an opportunity for extended social and ritual activities.[27]

The weather is hot, often well over forty degrees. Sometimes, it is too hot even for the Martu. At these times they buried themselves in the cool sand in the sides of sandhills to escape the heat of the day[28] and travelled more at night. When the salt lakes were too hot for their feet they made sandals from bark strips.[29]

Towards the end of *yalijarra* heavy rain, violent thunderstorms and huge displays of lightning can take place. For the Martu, all of this summer rain — the major source of water in the desert — originates in the Percival Lakes and is controlled by Wirnpa and the other rainmakers from that area.[30]

There is no guarantee of rain. In good years, though, water from ephemeral sources tends to be more widely available during this hot time, and so people would spread out across their country in small family groups, using water from claypans and small rockholes in areas that they would otherwise rarely visit. Fast-growing, temporary plant foods appear after the rains, but there was still a strong reliance on the desert staples of goannas and lizards.

Jawirli, the quandong tree (*Santalum acuminatum*). PHOTO: ROBERT MACAULAY, DATE UNKNOWN

The season called *wantajarra* runs from March until August. The daytime temperatures can be cold, sometimes with bitter winds and overnight frost. Rain is rare, more widespread and drizzly in character[31] and is strongly disliked.[32] Semi-permanent water sources may still be full from the summer rains. The relative abundance of water and some seeds and early fruits allowed small groups to combine with others and camp together. Goannas and lizards hibernate, however, and can be more difficult to find.

During this time Martu would try to escape any rain by sheltering behind anthills or sleeping in caves.[33] At night, they would sleep with fires between them, and Yuwali told of warming herself by sleeping with some of her three or four dingos.[34]

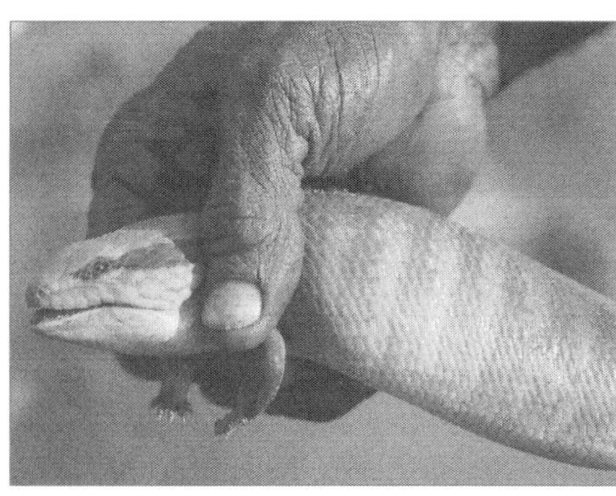

Lungkurta (*Teliqua multifasciata*, blue-tongue lizard).
PHOTO: SUE DAVENPORT 2003

Tulparra runs from August to December. This is the rich season: temperatures rise, and there is plenty of food as plants and animals become more abundant. There are fruits, tubers, reptiles emerging from hibernation and more large game. But as the season progresses and it becomes hotter, more stable water sources had to be relied upon, forcing people to travel back towards a main camp.

As they travelled, Yuwali's family would carry very little: light stone and wooden tools that fulfilled multiple purposes. A woman's main portable implements were a digging stick and wooden bowls, *piti*, which might be used at different times for carrying water, food or a baby, or for scooping, digging or winnowing.[35]

They would also carry firesticks — slow-burning sticks or bunches of spinifex that ensured they always had fire with them.[36] They burnt country as they went, because areas in which the spinifex and dead growth have been burned off produce larger numbers of food-bearing plants and significantly more food and game.[37] Firing the country makes it far easier to track small game and to find their holes, which are often under spinifex. It also allows people who have separated to hunt to communicate with each other.[38]

Yuwali witnessed a gradual emptying of the desert during the long droughts in the 1950s, and a further harsh drought between 1958 and 1962.

> [When I was a child] there used to be a lot of Martu [in the desert]. But they followed the people on the Canning Stock Route: my father's brothers and their families. [At Jigalong] they asked me: 'Are there any other people out there in the bush?' I told them, 'No, there's no one else out there'.[39]

The Western Desert was never heavily populated by European standards. It's estimated that the average distribution of people in this area prior to contact was one person per 200 square kilometres.[40] But from 1920 to 1960 the deserts gradually emptied of people as they moved towards fringe settlements, and Martu ranged over increasingly large areas.[41]

By 1964, Yuwali had been travelling in a group of twenty women and children for the past two to three years. They would separate into smaller groups to hunt but would come back together, particularly during *yalijarra*, the hot season.[42] The group, spanning three generations, was made up of four older women, several mothers with children, two young women of marriageable age, four boys (the oldest was about twelve), one girl and six very young children.

The Martu

This is the extended family group living in and around the Percival Lakes in 1964. The lighter boxes indicate family members who do not feature in the story (having either passed away or those travelling elsewhere at the time). The ages given are estimates made by patrol officers Long and MacDougall.

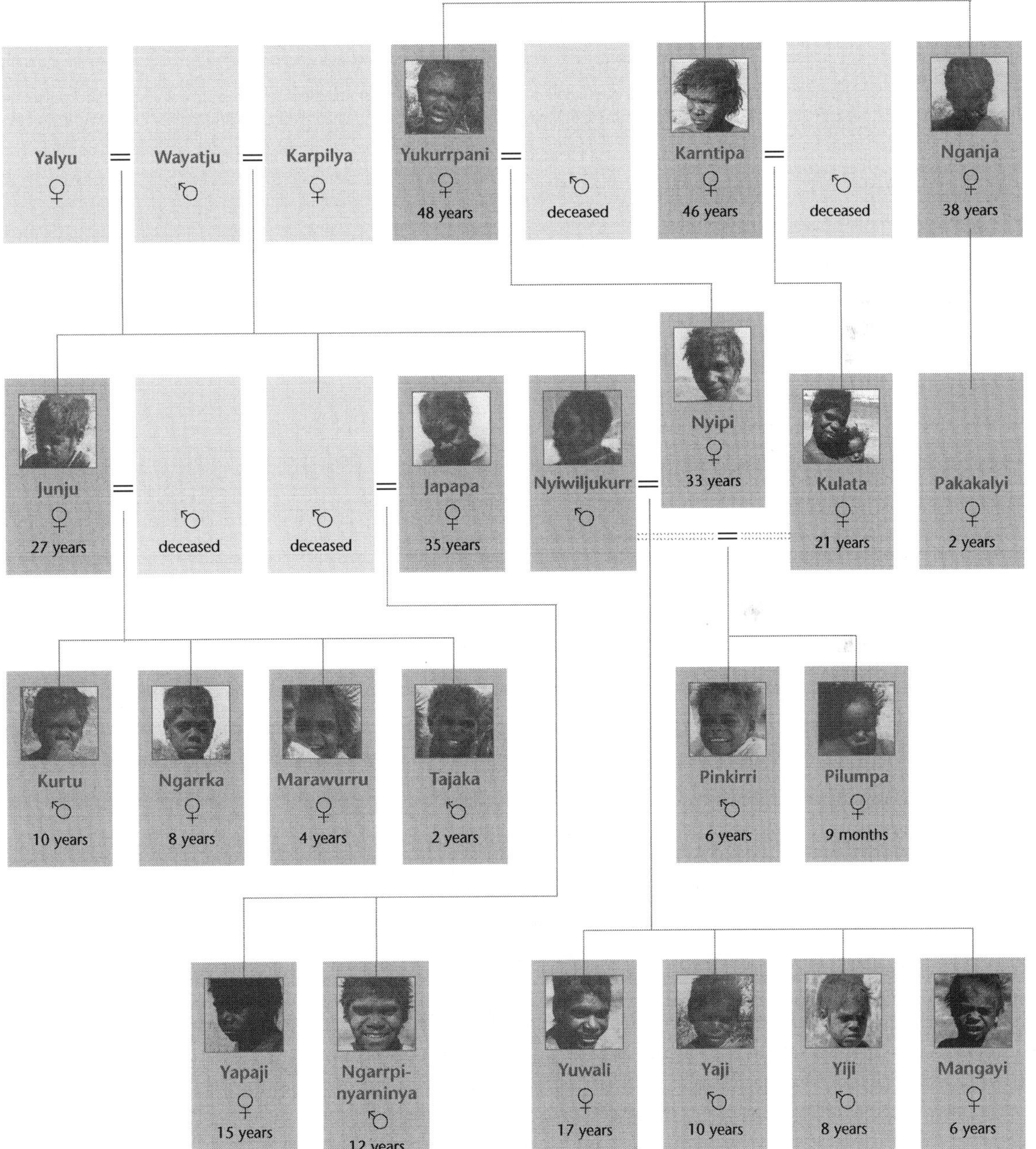

Nyiwiljukurr, Yuwali's father (far right), with some of the group brought in from Joanna Spring in 1967. PHOTO: MARGO TOOHEY, 1967

Each of the adult women had children, and some had grandchildren. Y uwali and her siblings were Y ukurrpani's grandchildren by birth. However, in accordance with the Martu system of kin reckoning, she would have called Y ukurrpani's two birth sisters — Karntipa and Nganja — *nyami*, or 'grandmother', as well.

Yuwali's mother, Nyipi, was married to Nyiwiljukurr, an older man who was blind by the time the events in this stor y took place. Kulata was also married to Nyiwiljukurr. Junju, a twenty-seven-year-old with four children, was Nyiwiljukurr's younger (birth) sister. At the time of the rocket launches, Nyiwiljukurr was travelling in the north, near Joanna Spring, with his other wives. Eventually , in 1967, he and his group were brought from Joanna Spring to La Grange mission, one of the very last groups to come out of the W estern Desert.[43]

It was highly unusual for a group of Martu women and children to travel alone for such an extended period. Men sometimes travelled in same-sex groups on ritual and religious business, but women did not.[44] Among all of the reports of Aboriginal people to have come in or to have been brought in from the desert, this stor y is unique.[45]

The men had disappeared over several years. Y uwali's father had separated and was travelling in the north. The husbands of Y ukurrpani, Nganja and Japapa had died. Karntipa's husband had been killed by a revenge party of 'featherfeet' (see below). Junju's husband had also been killed, speared in the ribs by 'men from the north' because he had eloped with Junju.[46]

Even apart from the killings of two of their husbands, there were many reasons for the women to be wary or fearful of strangers or unusual phenomena. Venomous

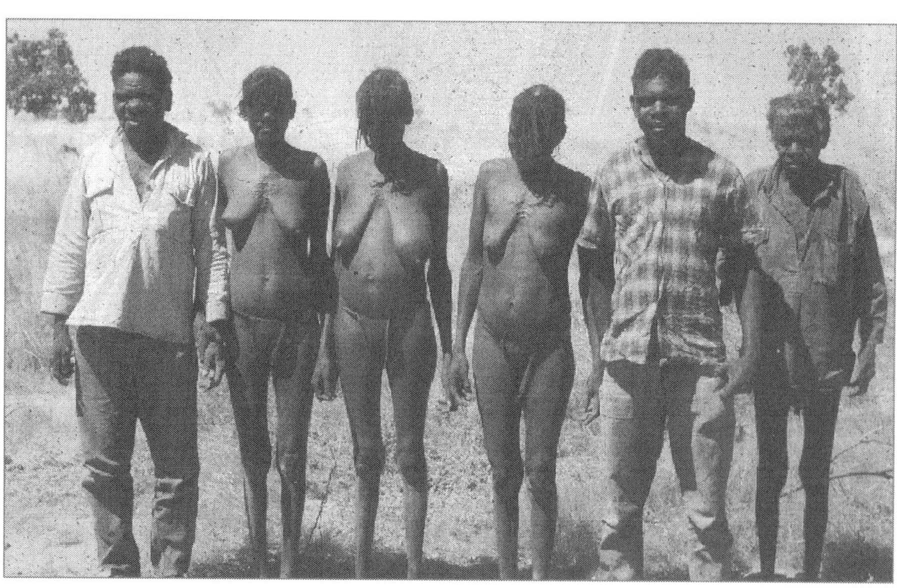

Other members of the group brought in in 1967. The three women are Nyiwiljukurr's wives, the ones who travelled with him while his other two wives remained with Yuwali's group at the Percival Lakes. PHOTO: MARGO TOOHEY, 1967

snakes and scorpions created the main need for conventional caution, but the more frightening sources of danger were spirits — and other people. Malevolent spirits provided cause for fear:

> The Martu include within their world view a range of harmful spirits (*malpu*) or 'devils' that are dangerous and can prey on people. These spirits are believed to have existed even before the arrival of the creative beings (*jukurtani*) of the Dreaming epoch. They are ugly, and frequently kill. They are believed to be able to take human form. *Mamu* are human in form, hairy and fanged.[47]

Writing about the neighbouring Pintupi, Fred Myers described a ubiquitous fear of strangers:

> Some informants have described traditional bush life as 'just like war', in reference to the continual raids between localities which seem to have engendered a fear of 'strangers'. Despite their sociability, the Pintupi felt most secure in the company of their closest relatives and most frequent co-residents, in their local groups and among neighbours. These were people one knew and whose intentions and motives one understood.
>
> Revenge expeditions of ten to twenty men often travelled hundreds of miles, well beyond the areas individuals knew from economic pursuits. It seems that periods of grievance between groups alternated with periods of more amicable relations, until an incident sparked off trouble.
>
> As a result, distance is a marker of social boundaries. 'Strangers' are suspect of malicious intentions and one's own countrymen, with whom one most frequently interacts, constitute a security circle.[48]

Featherfeet (*jinakarrpil*) from neighbouring or distant groups, seeking revenge for the direct or believed killing of relatives, are particularly feared. These revenge parties were a part of Western Desert life, and an obvious cause of fear and flight. Given the ways in which several of their men had died, a fear of these ritual killers would have been very real to the women in Yuwali's group.

> Feather feet are ritual killers who wear special moccasins and are said to be men, not spirits, who come from distant areas and lie in wait from their victims. They ambush, kill and revive them magically, then send them back to camp. The victim is said to remember nothing of the attack and has no visible wounds and yet within days dies and is unable to name his attackers. The fear of revenge expeditions or feather feet is certainly a real one and a big one in that people would flee. There is no question that people would want to put a lot of distance between them and any groups believed to be following them. Feather feet have a mission to kill and are therefore terrifying.[49]

The sudden appearance of strange beings in human form in one's country was therefore good grounds for fear. The usual response was flight and concealment, at which the Martu are adept.

Yuwali had never seen *kartiya*, white men. She had heard stories of such people from her grandfather, who had told her to be careful of them, but she had no idea what they were.[50]

Other women in the group would also have heard stories of white men. There is a possibility that some of these handed-down stories would have been harrowing, as early contact in the Western Desert often involved violence and mistreatment.[51]

Yuwali had, however, seen aeroplanes, which she thought were devils. When she and the others saw them they would hide or make a big fire to scare the planes away.[52] Yuwali's mother, Nyipi, had once seen what they later learned to be a motor vehicle:

> We came across a newly graded road and heard a noise. Nyipi went up the sandhill to have a look. She saw the vehicle. She was frightened. She ran down and told the group to run away, so we all took off. Nyipi talked about it looking like a rock — a rock that could move around. We didn't realise there was anybody in it.[53]

Just like her mother before her, in May 1964 Yuwali walked up a sandhill and suddenly saw white men and a truck for the first time in her life. In these strangers, she saw devils.

The story of those devils, and why they now appeared in the desert, had started at the same time that Yuwali had been born, but in a different world.

Posterity will prove the truth

> It will be apparent from the advances made by science in the methods of warfare that the guided weapon is a reality which we must face, that should war unfortunately occur again, we could be subjected to attack by guided weapons possessing far greater range and destructive power than the V1 and V2 used against England.
>
> Should we be forced to defend ourselves against aggression, it is imperative for us to ensure that we attain and maintain the technical initiative in the development of the scientific weapons with which we can be certain a future war would be waged.[54]

Even before the end of the Second World War, the British and Australian governments were discussing the siting of a missile range in Australia. The use of the V1 flying bombs and V2 rockets, launched by Germany against Britain, had foreshadowed the future of long-range and even intercontinental warfare. Both countries wished to arm themselves with this new class of weapon.

In late 1945 the Australian Minister for Defence, John Dedman, made the first official announcement of joint discussions on the possibility of using central Australia as a testing ground for guided missile research. By June 1946 there were reports of Britain's plans to locate the rangehead at Mount Eba in South Australia, and on 22 November 1946, Dedman confirmed Cabinet's decision to establish the guided missile range.

John Dedman, the Commonwealth Minister for Defence. PHOTO: NATIONAL LIBRARY 1947

The range was envisaged to extend diagonally north-west across the continent, from the rangehead at Mount Eba to the coast near Port Hedland. The rangehead was later moved to Woomera, however, because it was closer to established settlement, the transcontinental railway and some temporary lakes which gave an immediate supply of potable water.[55]

The range was to be constructed in two stages. The first stage was to cover only 300 miles, running north-west from Woomera but stopping short of the Central Aboriginal Reserve. The second stage would ultimately be extended through the Western Desert, over the Canning Stock Route and Percival Lakes, and on to a section of the northern coast of Western Australia between Port Hedland and Broome (later declared the Talgarno Prohibited Area).

In his statement to the House of Representatives in November 1946, John Dedman explained the limited impact of the full range:

> Except for a few pastoral leases at the firing point end in South Australia, the Central Aboriginal Reserves and a few more pastoral leases adjacent to the Ninety Mile Beach

> in Western Australia, the area of the range and that which it is proposed to reserve for eventual extensions is largely uninhabited.[56]

He also promised that the government would do '. . . everything possible to safeguard the aborigines from contact, or encroachment on any area of special significance to them'.[57]

This assurance, affirming the policy of segregation and protection which then applied to nomadic Aboriginal people, was in response to a vocal body of public opposition to the range plans. As soon as news emerged that the range was to be developed over unallocated Crown land and parts of the reserves, a small but active number of people supporting Aboriginal interests rose in opposition to it. They held public meetings, made representations to members of parliament and gained prominent press coverage.

The public opposition clearly concerned the chief executive officer of the Long Range Weapons Organisation, JF Evetts, who had been appointed by the British government[58]:

> [T]here is serious opposition being engineered, which is assuming larger proportions every day, on the ground of interference with the aborigines . . . So serious is the pro-aborigine movement that I am flying to Canberra tomorrow to spend Friday with the UK High Commissioner to discuss this problem.[59]

This public reaction prompted the federal Cabinet to try to defuse any sense of a threat to Aboriginal people. In their endorsement of the creation of the range, they added a recommendation:

> In view of the numerous representations which have been received in regard to the safety and welfare of aborigines in the proposed range area, it is suggested that the Australian Guided Projectiles Committee might be requested to report specifically on the measures necessary to ensure this.[60]

Prof AP Elkin. PHOTO: NATIONAL LIBRARY OF AUSTRALIA, 1955

The committee met in early 1947. As requested by Cabinet, they had co-opted a number of government specialists in Aboriginal affairs: the director of Native Welfare for the Northern Territory (a Commonwealth employee), the secretary of the Aborigines Protection Board in South Australia and the former commissioner of Native Affairs in Western Australia. Finally, they added the pre-eminent white authority of the time on Aboriginal culture, Professor AP Elkin of Sydney University. Elkin had long been an advocate for a shift in government policy away from segregation of Indigenous people and towards their assimilation into mainstream white-Australian society.

The committee had specific instructions from the Minister for Defence to hear two of the most influential opponents of the Woomera Range, Dr Charles Duguid and Dr Donald Thomson.

Dr Duguid was a physician who had worked for decades with Indigenous people in central Australia. He was instrumental in setting up the mission at Ernabella, and had organised much of the opposition to the range in South Australia. He sought preservation of the traditional Aboriginal way of life, particularly on the central reserves — a vast body of land straddling the Northern Territory, South Australia and Western Australia — which would be most affected by the range.

Dr Thomson was an anthropologist. He disagreed with Elkin's strong support for assimilation, advocating a form of self-determination. He saw the siting of the range as 'the violation of one of [the] last great strongholds' of the Indigenous people of central Australia.[61] Thomson was later to claim:

> I was invited, with Dr Duguid, to attend part of one meeting of the Committee. I received no warning and the invitation was conveyed to me by telephone only the night before the meeting. I had no adequate knowledge of the facts which were before the Committee and when I went into the room it was clear that my presence and that of Dr Duguid was a mere formality in deference to the instructions of the Minister.[62]

While Duguid objected to the range passing over the central reserves, his principal concern was not rockets and bombs falling from of the sky and onto the reserve: he was chiefly opposed to the observation posts that would be strung along the range. The construction and staffing of these posts would, he argued, inevitably lead to contact between range staff and the Indigenous inhabitants of the reserves, contact which would change the traditional life of the Aboriginal people.

Dr Charles Duguid at a public meeting, showing a map of the rocket trajectory. PHOTO: THE NEWS, ADELAIDE, 8 AUGUST, 1946

Thomson shared this concern about the effects of contact, and had particular concerns about the impact of the military's presence on Indigenous people. This was based on his service during the war in charge of a native patrol in the north of Australia. Thomson argued against the safeguards proposed by the committee, quoting 'concrete examples' from his personal experience to support his belief that the range 'must mean the doom of the aborigines in the territory concerned'. His argument was not, he realised, 'palatable to the committee'.[63]

Meanwhile, a member of the House of Representatives had given parliamentary voice to the concerns of the opponents of the range. On 16 December 1946, Mrs Doris Blackburn[64], an independent MP, had proposed a motion in the House in the following terms:

> That in the opinion of this House —
>
> 1. the proposal to establish a rocket bomb testing range in Central Australia is an act of injustice to a weaker people who have no voice in the ordering of their own lives; is a betrayal of our responsibility to guard the human rights of those who cannot defend themselves, and a violation of the various Charters that have sought to bring about world peace; and
> 2. such action is against the interests of the people of the Commonwealth. [65]

John Dedman publicly announced that the committee had been briefed to provide expert advice to the government in order to assuage such fears. In a statement released in response to Mrs Blackburn's motion, he said:

> It had always been appreciated that the construction of the range, as proposed, would interfere to an extent with inhabitants, either white or aboriginal, now living within the area selected, but, from the point of view of interference with aborigines, similar objections would apply in any other area that might have been chosen . . .
>
> I was very conscious of the need to do everything possible to safeguard the aborigines from contact, or encroachment on any area of special significance to them, and that instructions had been given that the Australian Committee on Guided Projectiles was to consult . . . and report on the measures necessary to ensure their safety and welfare.[66]

Dedman went on to quote the committee's conclusions. These outlined the extent and methods of protection that would be accorded to Indigenous people affected by the activities of the range. They included an illuminating exposition of their assumptions about the future of the Indigenous inhabitants of the desert:

> In the light of its examination [the committee] reached the following conclusions:
>
> (a) De-tribalisation of the aborigine is inevitable, and, provided the contacts brought about by the construction and use of the range are controlled and of a wholesome nature, their only effect would be putting forward the clock regarding de-tribalisation by possibly a generation.
>
> (b) On the basis of the statement of proposed activities as affecting the Central Aborigines Reserves, satisfactory arrangements can be made to ensure the safety and welfare of the aborigines in the proposed range area . . .
>
> (d) Interference with the aborigine by reason of . . . (iii) construction of roads within the Central Reserves . . . can be discounted entirely, as none of these courses of action is contemplated . . .
>
> (f) Any acceleration of the de-tribalisation which is now taking place, or interference with the habits of the aborigines and areas of special significance to them, which have existed from time immemorial, can be controlled by the appointment of patrol officers. Such patrol officers should be selected by the appropriate aborigine authorities, the Commonwealth providing the requisite funds.[67]

Dedman deferred to the expertise of both the committee (rather than that of its critics) and the state representatives to absolve the Commonwealth of any responsibility, accepting the committee's conclusions in full:

> From the foregoing, it will be seen that, in the opinion of those most competent to judge, it is considered that the construction of the range as proposed will not introduce effects detrimental to the aborigines, and therefore the proposal to establish the range cannot be considered rightly as an act of injustice to a weaker people who have no voice in the ordering of their own lives.
>
> As the authorities on native affairs representing the Commonwealth, South Australian and Western Australian Governments and Professor Elkin are satisfied with the measures proposed to be taken for safeguarding the interests and welfare of aborigines, the Government has accepted the conclusions of the report with which these authorities were associated.
>
> If, as has been stated, no injustice to the aborigines is involved, there can be no charge of betrayal of our responsibility to guard the human rights of those who cannot defend themselves, and therefore this aspect does not require further explanation other than to say that, as our efforts are aimed to ensure the preservation of our democratic ideals and mode of life, our actions, far from being a betrayal, are in the common interests of both white and black Australians.[68]

Dedman's statement, adopting the committee's recommendations, was to be the formal articulation of policy for the Commonwealth's treatment of traditional Indigenous people affected by the activities of the range for the next twenty-five years.

One committee member (FH Moy, the director of Native Affairs in the Northern Territory) illustrated its assimilationist disposition when writing to Elkin with criticism of Thomson:

> [T]he matter of preserving tribal institutions and customs within the framework of our society . . . savours too much of keeping a live museum and there are certain of our friends who dread the thought of the Australian aboriginal becoming a normal citizen — one in particular would miss [Thomson's] occasional ill-informed articles in the Melbourne *Herald*.[69]

Duguid later wrote that both he and Thomson, 'realised that reason and argument would have no effect against closed minds . . . The military mind was made up long ago. In my opinion, the people of Australia have been fooled'.[70]

Thomson publicly attacked the good faith of the government:

> I consider that the official statement made subsequently is a serious misrepresentation of the facts and of my own warning as to the inevitable outcome of the policy now proposed by the Government . . . Posterity will prove the truth.[71]

The committee had not dealt with the concerns raised, but had proposed a policy of controlled disruption of the lives of the area's traditional inhabitants.

The rec ommendations effectively entrusted the protection of the interests of Indigenous people to two patrol officers, yet to be appointed.

Soon after publication of Dedman's statement, Professor Elkin moved to justify the committee' s recommendations and outlined what he (and presumably the committee) intended that the patrol officers would actually do:

> The committee is to appoint, as soon as the project is under way, trained and recommended patrol officers whose business it will be to know all about the Aborigines within the stretches of the range for which each will be responsible. Such patrol officers will be kept fully informed as to times and range of experiments. Amongst other tasks, they will be required to warn Aborigines who are likely to be near the part of the range where and when projectiles are expected to fall, to avoid it for the time being. Those of us who know the Aborigines in the central areas of Australia and their way of life know that this can be done. [72]

An insurance policy

> [T]he sustained opposition which came from many parts of Australia had at least one good result. The Federal Government created a special appointment, an officer who would be responsible for the care and protection of the Aborigines in the Reserve and who would ensure that they had proper explanation and warning when rockets were to be fired. The appointment went to a man who was ideally fitted for the task: Mr Walter MacDougall.[73]

Walter MacDougall came to Woomera in November 1947. His appointment as native patrol officer (NPO) was one of the first in the weapons project. As a superintendent from the Woomera Range was later to say, he was 'an insurance policy'.[74]

MacDougall was a gentle, retiring, but quietly capable man. Very tall, with rough red hair, he had lived and worked in remote parts of Australia for fifteen years. He knew the desert well, navigated by the sun, and could travel vast distances safely. In his time as a patrol officer he regularly complained to his superiors about being sent into the desert with people who lacked appropriate equipment or any bush skills, yet worked easily with them.

Walter MacDougall. PHOTO: NORMAN TINDALE, AR̲A IRITITJA

Already forty at the time of his employment by the Weapons Research Establishment (WRE), MacDougall had worked in Aboriginal missions since 1931, first in north-western Australia at Port George IV (Kunmunya) and then at Ernabella Mission in central Australia. He had a great respect for Aboriginal people, and was passionately committed to their welfare. Having learned some Pitjantjatjara in his time at Ernabella, he had practical knowledge of the life, society and customs of Indigenous desert people.

MacDougall was employed on the recommendation of the secretary of the South Australian Aborigines Protection Board, based on his bush skills and experience.

Little, beyond being given the title of Native Patrol Officer, was done to define the job. The lack of detailed guidelines gave the new NPO scope to shape his role and he defined it broadly, consistent with what he saw as the breadth of the committee's original concern and good faith:

> I interpreted discussions at the time of my appointment to indicate that as the Range developed, I would be the aborigines' representative, and that my duties would be to:-
>
> (a) Prevent needless or avoidable interference with their way of life, thus minimising the inevitable acceleration of detribalisation.

> (b) Control contacts by selection of personnel as far as possible, and by accompanying reconnaissance and working parties which are likely to contact aborigines within and without the Reserve.
> (c) Plan measures necessary for their moral and physical welfare.
> (d) Patrol areas where contacts have been made.
> (e) Work in conjunction with State authorities where aborigines under their control are concerned.[75]

It would become apparent that his views on what would constitute 'needless or avoidable interference' and 'measures necessary for their moral and physical welfare' were more encompassing than those held by his masters.

MacDougall had first-hand experience of the gradual movement of nomadic Aboriginal people from the deserts to points of white habitation on the fringes: cattle stations, missions, ration depots and, on the far edges, towns. This shift had been occurring in the central deserts for fifty years, steadily increasing during the 1940s. In the west of the Western Desert the movement had come later, with a few people moving in to ration depots and stations in the 1930s, then a major wave in the 1940s. Nevertheless, significant numbers of people still lived a completely traditional life in the remote parts of the desert, many having had no direct contact with Europeans.

MacDougall's experience of this movement towards permanent settlement around 'whitefella' resources informed his views on the dangers that ensued for nomadic people. His early reports sought to inform his superiors about what he saw as the greatest threat posed by the range: uncontrolled contact by people who lacked the knowledge and experience to minimise harm.

> The tribe is held together by the elders of the tribe enforcing laws, evolved through the ages . . . Some of these laws are contrary to those found necessary for the well-being of the white race, and are therefore broken down of necessity when contact is made . . . They break down on contact with whites because:
> 1. it is seen that white people suffer no magical harm when they unwittingly offend against the law;
> 2. they can claim police protection from normal results of crimes against the tribe. Because of great distances to be travelled, the police will not enforce the law for petty crimes, but will do so for big offences such as murder.[76]

And,

> Contact with white men has so far resulted in degeneration of the aborigines. It is only necessary to patrol areas where detribalisation has started to see this process in full operation and to realise how many natives now exist without working or hunting. Because of their own socialistic way of life, the generosity of their friends and friends' employers, and government rations, they inevitably adopt the routine of moving from Station to Station for free food. The result is laziness, uselessness and

> loss of self-respect. They neither hunt nor work for their food and the evils of unemployment of able-bodied men are never brought home to them. [77]

Up until the mid-1950s the Woomera Range only extended 300 miles, or 480 kilometres. Its range fell entirely within South Australia, well away from the central reserves, and with limited intrusion into the desert. In the early years of his employment MacDougall's activities were similarly limited. He provided a variety of services to Aboriginal people in the vicinity of Woomera — particularly on local stations — and conducted field trips down the range to identify the numbers and situation of Aboriginal people within the range, and to determine the range's effect on their lives and any arrangements necessary for their welfare.

He also had an eye to the future extension of the range into country that was largely unknown, whose Indigenous inhabitants lived a traditional nomadic life. Prior to a 1952 reconnaissance trip, which would extend into the central reserves, he outlined the purpose of the trip:

> The objects I have in view are as follows:
> (a) Discover the number of aborigines living in that area.
> (b) How many of them, and to what extent they will be affected by future Range activity, paying special attention to ceremonial grounds and hunting areas within the Reserve. Ceremonial grounds and the homeland of different tribal groups are of paramount importance to tribal communities; hunting grounds to the physical welfare of the individuals.
> (c) If possible, determine the existence or non-existence of a tribe alleged to be living west of the Everard Range, whom it is reported have made very little contact with whites.
> (d) Collect information that will indicate what measures will be necessary in the future to ensure the welfare of abo communities within and without the Central Reserve; particularly the affect [sic] of contacts made by survey and working parties and the manning of [observation posts].[78]

One of MacDougall's primary responsibilities was to clear people from danger on the range at firing time. He worked to ensure that Aboriginal people were shepherded away from testing areas that could be dangerous. While this responsibility initially focused on the rocket range, it was later extended to cover the nuclear tests at nearby Maralinga, when the British and Australian governments embarked on that separate program of firings from 1956.

MacDougall and a second NPO were responsible for clearing the area in which nuclear devices would be detonated, and the wider area exposed to contamination from radioactive fallout. With their limited resources, the vast area that required protection and the limited knowledge of nuclear explosions and fallout at the time, the NPOs were not able to protect Indigenous people from harm. That history has been documented by a Royal Commission, articles and books. (The unhappy story

MacDougall with his International truck. PHOTO: BILL EDWARDS, ARA IRITITJA

of the nuclear testing program at Maralinga is outside the scope of this book.)

In 1955, when the extension of long-range testing into Western Australia became imminent, MacDougall had his first substantial cause for concern about its effect on desert people. The range would now cover a vast portion of Western Australia, cutting across the Gibson, Great Sandy and Little Sandy deserts.

To support the extension, the WRE decided to locate a permanent weather station 600 miles (965 kilometres) along the firing line from Woomera. The station would provide weather information for the nuclear tests at Maralinga and act as an observation post for the planned firings over the full length of the range.

The weather station was to be located in the Rawlinson Ranges in the Western Australian portion of the central reserves, and required roads to be built across the reserves. Both the building of the station and the creation of the roads were clearly contrary to the undertakings made by the Minister for Defence in 1947, a fact that was recognised by WRE's chief engineer:

> Any suggestion of road entering native reserve . . . will raise difficult administrative problem . . . When the original fuss was on about the Aborigines, in relation to guided weapons, the Minister for Defence stated that we would not be constructing roads in aboriginal reserves . . . Your proposed road would appear to violate the spirit of the Ministerial statement. I feel that we could obtain approval of SA Govt if we are sure we must have this road as you suggest it. Before approaching them could you please confirm that we really do need this road into the reserve.[79]

This was the first real test of the government's policy to minimise the impact of the range on nomadic Aboriginal people. The early reconnaissance plans for the range extension heralded the start of a brawl between MacDougall and his political masters. His increasingly strident correspondence on the subject shows MacDougall's passion and his philosophy on the proper treatment of nomadic Indigenous people. His sense of betrayal by WRE, as he watched principle abandoned for expedience, was palpable.

On 11 October 1955 he fired a memo to the range superintendent:

> It is extremely unfortunate that any reconnaissance or establishment is necessary in that area as there are primitive aboriginals obviously avoiding any contacts living there. Any essential post established should be outside the Reserve and as far from the boundary as possible, no matter how unsuitable the country, providing the purpose of the establishment is achieved. Problems, if any, must be faced from the aborigines' point of view or as near to the desires of these people as can be determined. No decision as to where posts are to be established or decisions on supply routes can justly be made before thorough investigation of the effect on natives has been made.
>
> My appointment as Native Patrol Officer was made because of a general protest from the public or by those persons of the general public who concern themselves with aboriginal welfare, to ensure that a minimum of adverse effect could result from Range activity and establishment — the above to be carried out according to the generally accepted principles of best interests of natives; this is segregation as far as possible, controlled contacts, and all possible precautions to be taken to prevent acceleration of detribalisation. I believe that this policy is not in the best interests of the people concerned, but it is the principle laid down.
>
> The forcible entry into this area and establishment of posts, with the inevitable contacts, along with [some mining activity then taking place in the Reserves] . . . completely destroys the Reserve as an area of any value to primitive aborigines and their way of life.[80]

MacDougall went to the press to vent his anger:

> The demands of prospectors and, to a lesser extent, of Defence are mortally threatening one of the last refuges of Australia's primitive aborigines . . .
>
> This was asserted yesterday by a well known native patrol officer Mr Walter MacDougall [who] said:
>
> 'About 2500 natives from SA, WA and the Northern Territory use these reserves, which cover scores of thousands of square miles and were intended to be inviolable to the white man. A few hundred of the natives have had virtually no contact with whites . . .
>
> 'I believe that what is happening to these natives is contrary to the spirit of the declaration of human rights in the United Nations charter. If no check is possible, they seem doomed to increase the number of displaced persons in the world — to become prideless, homeless vagabonds, living by begging, stealing and government handouts. Their only crime, of course, is that they are descendants of a strong, dignified, stone-age race not capable of adjusting themselves easily to our civilisation without special help . . .
>
> 'Whenever the white man finds something of value to him in any aboriginal area the aborigines are pushed aside,' he added bitterly.[81]

The WRE controller, HJ Brown, intervened and sought the urgent advice of Eric Cook, the secretary of the board of WRE:

> I have managed to have the article stopped temporarily, and it is urgent that we tell the newspapers whether they can proceed, or failing being able to stop them altogether of the changes . . . that we would wish made. [82]

Cook replied immediately:

> Your action in withholding publication is confirmed. Please take whatever action you consider necessary to continue the ban on publication until further advised. The Secretary is discussing the matter with the Minister immediately.[83]

The response was very sharp. Two days later, Brown issued an official directive to MacDougall, which came with the weight of both the minister and the secretary, to toe the line:

> I now wish to pass on to [MacDougall] the following official instruction:-
>
> No written or verbal discussions on affairs connected with Mr McDougall's work are to be passed on to members of State Govt Depts or any other body but must be communicated to me . . . for any necessary action to be taken by me.
>
> Mr McDougall is to realise that he is a Cmwlth officer and is bound to put any complaints concerning native affairs to me as head of the establishment and not to any other person outside of the Dept.
>
> This instruction comes not only from me but is being issued on behalf of the Secretary and the Minister of Supply.[84]

However, after accompanying the reconnaissance team to the Giles site, MacDougall's report to the superintendent on 17 December 1955 demonstrated his increasing anger and frustration:

> This so called reconnaissance was a rush trip made by [several WRE and state staff] to a pre-selected spot in the Rawlinson Ranges . . . There was no attempt to select a site that would interfere as little as possible with Aborigines occupying the Rawlinson Range.[85]

MacDougall supported his concerns by quoting an old Aboriginal man — one of a party camping close to the reconnaissance party — with whom he had spoken:

> The old man enquired for what purpose the strangers had visited his country and expressed anxiety when told that they intended establishing a post. The word used means fear (I have not a word for troubled or anxious but I gathered that he was more than just afraid. That he was worried and concerned). [86]

In fact, there were to be direct and early casualties of this incursion, in a tragic demonstration of the dangers MacDougall saw as flowing from contact. Within months of the trip MacDougall found a community in the area suffering from 'very bad colds' — which he believed had been picked up from the white men — and mourning an old man's death.[87]

MacDougall questioned the good faith of the Commonwealth Government and opposed the proposed siting of the weather station:

> The actions and attitude of the reconnaissance party also shows that there is no intention of fulfilling or seriously regarding the promises made by the Commonwealth to the Peoples of Australia. Mr Barr [actually Mr Bahr, of the Meteorological Branch of the Department of the Interior] stated that it was intended to interest and encourage personnel to prospect as a hobby thus further invading country reserved for Aborigines.
>
> Mr Barr also stated that some area in the Warburton or adjacent Ranges [i.e. outside the reser ve] would be just as good if not better than the site selected for forecasting weather.
>
> In view of this statement and of the fact that [a portion of the reser ve had been excised by the Western Australian government for the Giles project] . . . there is now no reason to establish a post or build roads or airstrips within the reserve. Any establishment in country which is necessary to Aborigines and their present way of life is contrary to their best interests, but where contacts have already been made is much the less of two evils.[88]

Aboriginal people living in the Rawlinson Ranges.
PHOTO: CHARLES DUGUID, ARA IRITITJA

This report was followed up with a sharply worded submission to the superintendent, outlining his sense that the WRE was acting in bad faith:

> When the Long Range Weapons project was first mooted there was genuine concern both in and outside Australia for the welfare of tribal Aboriginals . . .
>
> The Government had a choice of two alternatives:
>
> (a) to keep the tribal Aboriginals segregated
>
> (b) to make contacts — thereby automatically ensuring their detribalisation — and train them to fit into our civilisation and be useful and self-respecting citizens.
>
> The Government decided on the first alternative and issued a statement which, inter alia, included promises that:
>
> (a) there would be no roads in the reser ves
>
> (b) contacts would be made only by 'fully qualified native patrol officers'.
>
> In my opinion the wrong decision was made since it is obviously impossible to keep tribal Aboriginals segregated forever. However, it has been my duty to act in

> accordance with the decision taken, though I have made representations to the Aborigines Department proposing a change to the other alternative.
>
> I understand that the policy has now been changed though oddly enough I, as Dept. of Supply Native Patrol Officer, was not informed nor has it been promulgated in any way. The new policy appears to be a third and disastrous alternative whereby contacts are made by completely unqualified persons and no provision is made to train the Aboriginals to fit into the twentieth century. The result is certain to be a degeneration from self-respecting tribal communities to pathetic and useless parasites — it has happened so often before that surely we Australians must have learnt our lesson. [89]

As he often did, MacDougall finished with an appeal to the moral perspective that clearly underpinned his sense of his and the WRE's responsibilities:

> In addition, there is an ethical aspect in that the country under discussion belongs to the tribe and is recognised as such by other tribes. However, we propose to take it away from them and give nothing in return — we might as well declare war on them and make a job of it. It is considered we are morally bound to take some action to fit them for de-tribalised life. [90]

The Woomera Range superintendent, Jack Newman, in a teletype to the WRE controller, recommended that MacDougall examine the Giles project 'from a native welfare angle', adding:

> This follows from the aspect of his job that he is an insurance policy ensuring that the Department does not come under public criticism for interfering with tribal natives and that the government's original promises are not inadvertently broken. (Incidentally I would respectfully suggest that this angle has rather been overlooked lately).[91]

As a result of MacDougall's continuing and angry protestations, controller Brown prepared a full memorandum to the Department of Supply's chief scientist, Alan Butement:

> It is necessary to advise that the Native Patrol Officer, Mr W.B. MacDougall, is far from satisfied with a number of decisions . . . It should be emphasised that it is possibly not just a matter of Mr. MacDougall as an individual being concerned, but the fact that he regards himself as specially appointed by the South Australian government to look after the welfare of aborigines, coupled with the fact that it is known there are a number of other people in the community who would be only too ready to publicly raise objections to certain steps which are being taken . . . [I]t is clear that in his present state of mind, he is likely to take some extreme step to draw attention to what he regards as a breach of the promises made by the Minister for Defence in his statement to the House in 1946 [92] . . . In case he does take such an extreme step . . . I feel it expedient that you and the Secretary should be brought up to date on the steps which have been taken to date. [93]

Brown outlined the proposals for the location of the weather station and the construction of access roads, together with MacDougall's view that there had been a change of policy which had not been announced to the public. He repeated his warning that there was the potential for embarrassment.

Butement had come from Britain to Australia at the establishment of the project in 1947, and was now in charge. His reply was firm, laced with vitriol:

> It appears that the Native Patrol Officer is viewing his responsibilities in a different manner to that of this Department . . . [In] his sincere desire to protect the welfare of Aborigines, Mr. McDougall [sic] has overlooked the reasons for his appointment . . .
>
> Your memorandum discloses a lamentable lack of balance in Mr. McDougall's outlook, in that he is apparently placing the affairs of a handful of natives above those of the British Commonwealth of Nations . . .
>
> [H]e is out of step with current thinking, and the sooner he realises his loyalty is to the Department which employs him, and which is glad to take his advice on matters on which he is an expert, the sooner his state of mind will be clarified, and he will be enabled to carry out his duties without any sense of frustration or disappointment, as is evident in your assessment.
>
> There are doubtless many tasks upon which Mr McDougall's services can be more profitably engaged than in debating whether or not the policy enumerated by the Minister for Defence in 1946 is being correctly interpreted . . . Mr McDougall might be instructed to get on with the job within his sphere of activity, and leave policy matters to those whose responsibility they are.[94]

Brown forwarded this letter to Jack Newman, the range superintendent to whom MacDougall reported, along with the following instructions:

> I am enclosing a copy of memorandum received from the Chief Scientist . . . This letter is for your information and it is suggested that you should not pass on a copy or show this to Mr MacDougall, unless it's necessary to do so.
>
> I think it is sufficient at the moment to make it quite clear to Mr MacDougall that he has sole responsibility to W.R.E. and that he has no right to make any statements to the press or to write on any policy matters to any organisation outside our own. As long as he keeps within this general framework and sends any complaints he has through you to me for such action as we consider necessary, I think there can be no further difficulties arising.[95]

It appears that this was the end of MacDougall's objections. Ultimately, the Western Australian Department of Native Welfare excised 250 000 acres (101 171 hectares)[96] from the reserve to support the location of the weather station, to be known as Giles.

Controller Brown chose to enlarge an imperfectly sited but existing prospecting track for WRE's equipment to be taken in. In this way, he felt the WRE had complied with the spirit of the 1946 ministerial.[97] Nearly thirty years later, Brown said that, 'No firm long-term policy could ever be obtained and so no-one really knew how to act . . . Ministers' views were never definite except to say that the joint project must not be upset'.[98]

This whole episode was a defining moment in MacDougall's relationship with the WRE, and in the establishment of the latter's policy and practice in relation to Indigenous people. It appears from MacDougall's later reports that this fight settled, in his mind, the interpretation that the Commonwealth government would place on the 1947 'promises'. He no longer asserted his highly principled interpretation, which saw the interests of Aboriginal people as a paramount concern. He seems to have accepted that the government, while seeking to avoid direct harm to Aboriginal people, had little interest in the rigorous avoidance of damaging contact, particularly where avoidance of contact would frustrate or inconvenience the WRE.

Instead, MacDougall proposed that the Commonwealth (through WRE) take an active role in mitigating the effects of contact by creating opportunities for people affected by the range. The approach he advocated — setting up pastoral stations, training facilities and long-term tenure over workable land — was, in fact, closer to the style of controlled and supported assimilation that he had always preferred to what he saw as an unworkable policy of segregation. Where contact was inevitable, he felt that Australia owed the Indigenous people an obligation to set them up with a viable economic base which would ensure effective and dignified assimilation over a period of generations:

> The areas set aside have ceased to fulfil their purposes as hunting grounds, and should be developed in ways which will now be of benefit to those dispossessed and conquered peoples.[99]

For a time the WRE authorities entertained MacDougall's suggestion of the establishment (at Commonwealth cost) of a pastoral mission station, to compensate Indigenous people on the reserves affected by the range. Controller Brown actively supported MacDougall's proposal and sought a policy, 'for the future concerning the assimilation of the aborigines into station work throughout the country, rather than maintaining a central reserve with an impossible task of segregating them from the white people'.[100]

The scheme, which Brown also saw as a means of keeping nomadic people within known areas[101], was discussed sympathetically at senior levels within the Department of Supply. A contribution to the proposed stations from the British government was even considered. Ultimately, however, this came to nothing. Paul Hasluck, the Commonwealth Minister for Territories, who had responsibility for the Northern Territory, was firmly against the proposal on both philosophical and political grounds. The proposal, which would involve the Commonwealth Department of Supply, would blur what was currently his responsibility for Indigenous affairs in the Northern Territory.

Giles weather station under construction, 1956.
PHOTO: BILL ELLIOTT, ARA IRITITJA

The Commonwealth Government had demonstrated that its responsibility for the welfare of nomadic Aboriginal people did not extend beyond the avoidance of harm. It saw the welfare of Indigenous people as the direct responsibility of the state governments and was not disposed to independently fund any initiative in this field that would benefit inhabitants of the states. [102]

MacDougall correctly determined that the only people to whom he could look to take responsibility for ensuring the welfare and future of these nomadic people were those in state government. In W estern Australia, this was the Commissioner of Native Welfare, Stanley Middleton.

Beyond the confines of civilisation

> We in Western Australia have always worked on a policy of non-interference so far as our bush natives are concerned, and I think this is a wise policy because, until such time as we are going to offer them something better, we should not interfere with their present existence — even if it is only an existence.[103]

The terms of the federal government's policy for Woomera, spelt out by John Dedman in 1947, envisaged native patrol officers funded by the Commonwealth but pursuing the policy of the state or territory in which they operated. This solution recognised that responsibility for Aboriginal affairs rested with the states.

MacDougall therefore looked to Stanley Middleton, the Western Australian Commissioner of Native Welfare, for leadership in his protection of the interests of the Indigenous people still inhabiting the vast deserts of that state. He was, once again, to be disappointed.

Middleton had been appointed commissioner in 1948. He was a new broom, bringing with him the British Colonial Office system of native administration that he had learned in Papua. Over the next fifteen years he secured dramatic increases in funding for the portfolio, expanded and decentralised the staff and changed the guiding policy of the department from one of highly intrusive 'protection' to one of assimilation. He secured a shift in official focus from 'native administration' to 'native welfare' with the passage of the *Native Welfare Act 1954*. This replaced the *Aborigines Protection Act 1905*, which Middleton saw as abhorrent:

> We, who are charged with the unpleasant duty of administering it, regard it as repugnant to basic humanitarian and welfare principles, devoid of any common ground with the people we are trying to help and creative of more misunderstanding, dissatisfaction and abuse than any other piece of similar legislation known to the free world today.[104]

Middleton focused his administration on people already having significant contact

Commissioner of Native Welfare, Stanley Middleton, visiting the north-west of the state, October 1960.
PHOTO: UNIVERSITY OF WESTERN AUSTRALIA, BERNDT MUSEUM OF ANTHROPOLOGY

with the European world, and the manner of their assimilation into that society. He sought community respect for Indigenous people and their improved treatment, profoundly increasing departmental budgets and activities. But his policy on Indigenous people living a traditional desert life was confused and reactive. Throughout his tenure, from 1948 until 1962, this sector of the Indigenous population was served by a department that had little knowledge of them, no real policy no training, no understanding and no plan in relation to them. An uncomfortable remnant, their interests were best served by government inaction and their invisibility.

Immediately prior to Middleton's appointment, the official policy of 'protective non-interference' with nomadic people had been summarised in the department's annual report:

> [T]he central principles of the policy of this State [include]:
>
> Non-interference with full-blood tribal natives except in respect to medical attention or assistance as may be necessary. No objection is raised to the establishment of mission posts on native reserves as centres of relief or medical attention . . .
>
> Detribalisation is inevitable . . . Even so, we must lay a steadying hand on undue interference with tribal life by protecting tribal natives from molestation as far as possible, except to medical attention and food assistance as may be necessary when bush food is scarce through bad seasons.[105]

The central reserve was intended to be an 'inviolable' protected space that would enable nomadic people to live their traditional lives unhindered. By law, permits and verifications of health and good character were required to enter a reserve.

In practice, Western Australia's reserves served multiple political purposes. They enshrined the sentiment that traditional Indigenous life should be preserved and protected, despite the state government's official line that 'detribalisation was inevitable', which suggested that natural social processes would end that life. They held an inconvenient Indigenous population at arm's length from any demands on government resources, which arose as soon as they came in to a settlement. And, along with the missions and settlements that formed a 'buffer zone', they kept substantial numbers of Aboriginal people away from the politically embarrassing fringe settlements around towns.

In addition to the Western Australian portion of the central reserves, there were even larger tracts of the state that were vacant Crown land. Unknown numbers of Indigenous people lived and moved on this land 'beyond the confines of civilisation', as the department itself put it. The land was too arid to attract pastoralists. The only potential commercial interest was mining, but the lack of roads made the vast area difficult to access. This land, and the interests of the Indigenous people living on it, were to become increasingly significant after the rocket range was extended to the north-west coast in 1958.

Middleton's department concentrated on the welfare of Aboriginal people 'residing within the confines of white settlement'.[106] Their concerns were the

Native Reserve sign. PHOTO: BOB VERBURGT, DATE UNKNOWN

welfare of children, housing, health, hygiene and education. But the major focus of policy concern was the increasing number of people of mixed descent, the 'rapidly increasing hybrid population of the south'.[107]

There was a clear hierar chy of urgency in Middleton's mind. People of mixed descent who fell within the definition of 'native' in the Act (more than one-quarter part of Aboriginal descent) required urgent action. People of 'full' blood who were settled in contact with whites — in towns, government settlements and missions — were in less urgent need than those of mixed descent. Traditional, nomadic 'desert dwellers' were not a priority. On the whole, they could be left alone until, by coming in to settlements, they changed status and required attention.

MacDougall's appointment, with its focus on Indigenous inhabitants of the desert, was a bonus for the department. As the WRE increased its activities in the Western Desert, MacDougall provided the eyes and ears that the department lacked.

Once the weapons project announced its intention to extend the range to Broome, MacDougall and other WRE staff began to make regular reconnaissance trips into W estern Australia, including the central reser ve. Middleton facilitated these trips by giving MacDougall significant rights and powers under the W estern Australian legislation. He was appointed a Protector of Natives for W estern Australia, which empowered him to 'authorise any person other than a native to enter or remain, or be within the boundaries of a reser ve in Western Australia for any purpose whatsoever' and to 'exer cise any authority with natives of W estern Australia for their protection and welfare which is normally execised by a Protector of Natives in this State'.[108]

As a result of his appointment, MacDougall wrote reports on each trip into Western Australia to Commissioner Middleton, and additional submissions on issues to do with the welfare of nomadic desert people, including those in contact with missions. The department came to rely on his reports — and those of a second NPO, Robert Macaulay, appointed in 1956 — for information about the situation in the desert, as they quickly became the only white people with any significant and regular information on the state's desert areas and people.

MacDougall's reports to Middleton show his concern about the creation of new roads and the contact these incursions brought, hastening what he saw as a destructive process of unplanned desert clearance. He used his reports in an effort to enlist Middleton's support on issues where he felt that the activities of the WRE

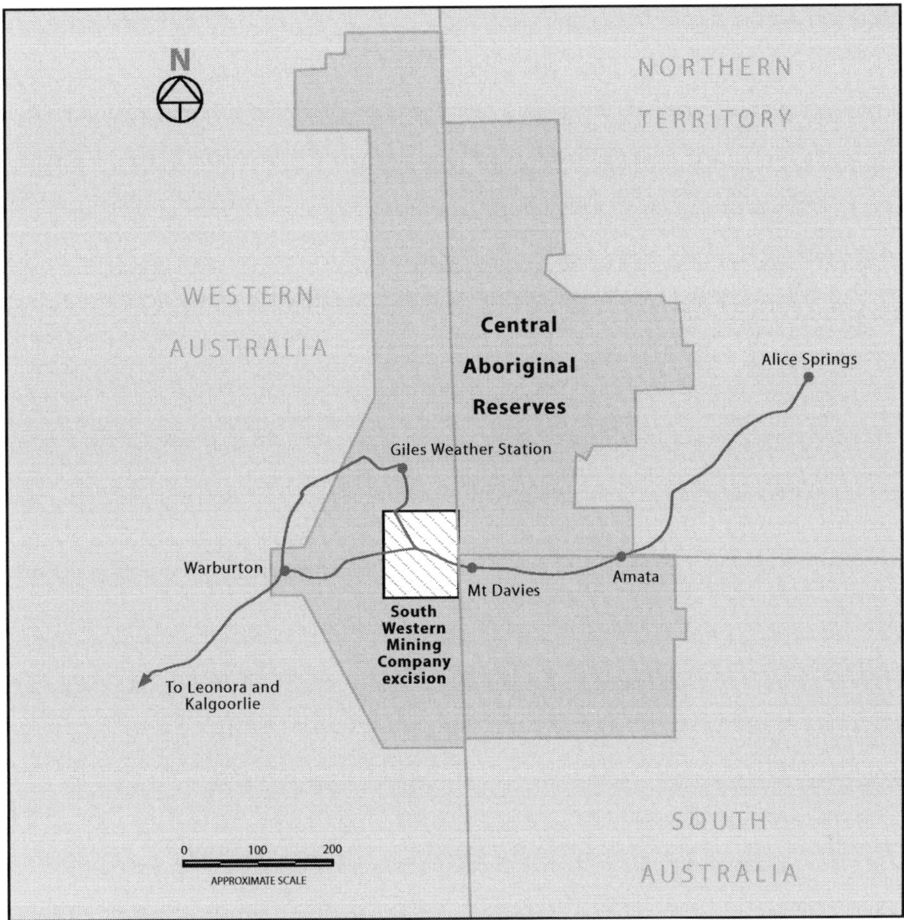

The Central Aboriginal Reserve (or Reserves) was the commonly used name for a group of reserves abutting one another at the borders of — and administered separately by — the Commonwealth (in relation to the Northern Territory), South Australia and Western Australia.

could endanger the welfare of W estern Australia' s Aboriginal people. The early reports also illustrate his assumption that the commissioner shared his views on the welfare of the desert people and what was required to protect their interests.

In 1955, after a patrol through the T omkinson Range, MacDougall wrote with alarm about an 'invasion of the Central Reser ve' by white interests. He was particularly concerned about the activities of the South W estern Mining Company, and the cumulative effect of roads that this company and the WRE had created:

> [I]t is now possible to drive along roads from Alice Springs to Kalgoorlie. This has opened up, and destroyed the value of, all the Reser ves South of the 26th Parallel as a Reserve.
>
> Almost all of the countr y that is of any value to human beings has been taken from the aborigines. This invasion shows that the policy of segregation is almost impossible to enfor ce and that no countr y, no matter how remote, can be kept for the sole use of the aborigines if the white man finds some profit in it or use for it. I

> realise that unless useful country is being used by the aborigines they cannot expect to keep it. For this reason I have for years advocated the establishment of pastoral holdings on which these people could be trained in stock work, station mechanics, etc., thus enabling them to earn what they want progressively and avoid increasing numbers of displaced people wandering about existing by begging, stealing and on Government benefits.
>
> I believe that the South Western Mining Co. are anxiously awaiting Western Australian legislation which will enable them to obtain a lease of a large area in Western Australia. Such legislation would further destroy any pretence of a Reserve for Stone Age aborigines. In view of this invasion of their territory, I believe a review of the best interests for aborigines' policy is urgently required.[109]

Middleton's reply summarised his position on the long-term outlook for the desert people. While sympathetic, the message was clear: it would be 'useless to attempt to hold back the economic development of large areas or attempt to forbid the use of them for scientific research'.[110]

On 18 November 1955, the Western Australian government excised almost five million acres (over 20 000 square kilometres) from its Central Aboriginal Reserve, granting a lease over it to the South Western Mining Company. MacDougall's intended response to Middleton's letter revealed his frustration with what he saw as further betrayal of the interests of Aboriginal people:

> I agree that it is useless to attempt to stop development of valuable land or the utilising of minerals, but I do object to it being done ruthlessly and without thought or concern for a people who have no say in the ordering of their way of life when contacts have been made, also to the very best parts of their reserve being withdrawn from their use and nothing effective being given in exchange.
>
> To withdraw the ranges would leave only sand and spinifex. Small mineral areas scattered along the ranges would be almost as bad because access roads would remove the difficulty of travel and entice adventurous tourists and other travellers.
>
> We had no difficulty in driving an International Utility from the Adelaide–Alice Springs Road to Mt. Davies and then to the W.A. Border. I believe there would be no great difficulty in driving any popular make of Utility from Alice Springs to Kalgoorlie. Because of the amazing speed with which the central reserve is being opened I have initiated an attempt to draw the attention of the public to the fact that the central reserve does not now meet the needs of the Aboes occupying it.[111]

The above archived letter is marked as 'Copy for S/R', presumably being for the range superintendent, Jack Newman, to whom MacDougall reported. The letter is marked 'Not sent'. Either MacDougall thought better of his language, or Newman intervened.

Middleton's letter had also informed MacDougall that the WRE's Senior Range Reconnaissance Officer had been granted the status of superintendent for the

Western Australian portion of the reserve to assist the reconnaissance teams in the area of the proposed Giles weather station. This appointment vested significant power in the WRE employee, giving him power to approve entry of his staff into the reser ve at any time and effectively overriding MacDougall's powers. The news inflamed MacDougall, who sought to have the appointment withdrawn by citing the statements on Aboriginal welfare made by the Minister for Defence in 1946 and 1947, and the public outcry at the time.

Desert road, 1967.
PHOTO: BOB VERBURGT, AṞA IRITITJA

His protestations were in vain. The appointment stood; it was convenient for the WRE and uncontroversial as far as Middleton was concerned.

The WRE sent two representatives to Perth to meet with state government officials about the proposed weather station at Giles: FP O'Grady , the chief engineer, and TR Nossiter, the senior range reconnaissance officer. O'Grady and Nossiter met with the permanent heads of all the significant departments (that of the premier , of mines, and of lands), the Commissioner for Main Roads, and Middleton himself, representing the Department of Native Welfare.

The significance of this meeting is highlighted by the fact that a detailed report was prepared by HJ Brown, the WRE controller , for Alan Butement, the chief scientist. Brown' s report expresses surprise and even delight at the extent to which Middleton, behind closed doors and in the company of his peers, advocated opening up the desert, despite any conflicting interests of the Indigenous inhabitants:

> Very briefly the policy is to assimilate the natives into the white man's way of living as quickly as possible. The Government of W estern Australia is opposed to the idea of segregating aborigines and leaving them in their original tribal state. Mr Middleton explained that, generally speaking, the only persons in favour of leaving the aborigines in their original state are anthropologists. In practice the Government in this State found it was quite impossible to maintain segregation. The setting up of native reser ves from which white people were rigidly excluded was difficult to administer.[112]

Middleton appears to have given unequivocal support to the primacy of economic and scientific interests over preser vation of the integrity of the reser ve:

> The attitude of his Department towards mining or other use being made of the reserve was to encourage such happenings rather than the reverse . . . He stated that

Road into Giles, 1959. PHOTO: BILL EDWARDS, ARA IRITITJA

> should this Establishment ultimately desire to use part of the reserve he would recommend to the Minister that a suitable area of land be excised to meet this Establishment's needs. He could see no objections of any kind to the proposed use of land in the reserve for such a purpose as a meteorological station. In the case of other possible needs along the centre line and finally along the North West coast, he indicated that a similar policy would apply. The Government of Western Australia would be most unlikely to raise any objections to this Establishment setting up works of any kind in any aboriginal reserve should such sites be found to be desirable for technical and similar reasons . . .
>
> Summing up the position as regards aborigines in Western Australia therefore, the position is now clear that this Establishment can choose its site for technical reasons without regard to the existence of any aboriginal reserves in Western Australia. Naturally care will be taken to see that sites are chosen in reserves only when they are really necessary . . .
>
> The visit [of O'Grady and Nossiter] . . . yielded results that were very good indeed.[113]

Middleton's readiness to accommodate the WRE was further illustrated when MacDougall objected to the proposed siting of the Giles station. While on reconnaissance, MacDougall sent a message through the WRE to Middleton suggesting that Giles be sited south of the Rawlinson Range. He clarified his reasons in a signal to WRE:

> Reference keeping installations south of the [Rawlinson] range. Some reasons are:-
> 1. Area is homeland of primitive aboriginals.
> 2. North side of range is favourite hunting ground.
> 3. Supplies of water on north side plentiful.
> 4. To fulfil partly the intention of the Commonwealth Government not to speed up detribalisation it is necessary to keep south of the range. There is no reason why buildings, water bores etc., should be installed north of the range. If you require further reasons there are countless reasons (too long to signal), please advise and I will write.[114]

The range superintendent at Woomera, Jack Newman, forwarded MacDougall's views to Middleton. Newman also sent a telegram, forwarding an additional request for assistance sought by MacDougall from Middleton:

> Consider a decision as to what is to be done in detail for the abo's in this area urgently required. Suggest you or representative visit area at early date.[115]

Middleton's reply directly undermined MacDougall:

Robert Macaulay, Rawlinson Ranges, 1957. PHOTO: MACAULAY FAMILY COLLECTION

> Insofar as natives Western Australia concerned, MacDougall's demands not supported. Have every confidence your field personnel's ability preserve any native interests and property . . . Visit by me or representative not possible and in circumstances not considered warranted.[116]

In fact, the WRE controller appears to have accepted MacDougall's recommendations: despite the reconnaissance team recommending a site north of the Rawlinson Range, it was located to the south.[117]

After the establishment of Giles in 1956, the WRE employed a second Native Patrol Officer to be based at the station. Robert Macaulay was a young man, recently graduated from Sydney University with an anthropology degree. Middleton had sought the advice of Professor Elkin on the appointment; Elkin recommended Macaulay, his former student.

Middleton provided the new NPO with written instructions on policy for dealing with Aboriginal people in the Rawlinson Range area. Because the department had no staff in desert areas, these instructions constituted the most specific and comprehensive statement of Department of Native Welfare policy to that point in relation to Indigenous desert people:

> It is not desired to embark on a programme of distributing Government rations and clothing to these natives. They are self supporting in a manner which has sufficed them for generations and it is not intended to sap their independence by encouraging them to rely on Government handouts. In cases of extreme emergency (e.g. threatened starvation through droughts) it may be necessary to institute special measures. In such cases the situation should be fully reported without delay.
>
> Natives are to be discouraged from contact with the Meteorological station and certainly from any tendency to settle there. There is little they can learn to their benefit from such contact and it is undesirable that they should come to regard the station as a source of supply. Any tendency on the part of station staff to give away food etc. to the natives would therefore be discouraged.
>
> So far as possible, it is desirable that any contact which does take place should be cushioned in such a way that the natives may continue to live their normal existence without unnecessary interference . . .
>
> Take such measures as you deem practicable and necessary to prevent natives suffering physical harm from scientific tests . . .
>
> It is well to remember that the natives of this area are living in 'blackfella' country, where there is little likelihood of assimilation in any foreseeable time. Until

> the means of assimilation do exist, it is preferred that their customary way of life be disturbed as little as possible.[118]

This statement highlights a policy hole into which desert Aboriginal people fell. The department's general policy under Middleton was strongly directed to assimilation. However, this statement expounded an explicit segregationist policy, 'until the means of assimilation do exist'. While speaking in protectionist terms, it was clear that Middleton's protection extended only to the avoidance of direct physical harm to individual people, rather than to the avoidance of social or environmental harm that resulted from any cause other than 'unnecessary interference'. That phrase perhaps conveys the political essence of the Middleton approach: the judgement of what was 'necessary', and the perspective from which that judgment was exercised.

Within two years of the founding of Giles, it became clear from the reports of the NPOs that the station's presence was having a marked effect on the lives of the Indigenous people in the area. Macaulay repeated the suggestion that an active policy be instituted for these people, and added that, 'The native menfolk have expressed concern that their land may be denied them in the future'.[119]

Charles Duguid, who had originally warned about the consequences of WRE activities when opposing the creation of the range in 1947, felt that his concerns about cultural annihilation were being borne out:

> They are losing cohesion and in a generation will have ceased to exist, except as oddments here and there, without any hold on life, unless something is done at once. No Government has yet made any suggestion as to how the tribal aborigines of the Reserve are to be helped to meet the new situation.[120]

In August 1956, a new source of tension for Middleton's department emerged. An independent member of the state parliament, William Grayden, raised questions in the Legislative Assembly about the impact the atomic weapons tests at Maralinga in South Australia would have on Western Australia's Indigenous people, particularly in the desert areas, and the extent to which precautions for their welfare had been taken. He closed with a comment on what needed to be done for the safety of any people displaced by the testing:

> [I]f we have to interfere with the natives, let us not deprive them of their tribal grounds from which they obtain their livelihood without providing them with a satisfactory way of life. It is up to the Government of Western Australia to obtain special assistance from the Commonwealth and to do something for the natives. The Government should provide natives in those areas with alternative accommodation, adequate water supplies and officers to provide medical attention. These are really the three essentials.[121]

Middleton prepared a briefing note for his minister on Grayden's speech, commenting:

People from the Giles area gather round MacDougall's truck, 1959. PHOTO: BILL EDWARDS, ARA IRITITJA

> It is difficult to know what Mr. Grayden has in mind when he so frequently refers to the natives of this State being deprived of their tribal ground . . . nor what he means by 'providing them with a satisfactory way of life'. I am certain that for them the most satisfactory way of life is that which they now enjoy; freedom of movement over thousands of square miles irrespective of reserve, State or other boundaries . . . freedom from daily and inescapable contact with the civic, social and economic orders of 'modern civilisation'; freedom of thought, speech and action. To take these from them and herd them into any form of institution or settlement, however well-equipped, well-intentioned and efficient it may be is, in my opinion, imposing on them something more lethal in its immediate effect than the exploding of atomic bombs within their sight and hearing.[122]

However, as a result of Grayden's actions, a parliamentary select committee was established to investigate the condition of the Indigenous people in the Warburton and Laverton regions, including those around the Giles weather station. The committee's report painted an unhappy picture of their lot. Its recommendations included significant investment in a number of initiatives, including the sinking of wells, and funding a pastoral and training station in the area.

Middleton's comments on the report were largely scathing:

> The questions which come immediately to mind are whether this one area — about which the chairman of the committee has only a cursory first-hand knowledge — is to become the focal point of a major Government effort; why a few of an estimated total of six thousand natives in this State are to be subjected to special treatment at great cost to the exclusion, for financial reasons, of the others.[123]

Middleton's argument was disingenuous, at least in its presentation. The figure of 6000 desert inhabitants was a spurious, anachronistic guess that was a relic of old

Patrol members meet with local people at Mitiga rockhole during the Warburton controversy. PHOTO: UNIVERSITY OF WESTERN AUSTRALIA, BERNDT MUSEUM OF ANTHROPOLOGY

and unfounded departmental population estimates. (Middleton knew this, and downgraded the official estimate in 1959, precisely because it was manifestly excessive. Moreover, within two years he would be asserting to his minister that a conservative estimate of the population of the desert was 250, when a low figure suited his political ends.)

After listing what he saw as the insurmountable fiscal and practical obstacles to the committee's proposals, Middleton added a note of defensive outrage:

> It suits the writer [of the Report] to be relieved of administrative responsibility for a scheme which is so fraught with complexities and problems; the lack of confidence, however, irrespective of my qualities, qualifications and experience, is characteristic of the chairman and many other Members of Parliament of to-day in respect to Government officers; but it does not in any way shake my confidence in my ability nor in any way diminish my firm belief that I know more about natives and native administration than he or they ever will.[124]

Grayden continued to conduct a campaign in the Assembly to alleviate 'the plight of the natives in the inland desert areas' of the state. In mid-1957 he took up the publicised (but largely unfounded) case of about forty people in the vicinity of Well 40 on the Canning Stock Route, near the Percival Lakes, reported to be starving and in need of help. This was at the start of a particularly severe drought, which was to last until 1962.

Grayden's activities had little direct impact on the policy of Middleton's department. However, his forays precipitated a steady stream of florid and frequently ill-informed parliamentary and press activity over the next few years which created a public image of emaciated, starving and dehydrated Indigenous desert people. This image would quickly excite politicians' fears of public outrage, and was easily exploited by opposition members. This combination of image and opportunism would shape the political context of the rocket firing nearly eight years later, in 1964.

To bolster his opposition to Grayden's report, Middleton sought the advice of the anthropologist Professor Ronald Berndt. (Berndt had founded the departments of Sociology and Anthropology at The University of Western Australia.) In dismissing Grayden's assertions, Berndt addressed the vexed issue of intervention.

Berndt believed that any intervention at any level (from food drops during times of hardship, to sinking wells, to 'rounding them all up') could not be seriously contemplated until the size of the desert-dwelling population was more precisely known.[125] He repeatedly recommended that a formal survey be conducted to discover the number of people and their condition, from which policy recommendations to Middleton and the government could be made.

Despite its fundamental significance to policy and practice, Middleton's department had never made a realistic estimate of the number of people living a traditional life in these desert areas. Between 1930 and 1958, the figure was regularly estimated at around 1000, despite the evidence of sustained movement from the desert to missions and settlements on the fringes throughout this period. At the same time that Middleton provided the politically expedient figure of 6000 people, Berndt was independently estimating the population as 250.[126]

In 1958, Middleton was forced by pressure from the Premier's Department to make an accurate assessment of the desert population.[127] Middleton's main source of information on the subject was the Surveyor General's office, which held information from surveys undertaken by state and Commonwealth expeditions between 1954 and 1957. These surveys had occasionally reported sightings of or meetings with Aboriginal people in these remote areas. The surveyor general, WV Fyfe, confirmed the figure of 250 people (the majority along the Canning Stock Route), based on the notes of five surveyors who had worked in the area.[128]

In reality, there was little government information on which estimates could reliably be based. Certainly, reliance on sightings by surveyors was at best naive, in view of repeated advice from MacDougall that Indigenous people would not be seen unless they wished it.

The department's annual report of 1959 spoke of the difficulties in estimating the nomadic population. The figure of 10 000 'unclassified natives' cited in 1948 was reduced to 2000 people 'living beyond the confines of civilisation', though the report admitted that, 'it is not improbable that this figure may also be a liberal one'.[129]

The lack of knowledge about numbers was just one aspect of the department's lack of interest in or engagement with Indigenous people in the desert. Its estimates of and policy towards Indigenous inhabitants of the desert were reactive and expedient. The department lacked the staff, the knowledge, the resources, the policy and the desire to investigate and actively pursue the long-term interests of these people. It simply relied on the WRE to provide information and take action to protect the interests of people in the desert.

This was highlighted in the record of a meeting the WRE controller, HJ Brown, held with Middleton and his South Australian counterpart. 'I called a meeting with Bartlett of S.A. and Middleton of W.A. . . . to ascertain and explore any native affairs matters worrying them in respect to our operations . . .' wrote Brown to his chief scientist, Alan Butement. 'They expressed their satisfaction with all that we were doing. With our two officers we are doing more to look after the natives than they could hope to do themselves.'[130]

In the decade from Middleton's appointment in 1948 to 1957, no departmental staff conducted or participated in any formal survey of the situation of these nomadic people. While the department had welcomed the appointment of MacDougall and Macaulay by the WRE, the scope of their patrols was limited by WRE interests, the vastness of the Western Desert and the lack of roads into the desert area.

But these limitations were about to change. In 1958, the WRE foreshadowed the full extension of the range and firings to the north-western coast. For the first time, rockets were really to be shot across the desert. Life in the desert would never be the same.

The prohibited area

> Missiles are now to be fired 1,250 miles across tribal territor y.[131]

Up until this point, most controversy about the WRE's activities had centred on the construction of the weather station at Giles, its major incursion into the desert. In mid-1958, however, the WRE announced the extension of the range to its full length, a 200-mile-wide (322-kilometre) swathe, reaching across W estern Australia to the north-west coast.

The implications of the extension, raised publicly by critics and privately by the NPOs, highlighted the W estern Australian government' s policy vacuum towards the state's Indigenous people. They were largely invisible because of remoteness, uncontactable because of the lack of roads, and irrelevant because of the lack of conflicting interests. The range extension changed all of this, and the government was not ready. Middleton acquired a host of new headaches as the desert people developed a political profile.

The prospect of extending the range had been discussed as early as 1955. At that time, Middleton had expressed his full support for the WRE' s activities[132], despite any impact on Indigenous inhabitants. In an illuminating internal WRE report, the state government's representatives appeared more cir cumspect about the effects of the extended range on any European interests. Brown wrote:

> The W.A. Government has been active in developing interests in the north-west coast area. Any suggestion of dispossessing large pastoral companies would therefore be unpopular for a number of reasons. It . . . was clear from their attitude generally that they would be alarmed at the prospect of losing large amounts of the more valuable pastoral lands along the coast.[133]

The vast area of W estern Australia covered by the range prompted critics to charge that this land had effectively been ceded by the state to the Commonwealth, along with responsibility for Indigenous people in the area. Critics of the WRE' s activities had a new focus for their outrage, criticising both the federal and state governments.

Charles Duguid was once again at the forefront of the protest. He now focused on the huge area of unalienated Crown land through which the rockets would pass:

> Missiles are now to be fired 1,250 miles [2011 kilometres] across tribal territor y. The only safeguard allegedly to be taken is to warn native welfare officers of the tests 'to prevent nomadic tribes of aborigines on walkabout from entering the test area'. Such an operation would take an army of welfare officers . . .
>
> To permit this flagrant disregard of fundamental human rights to continue must bring condemnation upon the people of Australia and deny the moral right of

> this country to condemn Russia, South Africa, citizens of Little Rock, or any other people who fail to preserve basic principles of justice.[134]

In the wake of the publicity following Duguid's press release, the Commonwealth Department of Supply moved quickly to reassure the state government. The Commonwealth secretary wrote to the Western Australian Premier's Department:

> The area . . . contains, to the best of our knowledge, no 'resident' aborigines who would be inconvenienced by the declaration. Aborigines in the area are confined to station employees, who have already had a period of contact with Europeans, and upon whom the proposed prohibition would have no effect . . .
>
> It is quite wrong to say that a few hundred natives will be deprived of areas from which they have eked out a difficult existence. In this connection, your Mr Middleton could be more knowledgeable than we are.[135]

When a South Australian group of citizens wrote to the Minister for Supply to express its concern, he gave them a number of similarly sweeping reassurances:

> Ever since the Woomera Range was commenced in 1947, the Australian Government has had very much in mind the effect such a range might have on the aborigines .. . The areas chosen for Commonwealth defence operations have taken particular account of aboriginal welfare, and areas have been chosen where aborigines are few indeed — perhaps not at all. In other words, the areas selected have been those where absence of water and natural game has made it difficult for tribalised aborigines to live.
>
> [You] can therefore be assured that the Government is conscious, at all times, of the need for preserving the welfare of the Australian aborigine, and has taken every step to conduct its operations without interfering with aboriginal life and customs.[136]

The minister did not indicate the basis of his assertions about Indigenous life. Yuwali and her group, which still included the men at this time, as well as other family groups, were still active throughout the prohibited area.

The controversy caused some concern in the Premier's Department. Middleton was asked for detailed information on the effect of the range. The Department of Native Welfare had never undertaken a field patrol into the affected areas, took no current action to safeguard the welfare of people there, and had little real idea of the number of Aboriginal people in the area.

Acting on the information (received earlier from the Surveyor General's office) that there could not be more than 250 Indigenous people in the Western Desert, Middleton confidently reassured the premier's under-secretary that the controversy was a beat-up:

> The Press statement released by the Federal Council for Aboriginal Advancement is . . . uninformed and misleading . . . I can see no reason for alarm or concern on the natives' behalf because with the facilities we will have at our disposal through the

> Commonwealth [i.e. the two Native Patrol Officers], we can take every precaution for their safety.[137]

Middleton's assurance that two NPOs could effectively patrol an area larger than France, thereby fulfilling the state's responsibilities for the welfare of the desert inhabitants, was accepted by the premier.

But tensions were rising with the very patrol officers upon whom Middleton relied so heavily. The department's lack of detailed knowledge or settled policy became an increasing frustration for them. MacDougall and Macaulay were both well aware of the public criticism of the department and of the controversy that was likely to attend the range extension. They were concerned about the extent to which the criticism directed at the department might now be directed at the WRE and, specifically, onto themselves. Given that they were required to operate in accordance with state government policy, they were alarmed by what they saw as inconsistent, inappropriate or non-existent policies.

In a report from Macaulay to the range superintendent, he outlined some of the issues that would face the WRE in safeguarding Aboriginal people affected by the range extension.

> Considerable local interest is taken in what is referred to as 'the problem of the inland natives'. There is every indication that there are natives inhabiting the area inland from Eighty Mile Beach at least as far as the Canning Stock Route, but I am not aware if this poses any problem from the point of safety . . .
>
> These inland natives have already been subjected to publicity from Grayden[138], and now that the Range has extended it is to be expected that Grayden will switch to his theme of starving natives being violated and not assisted by the Department of Supply.
>
> It is considered essential that the inland natives on and around the 'Centre Line' [the line running along the centre of the rocket firing line] be contacted and information gained as to their physical condition, welfare requirements, if any, and their movements. This could occupy a large part of the winter of 1960 for two Native Patrol Officers.[139]

The extension of the range into Western Australia also prompted Macaulay to provide additional, confidential information to WRE management about the relationship between the NPOs and the state government. This was prompted by two things: a Commonwealth proposal to appoint a third NPO at Talgarno[140]; and the exasperating efforts of dealing with Middleton's 'sweeping statements' and the shifting sands of his department's policy. As Macaulay stated, 'Unfortunately, "policy statements" by Mr. Middleton cannot be relied upon, and as the Range develops, the policy is likely to be modified or changed completely'.[141]

He went on to highlight the increasing political tension between the Commonwealth and the state department, tension which was being actively fuelled by the academics upon whom Middleton relied for advice:

> I detected a feeling in the Native Welfare Department, Perth, that the State Department feels itself being bowed down and partly superseded by WRE interests. This attitude has been influenced and probably fostered by Drs. Ronald and Catherine Berndt of the University of Western Australia. Reference is made to their mimeographed publication, last paragraph, pp 14–16 [142], and I quote:
>
> *'What is significant, however, is the increasing spread of such control of native affairs by the Commonwealth Department of Supply, thus virtually cutting away the central region from the Western Australian Native Welfare Administration.*
>
> *'In other words, all this region is becoming, or will become, for practical purposes, Commonwealth Department of Supply "territory".'*
>
> For example, Mr. Middleton asked me what is the WRE policy towards Reserve No. 17614 [the Western Australian portion of the central reserves]. I replied that there is no policy except to follow the State policy (and I felt like adding, whatever that is). Later I detected the suggestion that WRE Native Patrol Officers can be non-effective from the State view point as they do not, or cannot, present information which is relevant to the State Department, but which might be detrimental to WRE interests. All this, of course, is obvious. Actually, it is not a matter of WRE encroaching on State prerogatives so much as the State Department leaving everything to WRE, and then beginning to smart under criticism. [143]

In early 1960 Macaulay submitted another report to the WRE, providing a snapshot of the cumulative effect of WRE activities since the assurances given by John Dedman in 1947. His report covered the ongoing 'detrimental publicity over alleged interference with Aborigines', and the effects of the Giles weather station on the Indigenous people of the Rawlinson Ranges. Since its inception, the station had attracted local Aboriginal people because of the promise of relatively easy food, water and medical assistance. For large portions of the year, between thirty and 100 people camped within several miles of the station. 'Unless employment is made available soon,' said Macaulay, 'it could be said that the Weapons Research Establishment has not accepted the responsibility incurred in establishing a weather station in the Reserves.'

He also addressed the road construction program. By 1960 graded roads criss-crossed the reserve and had, 'increased the amount of contacts with Natives and has contributed indirectly to their partial de-tribalisation'.

The two people in the photo below were part of a group whose range covered a large part of the Talgarno impact zone. They were contacted in 1965, and were therefore considered 'resident', within the prohibited area until this time.
PHOTO: BOB VERBURGT, 1965

Party travelling through the reserve, 1957.
PHOTO: NORMAN TINDALE, ARA IRITITJA

> The number of white people using the roads over the past four years runs to several hundreds, and while it is true that some of these people would have penetrated the Reserves without roads, it is unlikely that the number of 'legitimate' permit holders would have been anywhere near as great. (By 'legitimate', I refer to those to whom the State Welfare Departments have found it difficult to refuse permits. They include personnel from the Lands and Survey Departments, National Mapping, Bureau of Mineral Resources, Mines Department, Frome-Broken Hill, other oil exploration groups, and miscellaneous ventures of 'National importance').[144]

Macaulay reiterated the deterioration in relations between the WRE and the Western Australian Department of Native Welfare, particularly the possibility that, 'Any major trouble in the Reserves might be laid at the feet of the Department of Supply for "opening" the Reserves, the more so as there is no uniformity in State policies and so no clear-cut statement of overall State policy for the guidance of the Department and its Native Patrol Officers.' This was an acute problem for the NPOs when dealing with Western Australia; relations with their South Australian counterparts were smoother and clearer 'because of the more definite policy of this State'.[145]

Macaulay expressed scepticism about the ability or desire of the Western Australian department to do anything to actively protect the interests of Indigenous people in the reserves affected by the WRE activities:

> The Western Australian Native Welfare Department has a rather vague 'ameliorative welfare policy' towards their Reserve, and personal contact with that Department has led to the conclusion that nothing will be done for the inhabitants of the Reserve unless the Commonwealth initiates and guarantees a Commission to develop the Reserves. It is believed that the finances of the Welfare Department are so strained that the burden of initiating large-scale pastoral development is beyond the resources available to the Welfare Department . . .
>
> The question of whether 'ameliorative welfare' includes a protective policy of safeguarding Natives against uncontrolled contact by whites was one on which the Western Australian Department could not be drawn out. However, the fact that tourists are obtaining permits for the express purpose of 'touring the Reserve' speaks for itself. The Commissioner of Native Welfare, Mr. S. Middleton, has stated that he cannot see the mechanics of 'policing' Reserves against unauthorised entry, and that

> the South Australian policy of enforcing permits is impracticable and needless. He has further added that it would be a 'good thing' if a main road goes through from Laverton to Alice Springs. There are also some newspaper references to make a Western Australian National Park Reserve from the better parts of the Native Reserve.[146]

Len Beadell, 1960.
PHOTO: BOB MAJOR, ARA IRITITJA

While opposing active measures to support Indigenous people displaced by the WRE, and despite the increasing bureaucratic tension and public scrutiny that Macaulay had reported, Middleton continued his active support of the range opening up inland Western Australia.

This was confirmed when the Commonwealth Director of Works wrote to him in early 1960, outlining the network of reconnaissance tracks to be constructed by a team led by Len Beadell, a WRE surveyor. Middleton replied, saying that he had, 'no objection to the construction of reconnaissance tracks in the portion of Western Australia to which you refer'.[147]

Beadell later recollected:

> I didn't know at the time, but this centre line [i.e. from Woomera to 80 Mile Beach] would govern the future of central and Western Australia forever; because I was later to open up a network of access roads to place instrumentation and carry out special surveys for satellite tracking stations, impact areas and target areas.[148]
>
> We were on our way to make a network of outback roads 4,000 miles [6437 kilometres] long . . . Our aim was to open up over 1,000,000 square miles [2 600 000 square kilometres] of central and Western Australia, which had hardly been touched by a white man barring a few explorers.[149]

In fact, these roads were to give the department access to the desert regions for the first time: extended patrols of the northern half of the Western Desert became possible. These patrols provided the department, over the next four years, with its first authoritative basis for policy on the nomadic inhabitants of the desert.

As Beadell claimed, the roads opened up central and Western Australia, and they continue to shape the future of the desert and its inhabitants.

Moving in

> Certainly, in his traditional setting, the Aboriginal is a resourceful, self-respecting and self-sufficient individual, living to a strict code of ethics in apparently perfect contentment. However, it is a harsh, hazardous life, and it is hardly to be wondered at that when he hears of another way of life he should decide to investigate. He is perfectly free to return to his tribal country should he wish to do so and it seems probable that he intends to do this in most cases. However, having sampled a life of comparative ease, with its readily available food and medical attention, he rarely does return permanently. At times he may pay brief visits to the land of his ancestors, but even these become further and further apart and often eventually cease altogether.[150]

Everything was changing.

As the WRE's plans to extend the range through Western Australia continued, the scale of the area affected, the potential for impact on Indigenous people and the likely responsibilities of the NPO's began to hit home. In a very real way, the WRE was going to open up the desert.

The roads that the WRE constructed through the late 1950s and up until 1963 made travel into the desert possible, and made its inhabitants visible to white Australia. Where the state government had previously been able to wash its hands of these invisible people, new problems quickly emerged. With access came knowledge and, with knowledge, responsibility. This responsibility was made difficult by a policy conundrum: what exactly should the government do about Indigenous people living in the desert; when should it do nothing, and when should it intervene?

Meanwhile, the piecemeal policies that different governments had pursued in relation to the central reserves and the inhabitants of desert areas were becoming less viable. For the first time, the governments of the Northern Territory, Western Australia and South Australia decided that they needed better information, and some coordination of policy. In 1961, they formed the Standing Committee on the Central Aboriginal Reserves. Greater cooperation also created greater visibility of government practices, accompanied by some accountability.

The NPOs were active players in all of this change. After participating in an aerial survey across north-western Australia in 1960, Macaulay observed that the north-west road-building scheme would, 'bring increasing numbers of whites into new areas where contacts will be made with a variety of natives, tribalised and otherwise, nomadic, mission, and station types'. As the reserves decreased, 'in importance and function' the responsibility and workload for the NPOs would dramatically increase.[151]

The Northern Territory's welfare officers had travelled on patrols into the west since 1957, but the major roads through the Western Australian portions of the Western Desert constructed between 1960 and 1963 provided vastly greater reach. By 1963, they provided the capacity to travel from the Northern Territory across to the north-west coast. Several exploratory patrols were conducted during 1963 and early 1964, which later attracted substantial and unwanted political interest.

Len Beadell's road-making crew. PHOTO: FROM THE COLLECTION OF THE NATIONAL ARCHIVES OF AUSTRALIA

In July and August 1963, a Northern Territory research officer, Jeremy Long[152], conducted a survey through the northern portion of the Western Desert, 'to make a more accurate and complete assessment of the numbers and needs of the people still living in the desert areas'. [153] He travelled west from Papunya on one of the new WRE roads, which allowed him to travel as far west as the Canning Stock Route, close to the Percival Lakes, far within Western Australia. The Western Australian Department of Native Welfare (DNW) had no experience of this country, and no real idea of the number of people living there.

Long contacted eighteen Indigenous people, and estimated that there were about seventy-four altogether in the area between the Western Australian border and Jupiter Well. He reported:

> Mr MacDougal [sic] had met last year two men of these western groups but until this month no satisfactory contact had been established. The contact established last week has revealed (1) that the group is inadequately nourished and many of them are sick; and (2) the group is less numerous and more isolated than information gathered last year had suggested. The children in particular are in poorer condition than any I have met on previous visits to nomadic groups in the desert areas. The next trip should reveal whether this poor condition is general, but the health of the children is a strong argument for acceding to the wish of the people met so far to be taken out of the desert. It is now evident that this group is no longer part of a viable society.
>
> The remoteness of these groups from either Papunya or Giles and the difficulties of the terrain make it very difficult to maintain any oversight of their welfare where they are. On the other hand it would it appears be inhumane to leave them

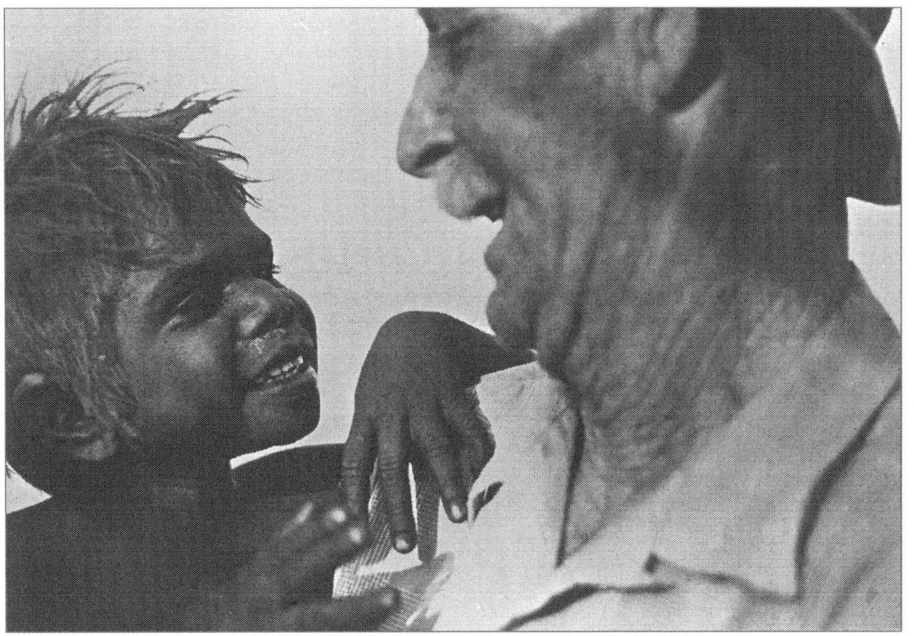

Walter MacDougall with Karparti at Jupiter Well, November 1963.
PHOTO: JOHN ALLAN. UNIVERSITY OF WESTERN AUSTRALIA, BERNDT MUSEUM OF ANTHROPOLOGY

> there to die out as they surely will in time. I have elsewhere suggested the sinking of bores . . . to provide for the needs of the Pintubi people and in particular those who remain in the desert or have recently left it for Papunya. The condition of the people seen last week together with the fact of the recent emigrations to Papunya give this project an added and a high degree of urgency. If it is humanly possible at least two bores should be sunk and equipped in the next six or eight months and a ration depot which could be visited fortnightly from Papunya or Alice Springs should be established. Meanwhile I strongly recommend . . . that transport should be provided to bring the people in from Jupiter Well/Likilnga to one of the western bores on the Haast Bluff run where they could be visited weekly or fortnightly from Haast Bluff and rationed and could be helped to hunt the great numbers of kangaroos in these areas.[154]

After a second patrol, Long filed a further report, intended for discussion with the Western Australian department:

> An effort was made to find out what these people themselves want to do or want done for them. It is, however, impossible for them to make an informed decision. If it appears at times that some have not been seeking, if not actively avoiding, contact with these patrols, there is never any suggestion of hostility to the intruders nor to proposals that they might be better off living elsewhere. Requests for transport to Papunya in fact invariably precede any suggestion by me that they might move in and it is only the refusal of a lift that disappoints and, in one instance, obviously annoys. In later discussions the possibilities —

(a) that transport might be provided to bring them East; and

(b) that waters might be provided for them . . . have been raised and apparently approved. The suggestion made was that transport might be provided next autumn if all the authorities approved. Some made it fairly clear that they would walk in before then and because they were enquiring whether there was water at Sandy Blight Junction, I left some 25 gallons there . . .

These people are not as isolated as information obtained on the first patrol suggested but, as was revealed by last year' s patrol, there are not enough people left for the social system to function effectively: young men cannot be initiated and young women cannot find appropriate husbands. The death rate is evidently high: 34 people were seen last year and twelve months later two of these were dead and this in groups obviously better nourished than those seen for the first time this year. All children over 18 months or two years are more or less severely under-nourished and four out of 10 children under 10 years of age seen in the western groups had yaws. Given the evident keenness of these people to come in to a place where good food and warm clothing are readily available these reasons appear sufficient to justify interference in the situation.

These people are living too far from the main field of work of the WRE Officers for these men to effectively look after their welfare . . . Most of their closest relatives are at Papunya and others are at Y uendumu and Balgo Hills.[155]

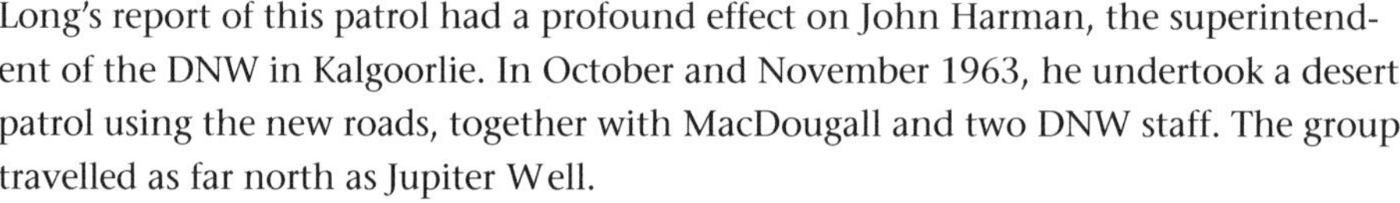

Long's report of this patrol had a profound effect on John Harman, the superintendent of the DNW in Kalgoorlie. In October and November 1963, he undertook a desert patrol using the new roads, together with MacDougall and two DNW staff. The group travelled as far north as Jupiter W ell.

John Harman.
PHOTO: ROBERT MACAULAY, DATE UNKNOWN

Middleton had retired from the department in 1962, and was succeeded as commissioner by Frank Gare. In a report on this desert survey to the new commissioner, Harman spoke of the implications of their contact with people in the vicinity of Jupiter Well and of the Long report.

Until receipt of Mr . Long's report I had formed the impression that these natives often referred to as 'Pintubis' were living in countr y which although in W estern Australia was quite close to the Northern Territory border . . . [However] Jupiter Well is 383 miles [616 kilometres] from Papunya and 186 miles [300 kilometres] west of the N.T./W.A. border. Well 35 of the Canning Stock Route is 320 miles [515 kilometres] west of the N.T ./W.A. border. It is possible that the people contacted at Jupiter Well and surrounding areas are not even Pintubi people. The fact remains that these people are so far inside Western Australia, that I feel we cannot now rely entirely on the assistance of the Northern Territory Welfare Branch and these people must therefore, become of prime importance to this Department in W estern Australia.

At this stage, insufficient knowledge of these people and the countr y they traverse is known to us and it is suggested that this Department organise an expedition to the area and remain there for at least one month.[156]

Harman's survey was the first substantial exercise in which DNW staff had ventured into the desert to learn about the numbers and situation of people living outside the settlements, missions and stations that were their normal focus.[157] It was also the first time that any question of departmental responsibility to nomadic people as yet uncontacted had really been raised internally.

In its consideration of the Long and Harman patrols, the standing committee on the Central Aboriginal Reserves, meeting at Woomera in December 1963, concluded that, 'There are probably thirty or forty persons south of Jupiter Well who have not been contacted recently'.[158]

The committee considered Harman's suggestion of a joint patrol, and what should be done with nomadic people discovered in future patrols. Its delegates agreed that, 'movement into settlements is inevitable but that the movement should not be hastened'. It also recognised that a medium-term (five- or six-year) plan was required, 'to give the people some option as to where they may go'.[159]

It also agreed that a joint patrol would be mounted in April 1964. This patrol was to prove the committee's assumption that 'most Aborigines have been contacted' wrong.

Meanwhile, the NPOs continued to patrol the range, bringing people in to missions when they requested or required medical treatment. The NPOs followed what they believed to be the policy of the DNW: to leave Indigenous people living in the desert unless they required assistance.

Convoy of vehicles from the joint Northern Territory and Western Australian patrol 1964. PHOTO: IAN DUNLOP, AIATSIS

Despite assertions from the department that there was no official policy to bring people in, there was at best an ambiguous policy in the field. Tom Murray (a Commonwealth police officer at Maralinga who participated in WRE field patrols into Western Australia in April 1964), reported to his senior officer:

> I understand that it is the intention of the Native Affairs Department [sic], W.A. to completely depopulate the Great Western Desert, W.A. if it can be effected without upsetting the groups, as some dissention [sic] is always shown by the older people. The intended move is due mainly to the various known groups being reduced in numbers through migration to missions and some concern is felt regarding recent deaths that has occurred [sic] over the last year or so and which may have been avoided if contact could have been made and medical aid administered.[160]

The Western Australian contingent of the April joint patrol was led by John Harman. Its members included anthropologist Bob Tonkinson, from The University

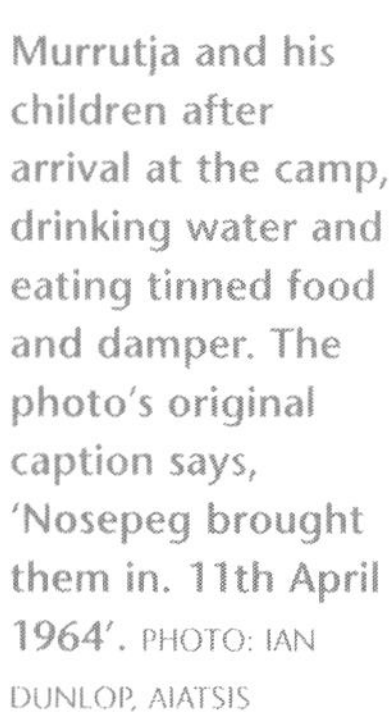

Murrutja and his children after arrival at the camp, drinking water and eating tinned food and damper. The photo's original caption says, 'Nosepeg brought them in. 11th April 1964'. PHOTO: IAN DUNLOP, AIATSIS

of Western Australia, as well as medical, welfare and scientific representatives, an Indigenous guide and an interpreter. This group was to meet a Northern Territory contingent — including Jeremy Long, MacDougall and Macaulay — at Jupiter Well.

The Western Australians explored the country from Jupiter Well west through the Canning Stock Route and almost 300 kilometres further west past the Percival Lakes, while the Northern Territory contingent worked to the east of Jupiter Well, but still chiefly within Western Australia.

Jointly, the patrol met over seventy people and gathered information on at least thirty-six others who remained in the area. They also brought forty-two people out of the desert, taking them to Papunya. The various reports on the patrol highlight some difference of opinion on the number of people still living in the desert. Jeremy Long's estimate was conservative: 'A further thirty-odd people remain in the desert who are likely to emigrate within the next few months'.[161]

Phillip Playford, a geologist who accompanied the group, gave a disinterested report on what would later be a contentious issue: the health of the people contacted. He made what was ultimately an accurate assessment of the likely numbers of people still living in the desert:

> Some 71 nomadic Aborigines were contacted by the joint parties on the expedition. All of these were living in their traditional way, virtually untouched by white influence. Some had never before seen Europeans, though of course they had heard of them. These people live a completely nomadic existence, moving from one well or water hole to another, hunting and collecting vegetable foods . . . Most of the

area visited benefited from cyclonic rains early this year and the natives were on the whole well fed. Their health also appeared to be good, though two cases of active yaws were observed and some of the women had decayed teeth. Trachoma was present, but it did not appear to be serious, no cases of blindness being observed.

A total of 42 of them elected to be transported by truck to the Papunya settlement in the Northern Territory, but the rest preferred to remain in their own country.

The welfare parties were informed of the existence of at least 30 more natives in the area, and my own estimate is that several hundred probably remain in the Great Sandy and Gibson Desert areas. The present groups have only been encountered because roads have been cleared past their own particular water holes and wells, but these roads are very widely spaced in such a vast area. [W A Petroleum] parties have reported seeing abundant signs of natives in the Joanna Spring and Percival Lakes areas.[162]

John Harman's report highlighted the issues for the DNW that were raised by the existence of the new WRE roads and the findings of the patrol:

The provision of roads by the Department of Supply as access routes for National Mapping has made it possible for patrols to contact these natives. It is indeed interesting that this patrol which only travelled in comparison a few miles (twenty to thirty [32 to 48 kilometres]) off the made roads, contacted 71 natives. The question to be asked is how many nomadic natives are living within the areas, bounded by roads which area is approximately 30,000 square miles [77 700 square kilometres] . . . It would seem certain from our investigations to state that the area is populated but certainly very difficult to estimate a number.

It is anticipated that in the very near future further natives will be sighted and contacted by personnel from oil search parties and road construction parties. A report was received on this patrol of road construction workers driving into a nomadic native camp site with a bulldozer . . .[163]

Climbing aboard the truck to Papunya, men sit on the drums in front and the women behind on the floor; 19 April 1964. PHOTO: IAN DUNLOP, AIATSIS

When the findings of the joint patrol — and particularly the fact that forty-two nomadic people had been taken in to Papunya — became public several months later, there was once again a public outcry about government treatment of desert people. But this time it was mixed with some new ingredients: indignation alleg-

Blue Streak rocket launcher. PHOTO: FROM THE COLLECTION OF THE NATIONAL ARCHIVES OF AUSTRALIA

ing direct harassment of Indigenous people by the WRE, and questions about where the first WRE rockets were actually going to land.

The interest in the Blue Streak firings wasn't just domestic: the whole world was watching.

The firings represented the first (and last) time that the full rocket range across Western Australia would be used. They represented a new and exciting stage in Woomera's history: participation in the space race. The British terminated the testing of military weapons at Woomera suddenly, in 1960. The range then found a new use: as a testing ground for rockets ultimately intended to fire satellites into space. The Blue Streak firings were conducted for a European consortium that had adopted the untested British rocket technology, originally intended for weapons, to pursue their space aspirations. The intended payloads may have changed from weaponry to satellites, but the implications on the ground remained the same.[164]

Three firings were planned: F1 in May 1964, F2 in October, and F3 in early 1965. The rockets were intended to fly over the Western Desert, rising to a height of 170 kilometres and travelling at over 10000 kilometres per hour. They would travel almost 2000 kilometres in around ten minutes and substantially burn up on re-entry, with any remnants landing in the 'uninhabited' Percival Lakes, 1900 kilometres up the range. The trip would be tracked by cameras and radar placed along the range. In each case, the NPOs were commissioned to search the impact area in which the rockets were intended to land, and to clear Indigenous people to save them from harm.

On 12 May 1964, MacDougall left Woomera for the Percival Lakes, to prepare for F1.

PART TWO

THE FIRST PATROL

Before the first patrol

Walter MacDougall's job was to protect Indigenous people from any harm arising from the activities of the WRE rocket range. In particular, he and his fellow officer, Robert Macaulay, were responsible for ensuring that rocket firings did not lead to injury or harm.

An impact zone was identified for each firing; this zone had to be cleared before any tests could go ahead. It was the NPOs' task to clear the area, provide an all-clear immediately before the firing, then patrol the area to ensure that it remained clear.

For the Blue Streak firings MacDougall was to be accompanied by Terry Long, a Department of Native Welfare officer. Long was stationed in Port Hedland and had no experience of travelling in the desert, nor experience of nomadic Indigenous people. Like virtually all other officers in the department at the time, he worked predominantly with people living in settlements, townships, missions and stations.

Long took Gordon McKay as the patrol's interpreter and guide. He was an old man, but was reputed to know the country around the Percival Lakes. Once on patrol, however, he became uneasy. This wasn't his country at all.

Yuwali, Junju and their extended families were living in the Percival Lakes area at the time of the Blue Streak firings, completely unaware of the goings on at Woomera.

There were twenty women and children in the group, most of them related in one way or another. They straddled three generations (see page 13 for a complete genealogy).

FAR LEFT: **Alec Oliver, Gordon McKay, Walter MacDougall.** PHOTO: TERRY LONG. 1964

LEFT: **Terry Long.** PHOTO: PHOTOGRAPHER UNKNOWN, DATE UNKNOWN, FROM TERRY LONG FAMILY COLLECTION

The edge of the Percival Lakes, seen from the air. PHOTO: ROBERT MACAULAY, 1964

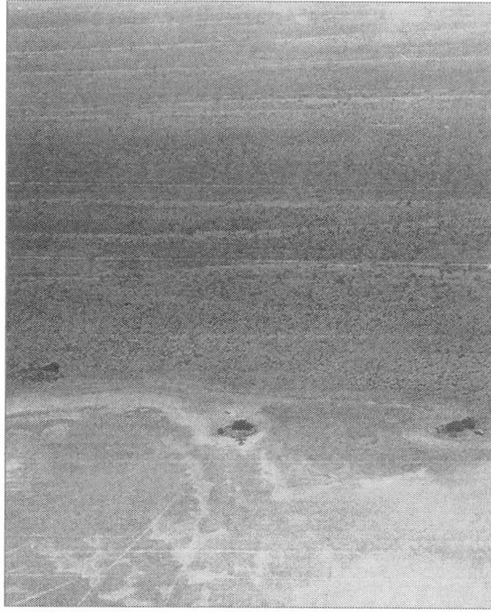

The bubbling spring at Kurtararra, seen from the air. PHOTO: ROBERT MACAULAY, 1964

The oldest four women were Yukurrpani, Karntipa, Nganja and Japapa, their ages ranging from about thirty-eight to fifty. In the middle generation were Nyipi, Junju and Kulata. Nyipi and Kulata were both married to Nyiwiljukurr, who was travelling further to the north with his other wives. Junju was Nyiwiljukurr's sister. Then there were the children. At seventeen, Yuwali was the eldest, but there were twelve others ranging in age from fifteen to less than a year old. All of the men in the group were either dead or elsewhere; the women had been travelling alone for at least two years.

These families wore only traditional coverings, had only traditional tools and, other than Nyipi's sighting of a vehicle, had never seen white people before 1964. Their foraging range in 1964 was approximately 2000 square kilometres, centred around the Percival Lakes.

The Blue Streak firings represented the first time that the full range would be used. The first rocket, F1, was to be launched on 25 May 1964. The impact was to be in an area 195 kilometres long and 145 kilometres wide, directly around and south of the Percival Lakes.

While the chance of the rocket hitting anyone was considered to be extraordinarily slim, the NPOs were required to identify — through aerial and ground patrols — whether any Indigenous people were present in or near the impact area and to move them out of the area for the duration of the firing.

On 13 April 1964 Frank Gare, the Commissioner of Native Welfare, received a telegram from his district officer in Kalgoorlie, John Harman. The telegram alerted the commissioner that an oil exploration team from Western Australian Petroleum

Ltd (WAPET) had recently seen evidence of Aboriginal activity in the south west of Lake Percival, near a hill they knew as Picture Hill. This alerted both the DNW and the WRE that a patrol would be necessary prior to the firing of F1.

So, in early May 1964, Walter MacDougall and mechanic Alec Oliver left Woomera for the Percival Lakes area. MacDougall arranged to meet Terry Long to the west of Percival Lakes.

To MacDougall and his party, the Percival Lakes were simply a series of salt lakes within the F1 impact zone. To Yuwali, the area was her birthplace and her source of livelihood.

Yulpu, Yuwali's birthplace, is a soak located approximately 50 metres from the edge of Lake Percival (the largest and most central of the Percival group). It has a grove of acacia and tea trees close by.

Yimiri is a bulrush-covered mound containing two soaks, or springs, in the middle of Lake Percival, and lies to the east of Yulpu. The springs at Yimiri provide large amounts of fresh water in the middle of a very large salt lake. Known as 'mound' springs, their presence is attributed to calcrete rock — a type of limestone that is a very effective aquifer — in which the watertable remains quite high (at least 3 metres), resulting in a permanent water supply.

The thick bulrushes surrounding Yimiri act as a natural deterrent to animals such as camels, thus keeping the spring in good condition. To get to the water the Martu had to push back the rushes to form an entrance. The spring is almost in the middle of the rushes, and a person hiding in the middle of the bulrushes would be invisible to people on the outside.

A further two bubbling springs are located at Kurtararra on the north-eastern shore of the same lake, across quite a narrow neck. A well-worn path connects these two important water sources. Both springs are surrounded by water, with acacia

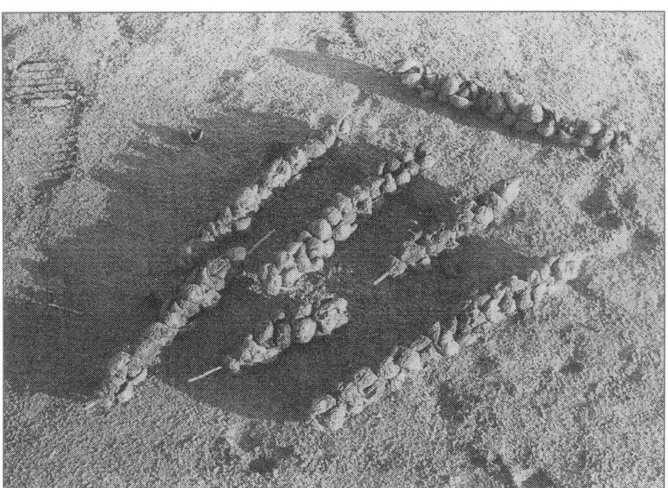

TOP: *Wamurla* (bush tomato, *Solanum diversiflorum*) are round fruit, the size of small tomatoes. The fruit is sweet when ripe and can be baked in the fire or dried and threaded onto a stick for keeping. PHOTO: SUE DAVENPORT, 2001

BOTTOM: Dried *wamurla*. PHOTO: VIC SURMAN, 1964

Collecting *wamurla*. Interviewed in 2000, Yuwali said: 'In winter time after it rained, people went out to other water in the surrounding area. In the hot time we stayed around Kurtararra, Yimiri and Wirnpa.' PHOTO: BOB VERBURGT, 1965

trees providing good shade. Y uwali's family camped at the base of a large sandhill, which ran along the shore of the lake.

In May 1964, Yuwali and Junju's families were camped at Kurtararra. They separated into two groups to go hunting: Junju took one mob far to the east; Y uwali and Nyipi initially went west, but ended up at a northern camp called Y uwin. The reason the group separated was to make the most of the available resour ces.

In the story below, Yuwali refers to 'four people' travelling east. In so doing she avoids mentioning *all* the people who went east as some of these have since died and their names cannot yet be mentioned. The actual group who went east were Junju, Marawurru, T ajaka, Y ukurrpani, Karntipa, Kulata, Pilumpa, Nganja, and

Pakakalyi. Yuwali's group consisted of the women Nyipi and Japapa, and the children Yaji, Yiji, Mangayi, Ngarrka, Kurtu, Yapaji, Ngarrpinyarninya and Pinkirri.

> We stayed at our main camp, Kurtararra. While we were staying there, we were eating *wamurla* (bush tomato) during the hot time. We stayed there for a long time, in our waterhole, in our place.
>
> Then it was winter. Four people went to the east: Junju, Karntipa, Yukurrpani and Kulata. They went towards the east.
>
> We went westward; Ngarrka, Yiji, Mangayi, and me. We went to Yuwin, on our own. We had separated from the others.
>
> We went towards the north. We climbed up to the lake. We ate some frogs that we caught from the sandhill, and in the afternoon we went to the water at Yuwin.
>
> We collected some bush tucker from the *mantawaruwaru* [acacia] trees around our camp.
>
> We ate some dry *wamurla* and we made camp, and rested and slept there until morning.[1]

Meanwhile, MacDougall's party approached from Woomera to meet with Long's Port Hedland party at Swindells Field.

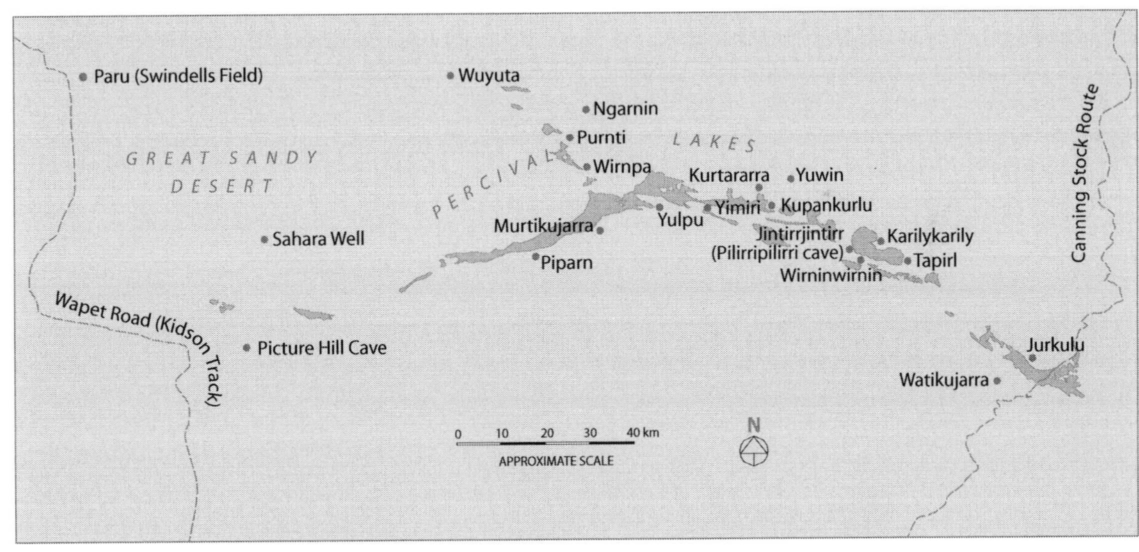

In the following section, Yuwali's story is aligned with extracts from the original patrol diaries kept by Walter MacDougall and Terry Long in 1964, and with an interview with Long in 1999. The map above shows the area in which the action takes place and many of the waterholes and soaks visited by Yuwali's group.

Sunday **17 May** 1964

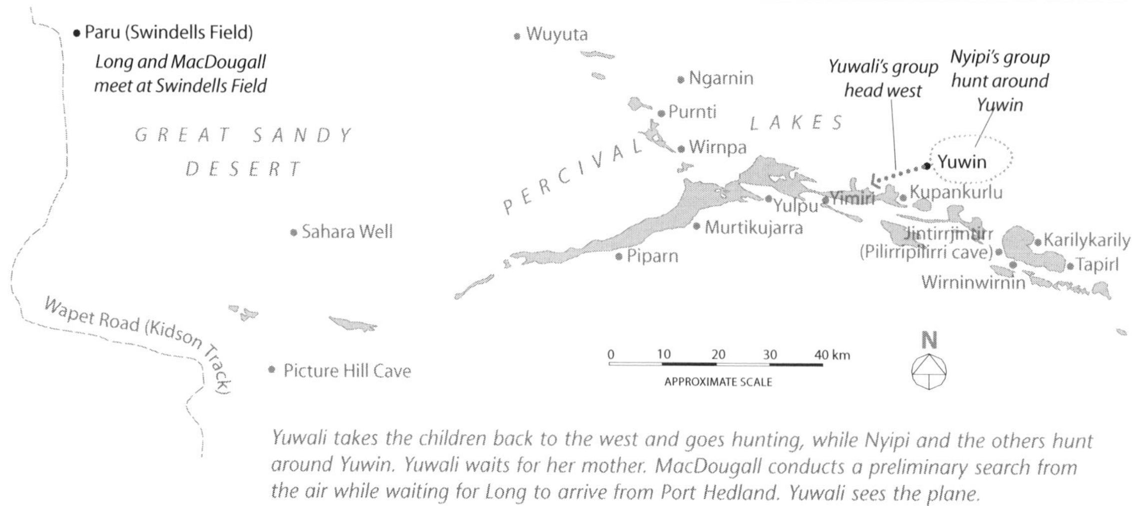

Yuwali takes the children back to the west and goes hunting, while Nyipi and the others hunt around Yuwin. Yuwali waits for her mother. MacDougall conducts a preliminary search from the air while waiting for Long to arrive from Port Hedland. Yuwali sees the plane.

Yuwali

I was responsible for Ngarrka, Mangayi and Yiji.

We walked west, then I stopped and made my little brothers and my sister sit and wait for me while I went looking for lizards. I left them there in the morning and went east to get meat.

I heard an aeroplane. I went to some trees and I stayed under them. I came out when the plane went away.

I came back with four lizards. The kids were all crying for meat. I cooked them and gave them to my little brothers and sister. We ate all the lizards, then we got up and started walking.

We walked up the sandhill. We were all sitting down and then we were all playing. (We used to go and run up the sandhill, jump down, roll in the sand. We used to play hide-and-seek and climb the trees.[2])

We got up and walked off again, to the next sandhill. We were waiting and looking for my mother, who was getting meat and some food. We waited all day till sunset. Then we left. We went down and found some *wamurla*, which we ate.

Cat and lizards stored in a tree. PHOTO: BOB VERBURGT, 1960s

Lizards. Despite its aridity, the Western Desert has one of the richest reptile faunas in the world. Reptiles (particularly lizards) are probably the most reliable source of meat. Most lizards are nocturnal. There are four major lizard groups: geckos, skinks, legless lizards and goannas. They live in grasses, burrows, rocks or trees. Lizards and goannas are dug out of burrows in the sand, logs or trees and are killed by having their heads hit against something hard. Their legs are dislocated and intestines removed, then they are thrown onto a fire. Their scales are removed after a few minutes and they are buried in hot sand with coals placed on top until cooked. PHOTO: SUE DAVENPORT, 1987

Long's journal

An air sweep was made on Sunday just prior to us going in by land. Fires had been seen to the north-east of Lake Percival and what appeared to be a large circular ring of bulrushes [Yimiri]. Because of the absence of any signs of life elsewhere in the 100 x 90 mile dump area [the area in which the rocket was intended to land] it was decided to search this sector on the ground.

To carry out a really competent search of the target area would take 6 months, and would require 2 vehicles, plus a supply unit to ensure petrol and water was always available to searchers.

I left for Swindells Field, accompanied by Trainee District Officer Webster and Mr. Gordon McKay, a native interpreter. After a trip, over fair roads of 400 miles [643 kilometres], we rendezvoused with Mr. MacDougall of the WRE and the RAAF Dakota aircraft, Lima Mike Foxtrot.

MacDougall's journal

The RAAF reported having seen two fire systems actually burning, one within the prescribed area and the other just outside [to the north].

Whilst waiting for Mr. Long I went flying to discover the best way to approach Lake Percival. From this lake I could make an attempt to contact the group living at a soak on its northern shore.

Whilst flying I discovered that WAPET had established a road from Swindells Field to a stony outcrop. This outcrop is within 8 miles [13 kilometres] of the southern shore of the lake. I decided to make my approach from there.

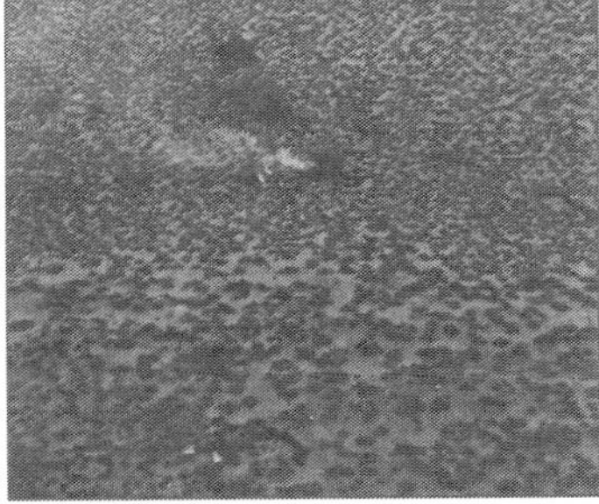

The Martu use fire extensively when hunting, to communicate with each other and to ensure regeneration of growth that attracts game. Looking for fire was a standard method of locating groups of people in the desert. PHOTO: ROBERT MACAULAY, 1964

Air sweeps were made in a Douglas DC-3 to try to spot any signs of life on the lake. Both MacDougall and Long did separate sweeps, spotting Yimiri and the general direction of fires. Swindells Field was an airfield and fuel dump created by West Australian Petroleum and used by the patrol for collecting fuel and other supplies that needed to be flown in. The Martu names for this place include Paru and Papija. PHOTO: ROBERT MACAULAY, 1964

Monday **18 May** 1964

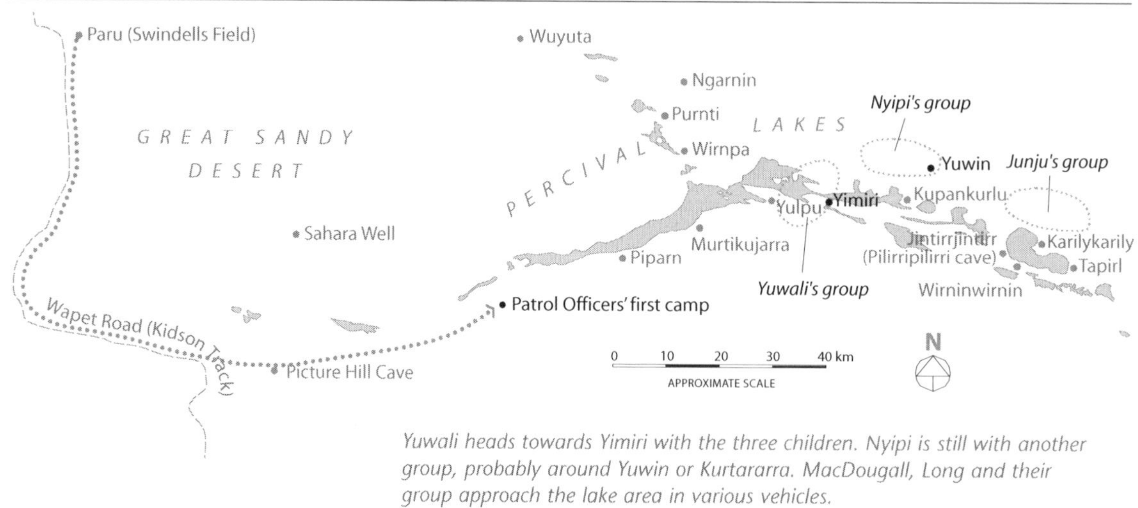

Yuwali heads towards Yimiri with the three children. Nyipi is still with another group, probably around Yuwin or Kurtararra. MacDougall, Long and their group approach the lake area in various vehicles.

Yuwali

In the afternoon we went west to collect bush tucker from the *mantawaruwaru* tree. We were collecting *lunki* (witchetty grubs) and *mankutingu* (thorny devil) We cooked them.

We climbed up the sandhill, we girls. We cooked some meat. We were playing. We went back along the sandhill to the east.

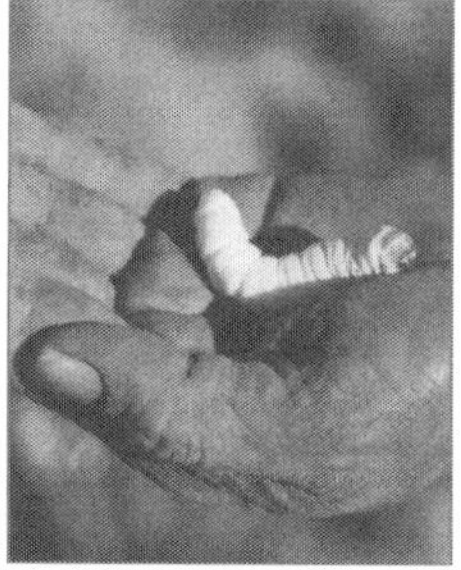

Mankutingu, or thorny devil (*Moloch horridus*) is a type of lizard which lives in shallow burrows close to the desert surface. They are extremely spiny and can look fierce, but are placid and are often played with as temporary pets. Their thorns are removed before they are cooked. PHOTOS: ABOVE: SUE DAVENPORT, 2000; RIGHT: FIONA WALSH, 1987.

Lunki is the Martu name for witchetty grubs, an important source of protein. They are found in the roots of certain acacia bushes and eucalypts. Their presence is indicated by a sawdust-like heap of excreta on the ground at the base of the tree. The women then dig up the roots with crowbars or digging sticks and crack the roots open if a swelling indicates the presence of the grub or if the root sounds hollow when tapped. Several grubs may be found in the one root. They can be eaten raw (tasting like raw eggs) or toasted in hot ashes, giving them a rich egg and nut flavour. PHOTO ABOVE LEFT: SUE DAVENPORT, 2001

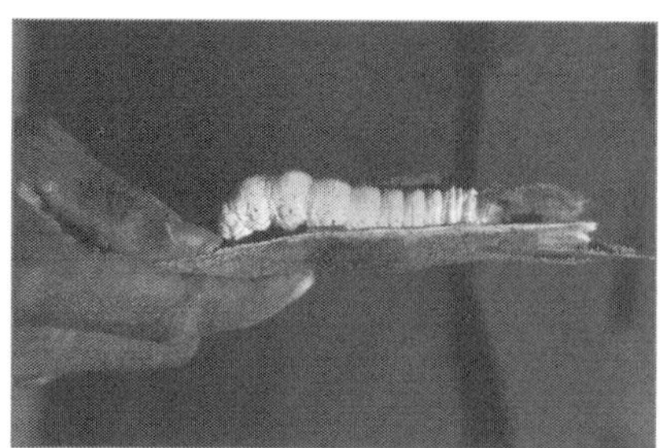

Long's journal

MacDougall and his mechanic Alec Oliver in the International and Gordon McKay in the Land Rover left Swindells Field at 8.00 am for Lake Percival.

There was a rough track put down by WAPET to an area we knew as Picture Hill, where there was a cave with paintings in them, which was 80 miles [130 kilometres] south of Swindells Field.

Picture Hill was reached at 1.00 pm. From here a rough track meandered towards Lake Percival, then cut out some 12 miles [19 kilometres] from the lake.

We left the Beadell Road at 4.00 pm heading north east and camped in sandhills at 5.30 pm, 8 miles [13 kilometres] south of Lake Percival. Broad valleys run north-east by south-west and end just short of the lake in a jumbled wall of sandhills running in every direction.

There were a lot of dingoes about. They were in a starving condition. You dare not leave your shoes or your boots outside your swag else they'd have been taken too. You had to keep everything under your pillows — there were a lot of dingoes there.

The International is a make of truck that MacDougall, Oliver, Meakins and Surman drove. It was very heavy and had a cabin and tray back. Len Beadell, referred to in Long's journal, was the chief surveyor of WRE. From 1951–63 Beadell surveyed and constructed a network of roads spanning over 6000 kilometres in length. These access roads were constructed to enable placement of instrumentation and special surveys for satellite tracking stations, impact areas and target areas. PHOTO: TERRY LONG, 1964

Picture Hill is located to the south-west of Lake Percival. It has a cave that has extensive drawings of a snake. PHOTO: BOB VERBURGT, 1960S

Dingoes are significant to the Martu. People slept close to them to keep themselves warm on cold winter nights and protect them from evil spirits. Dingoes can also sense the presence of strangers, 'featherfeet' and revenge expeditions. During the second patrol to the Percival Lakes in September and October 1964, MacDougall's boots were stolen by a dingo. PHOTO: BOB VERBURGT, 1960s

MacDougall's journal

In discussion, it appeared that Mr Long's instructions were not so much to assist in the search, but to act as an observer, and to ensure that WRE Patrol Officers did in fact remove all natives found in the dump area — an impossible task without proper organisation and time.

I found Mr Long an ideal companion for the type of work in hand. He was quick to learn the special techniques necessary in such difficult terrain, and was at all times ready to do his share of the work involved in the subsequent trials and tribulations imposed by inclement weather, difficult country and confusion.

Tuesday 19 May 1964

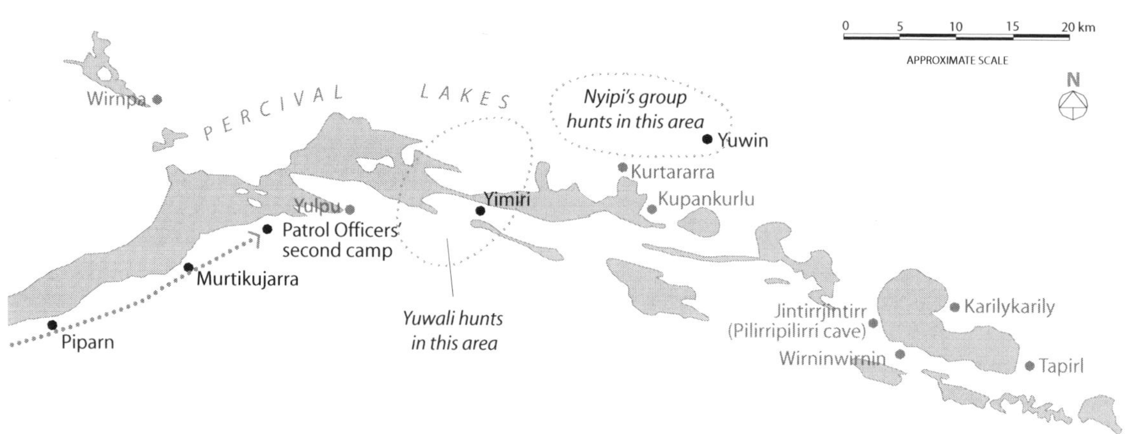

MacDougall's journal

We arrived without much difficulty on the southern shore of Lake Percival. I found it impossible to cross the lake so drove along its shore to the east.

Macdougall's heavy International quickly became bogged on the salt lake.
PHOTO: TERRY LONG, 1964

Long's journal

Carried out an attempt to get around the lake from the south shore to the other side.

It was decided to risk the surface of the lake. After an anxious half hour or so, we came out on a length of hard brown salt, which proved to be most stable where a brown and white mosaic pattern existed.

Both vehicles were soon travelling at an exhilarating 40-mph [65 kilometres per hour] and our confidence in this mode of travel began to rise.

Becoming unwisely venturesome, the two cars raced across the wide mouth of an extensive bay, and I was dismayed to see the International subside into a black morass of clay. We spent the next 3 hours assisting MacDougall to extricate the vehicle.

Despite every future care, conditions on the lake defied safe classification, and we were to spend many hours towing, digging, jacking and extricating both vehicles in the two weeks that followed.

After that we had to be very careful about where we went.

It was heartening to see spinifex fires burning ahead of us to the north-east. We camped that night, confident that we were in reach of a hitherto uncontacted group of Aborigines.

Fires in the distance, seen from the NPOs' camp at Yulpu. PHOTO: WALTER MACDOUGALL FILM STILL, AṞA IRITITJA, 1964

Wednesday **20 May** 1964

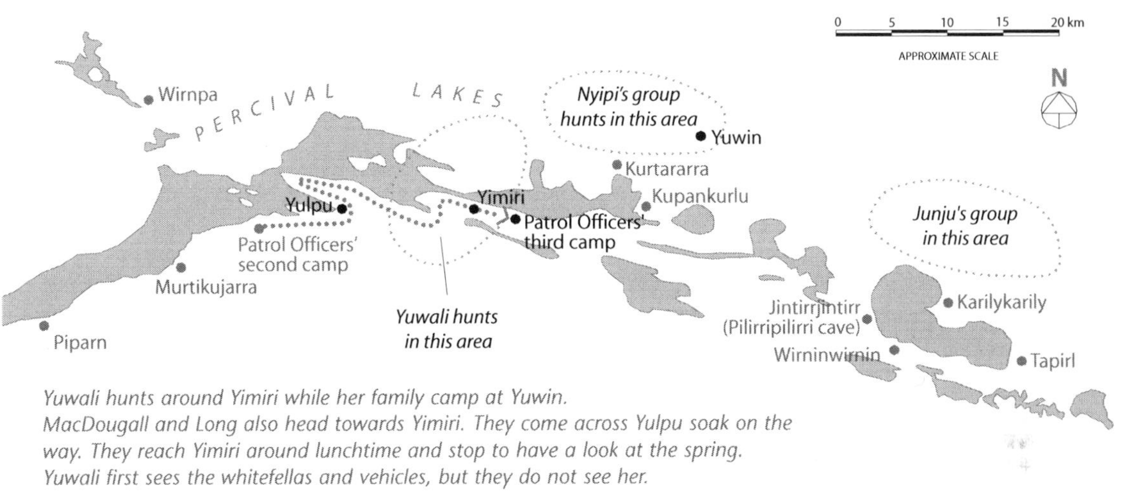

Yuwali hunts around Yimiri while her family camp at Yuwin. MacDougall and Long also head towards Yimiri. They come across Yulpu soak on the way. They reach Yimiri around lunchtime and stop to have a look at the spring. Yuwali first sees the whitefellas and vehicles, but they do not see her.

Yuwali

I left the kids. I walked, then I saw this . . . it was like a rock. And I thought to myself that it was a big rock at Yimiri.

[The whitefellas] were eating dinner, in that place of the dreamtime kangaroo.

I went running back fast and climbed a tree. I saw the kids and they were all right. I ran back and told the kids, 'I saw a big rock back at the camp and it's getting bigger.' I told the kids 'Stay here, don't cry, don't make a noise.'

I ran back and I went up a tree. I was looking at it. It was a motor car.

Then I came down from the tree. I went back to the kids and told my little sisters and brother.

We ran west, then we stopped. We had no water to drink.

We decided to come back. The sun was almost going down. We went back, and I made my little brothers and sisters stop, and I went on.

I crept up; I was crawling.

Yuwali had never seen a vehicle before. In 2000 she said, 'It was the first time [I'd seen a car]; I thought it was a rock moving around.' PHOTO: TERRY LONG, 1964

MacDougall's journal

The first tracks were seen at a soak situated a few chains south off the shore [a chain is an imperial measurement, 66 feet or about 20 metres]. There were some weeks old human tracks, which led to a disused humpy near the soak. An old bark sandal was found there.

Footprints leading to Yimiri. PHOTO: TERRY LONG, 1964

Yuwali's group used sandals made from bark strips for walking on the coarse crust of the salt lake. In summer the sand becomes very hot and feet need protection from burning. When, on the second patrol, a dingo stole MacDougall's boots, Yuwali made him a pair of these sandals, which he wore and later gave to the curator of the South Australian Museum, Norman Tindale. PHOTO: TERRY LONG, 1964

Long's journal

Late in the afternoon, we came across human tracks — fairly old — both male and female and also of children, and they led us to a deep soak, six feet under a wattle tree [Yulpu]. The whole area had been extensively occupied and was littered with flints and pieces of charcoal.

The patrol then moved on from Yulpu to Yimiri.

Long speaking in 1999

We were in the vicinity of the soak [Yimiri], which appeared to be over 1 mile [1.6 kilometres] from the shore — almost at the centre of this narrow neck. The footprints were very visible there and we walked out to the soak — quite a big well and a spring in the centre.

The winter campsite is essentially a windbreak comprising rows of acacia boughs laid flat on the ground. In 2000 Yuwali explained: 'We had to make a windbreak to keep the place warm and we used to keep the fire going at night to keep us warm.' PHOTO: TERRY LONG, 1964

Yuwali

I crawled around and then climbed a big tree. I was looking, I didn't know anything.

The whitefella had left the motor car there in our camp [Yimiri]. I asked the children, 'What's that thing rolling down in the camp? There is something like a rock cracking in the silence [the crashing gears of the International].'

Ngarrka was crawling up towards me. I told Ngarrka to have a look up here. There was a man standing there, he had a dish on his head. It was a hat.

They were looking at the smoke in the east. That smoke belonged to Junju's mob.

We stayed for a little while, then we got frightened and moved north when the sun was setting. We had a drink of water [probably at Kurtararra]. We made a firestick for a light.

Smoke was an important means of communication. Yuwali, interviewed in 2000, said: 'You might go and separate for a few days, or a long time and come back afterwards, in the hot time when everything is dry. We would come back and meet together as one. We knew where Junju was because of the smoke. The smoke was a signal to come and meet together in one place. That's how you knew to meet together in one big place, a place like Kurtararra or Yimiri. It was a special kind of smoke made with spinifex, a big smoke to say, "We're here, we're coming back".'
PHOTO: WALTER MACDOUGALL FILM STILL, AṞA IRITITJA, 1964

MacDougall's journal

Smokes from five separate fires were seen to the east late that evening.

I made camp knowing that I was opposite and in view of the natives who were camped on the opposite side of the lake some 3 miles [5 kilometres] away. I did this deliberately with the intention of demonstrating that I was not trying to take them by surprise.

Wednesday 20 May 1964 Night

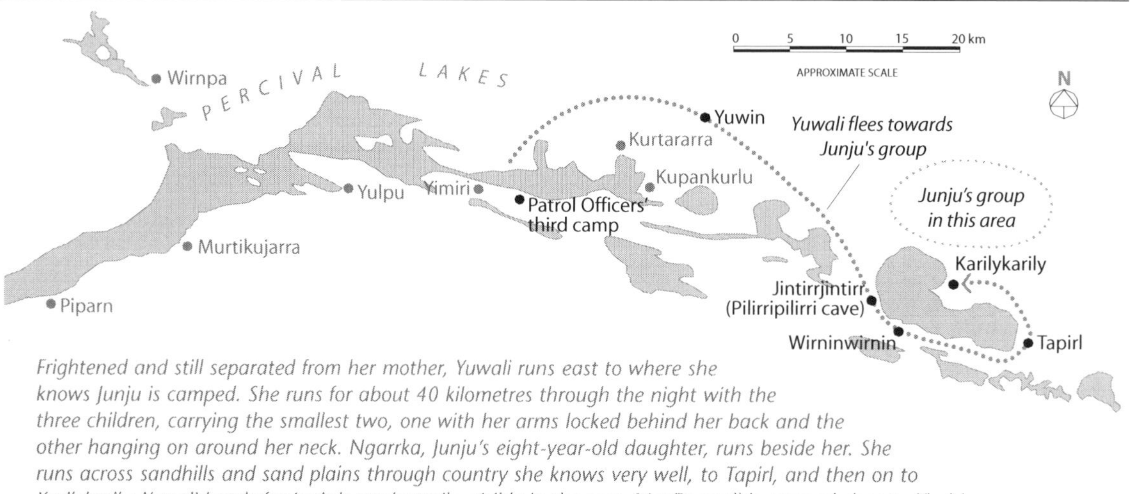

Frightened and still separated from her mother, Yuwali runs east to where she knows Junju is camped. She runs for about 40 kilometres through the night with the three children, carrying the smallest two, one with her arms locked behind her back and the other hanging on around her neck. Ngarrka, Junju's eight-year-old daughter, runs beside her. She runs across sandhills and sand plains through country she knows very well, to Tapirl, and then on to Karilykarily. Yuwali heads for Junju's smoke trails, visible in the east. MacDougall is camped close to Yimiri.

Yuwali

We went north in the night. We left and ran away, we were all running up the sandhills and down the sandhills. We had no water to drink so we decided to come back. The sun was almost going down. Then we walked back to the same waterhole. We went twice back to the sandhill. We were still waiting and looking for our Mum. We didn't have a drink of water. We stayed there, beside our fire and a tree.

We made some firesticks, then went back in the middle of the night to get some water [at Yuwin]. They [the other Martu] had covered our waterhole. We felt around but couldn't find the water — nothing!

Tapirl is a rockhole at the base of hills 100 metres from the edge of a small lake in the Percival Lakes group. PHOTO: SUE DAVENPORT, 1999

The Martu covered up springs and soaks to stop animals and birds fouling the water. PHOTO: TERRY LONG, 1964

We went back towards the north, climbing a sandhill. After sitting on the sandhill, we said to each other, 'Let's go quickly.' We got up and started walking up the sandhill towards the west, then back towards the north, then back around. I said, 'We are going towards the waterholes.'

We came to Tapirl in the night, lighting our way with firesticks. We had a drink at Tapirl. We made some more firesticks, and then got up. There were just the four of us, Ngarrka, Mangayi, one brother and myself. We went east. We stayed together in one group, walking in the night around Yarrkayija. We continued going west until it was dawn.

Thursday 21 May 1964

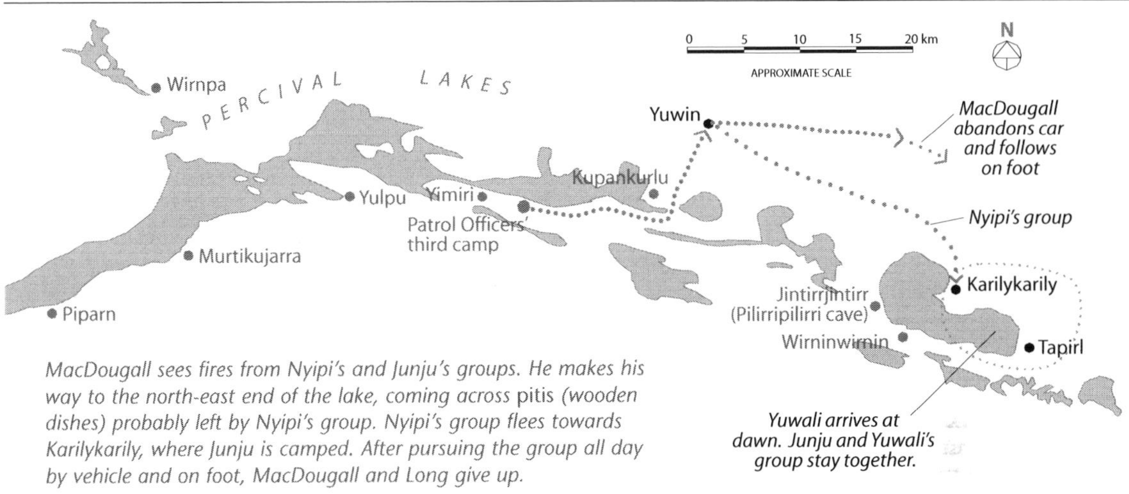

MacDougall sees fires from Nyipi's and Junju's groups. He makes his way to the north-east end of the lake, coming across pitis *(wooden dishes) probably left by Nyipi's group. Nyipi's group flees towards Karilykarily, where Junju is camped. After pursuing the group all day by vehicle and on foot, MacDougall and Long give up.*

Yuwali

At dawn we arrived at Karilykarily.

We were looking around where the *minyarra* [wild onion] grow; we were looking for Junju and three old grandmothers. We went east and we saw the smoke over in the sandhills.

When the morning came, we caught up with Junju and the others. When we arrived my mother was cooking some *wamurla*. They [Junju's group] were watching us come from the west.

We climbed up to them very early in the morning, after walking all night. They were all crying. Then we told Junju everything: 'We thought it was a rock!' We told her everything about what we saw — 'Must be a rock — a big rock! Must be!'

Then she was frightened. We were all frightened. We told them that devilmen were after us in the motor car. We thought that the motor car was a devil. We had never seen a motor car before.

MacDougall's journal

The invasion from the unknown was too much, and they moved to the east.

Long speaking in 1999

In the morning we saw these columns of smoke rising as if people were lighting fires deliberately.

Long's journal

We were now attempting to pursue them, the lighters of the fires. Both vehicles attempted to make a fast passage to the eastern end of the lake but were bogged 5 times in the mouths of creeks, which entered the lake every few yards.

MacDougall's journal

I found very fresh tracks leading east from the eastern end of the lake. These I followed to a soakage 6 miles [10 kilometres] from the lake and the first signs of panicky flight were seen. Wooden dishes were abandoned, a lookout posted on nearby hill, no more fires were lit, impulse food hunting was stopped and there was always a single track between me and the tracks of the main group.

Women and children collecting ***minyarra*** (wild onion, *Cyperus bulbosus*) in *pitis*, just as Yuwali and her group would have done. *Minyarra* is a small bulb of a sedge-type grass. To harvest it the soil is pounded with stones and then carefully scraped away and sifted by hand. The bulbs are then picked out one by one. They can be eaten raw or cooked on the fire, which makes them a little sweeter. PHOTO: BOB VERBURGT, 1960s

Yuwali

We had a little bit to eat, then Junju asked us to go [with her]. My mother told us Junju could take us to another place. We went on the lake; we walked on the side till we found some wild onion. We had a drink of water. They [Junju's mob] took us with them in the night.

Long's journal

Hunting fires were springing up in an area which appeared to be in the extreme north-east of the lake, and this arm was reached about 2.00 pm.

A fire sprang up within a quarter of a mile of the vehicles. We then made haste to round the last two sandhills into a broad valley, which had an unusual covering of blackened ironstone. The whole of the area looked as if it had been blasted by some volcanic action: it was blackened with almost a surface of stone on it.

Then we saw fires further to the east and it was obvious that people were now running from us.

TOP: **The abandoned camp** discovered by Long. PHOTO: TERRY LONG, 1964

BELOW: **Smoke** across the lake. PHOTO: SUE DAVENPORT, 1999

MacDougall's journal

The vehicles could not cross the sandhills at the point where the natives crossed and many detours were necessary. As they were travelling almost due east, I followed them until they were out of the prescribed area.

MacDougall holding a *piti*. *Pitis* were made by the men and used by the women to collect water, food and carry objects and even, at times, babies. The dishes ranged in size from small drinking bowls to large containers. PHOTO: ROBERT MACAULAY, 1964

Long's journal

We were now convinced that the group was running from us and were very frightened.

Four miles [6 kilometres] up this valley we found a well-used soak in a rock catchment with a dampened *piti* which had obviously just contained water, and other shallow digging tools all damp from recent use.

From here we followed fresh tracks which led up the valley for a further two miles [3 kilometres] and then went over three sandhills in the direction of a small kidney-shaped lake to the south-east.

We followed on foot but saw no sign of life and returned to the vehicle at dark. It was obvious that the party of eight people, including two children, had been surprised by our sudden appearance in the valley and had disappeared in sheer panic.

Gordon McKay and Alec Oliver drink from a *piti* abandoned by Yuwali's group. PHOTO: TERRY LONG, 1964

Long speaking in 1999

We followed them as best we could but it was obvious we weren't getting any nearer and we weren't really accomplishing anything.

We decided that we needed another method to contact them. We felt we were frightening them.

We made a decision that we would not be able to make face-to-face contact and that this should no longer be the aim of the patrol. We decided to keep following them to keep contact with the group's position and to try to make sure they were not in the prescribed area at the time of firing.

Yuwin soak with abandoned *piti*. PHOTO: ROBERT MACAULAY, 1964

Friday **22 May** 1964

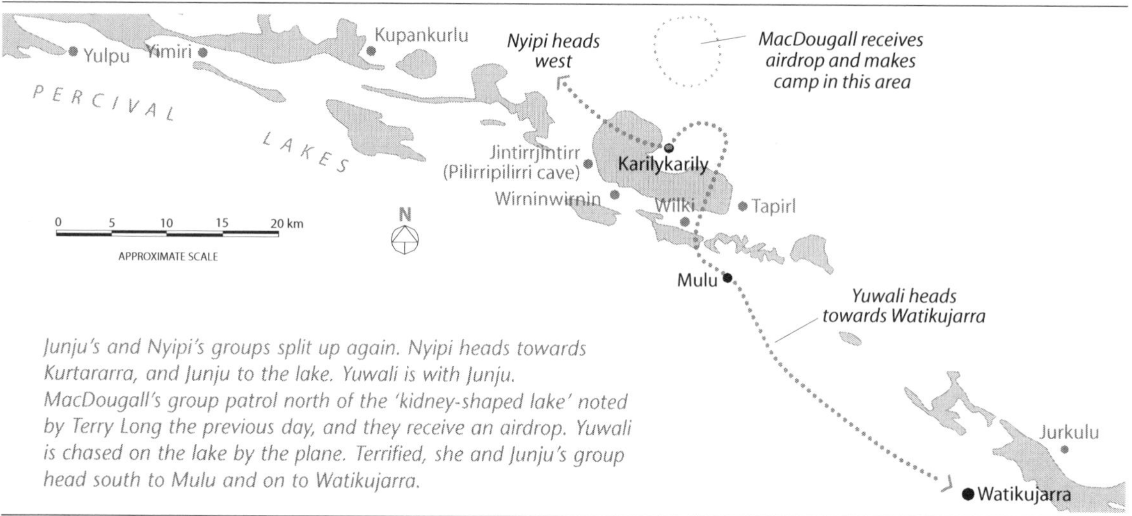

Junju's and Nyipi's groups split up again. Nyipi heads towards Kurtararra, and Junju to the lake. Yuwali is with Junju. MacDougall's group patrol north of the 'kidney-shaped lake' noted by Terry Long the previous day, and they receive an airdrop. Yuwali is chased on the lake by the plane. Terrified, she and Junju's group head south to Mulu and on to Watikujarra.

Yuwali

We went north, then came down to the lake and went south. We ran across the lake and up a sandhill. We ran towards Karrpinyupungu in the east. We were running but there were no trees on the lake. We saw an aeroplane coming towards us on the lake. It came close over us. We didn't know where to run. It chased us and we tried to hide in some small bushes, but our attempts were no good. We lit a fire and left. The plane lifted up after a long time from the smoke.

We ran to water, we came to Mulu. Junju dug out the soak. We were thirsty.

Soaks are a very important source of water in the desert. Sand or mud is scooped out, often to a substantial depth, until clean water gathers in the base of the hole. The precise location of each soak must be known. PHOTO: BOB VERBURGT, 1965

MacDougall and Long's vehicles seen from the plane making the airdrop. PHOTO: ROBERT MACAULAY, 1964

Long's journal

An airdrop was made to us.

The difficulties inherent in the task of an aircraft spotting human life in such surroundings was very evident. Although both vehicles were parked on the top of a sandhill, the plane had to be talked in to us and we learnt that we were not sighted until the very last moment.

For the next two days an attempt was made to follow them in the direction of a string of small lakes eastward from Lake Percival and they were tracked to a position on, or near, the perimeter of the dump area.

Long speaking in 1999

❛ We were still slowly following the signs of the fires, which were still being lit. Gordon McKay felt that they were watching us, that they were moving away. He felt a bit frustrated by it all, as he felt he could talk to them.

He was an old man, though. He couldn't really race about and he was only there to interpret really. We needed someone younger that could, if necessary, run them down.

We felt that it would be a mixed group of males and females and they were probably not wanting to go back to a mission or government station. We had no idea, of course, that they had had no contact with anybody at all for years. We really had no idea what sort of people we were up against.

Once it was obvious that we weren't getting anywhere, that we were perhaps making things worse for ourselves, we decided to stop.

MacDougall's journal

❛ Considerable air activity and, to them, a very rapid approach by land vehicle frightened the natives into retreat. Difficulty was experienced in sandhills. This prevented me from running them down.

Yuwali

❛ [Later] we went back towards the west. We stayed on a sandhill and made a fire and we sat down and had a rest. My mother was still back at Kurtararra. She was looking for us. But Junju had all of us kids; she was keeping us.

It rained hard on us. We heard a noise: it was the motor car! It was following our footprints. We got up, running. We were running towards the south. We sat under the shade in the day. When it was dark we walked over to the big hill Watikujarra. We slept there.

The weather began to change. Over the course of the next few days it became extremely cold, rainy and windy, making the salt lake very slippery and boggy. This bad weather remained for a number of days. PHOTO: SUE DAVENPORT, 2002

The twin springs at **Kurtararra**. PHOTO: TERRY LONG, 1964

Signal from MacDougall to WRE.

A group of natives are making contact in the [Karilykarily] area. Just crossing big sandhills in an easterly direction. I have travelled to north-easterly boundary. I recommend and will stay in this area if authorised until the firing plus one day.

Friday 22 May 1964 Night

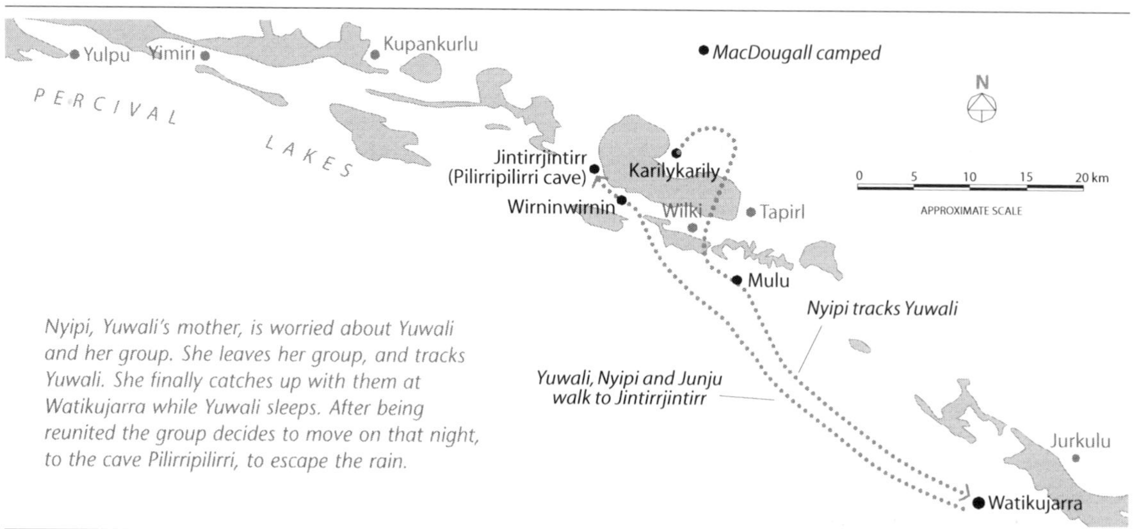

Nyipi, Yuwali's mother, is worried about Yuwali and her group. She leaves her group, and tracks Yuwali. She finally catches up with them at Watikujarra while Yuwali sleeps. After being reunited the group decides to move on that night, to the cave Pilirripilirri, to escape the rain.

Yuwali

While we were asleep, we heard a noise in the middle of the night. A noise like someone crying. It was Mum. She was crying for us. She followed our tracks — all the way while we were asleep she came to us. She was crying all the way, looking for us and following our tracks.

We got up in the night. We didn't want to stay there. We made firesticks and went back towards the west and then north. We came to Mikara, and we had a drink and a sleep, and got up. And we returned to the west.

After walking all night, some went towards the south. We went to the hill Jintirrjintirr, the dreamtime place, and Pilirripilirri cave and stayed there for the night.

Yuwali believed that the vehicle, a devil, could track their footprints. That night they camped on a sandhill: when winds are not too strong, the tops of high dunes are preferred as campsites that afford a clear view in all directions. The Martu's dislike of camping in hilly country or any partly enclosed areas relates to fears of attack by revenge expeditions. PHOTO: SUE DAVENPORT, 1999

Saturday **23 May** 1964

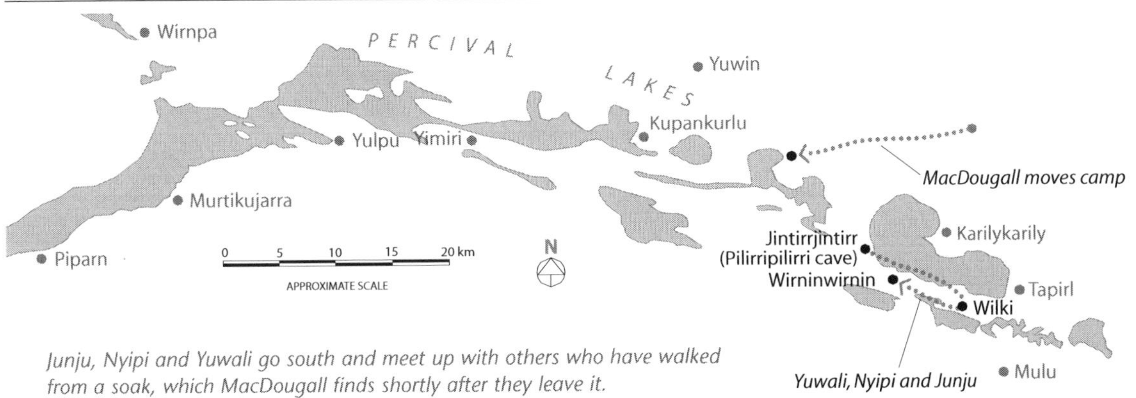

Junju, Nyipi and Yuwali go south and meet up with others who have walked from a soak, which MacDougall finds shortly after they leave it.

Yuwali

We slept all day till the afternoon in that cave. When it was the afternoon we went looking for food. We got some *wamurla*. We were eating.

The motor car was still looking for us around in the east near the lake area.

We slept till the afternoon in the cave.

The party's Land Rover seen from a cave. PHOTO: BOB TONKINSON, 1964

Long's journal

On the 23rd more tracks were found near the boot-shaped lake just within the [prescribed area]. A well-used soak was found here and evidence of yet another group of about 6 people [The group that returned to Kurtararra]. All tracks went off in a westerly direction and we followed.

This lake was almost entirely mud and clay and both vehicles were badly bogged in the treacherous surface around the shoreline. There was an awful lot of work extricating the vehicle.

Both vehicles were finally freed at 8.00 pm and we camped on the spot.

The International: bogged yet again. PHOTO: VIC SURMAN, 1964

Signal from MacDougall to WRE

All of the area north of the Beadell Road is clear with the exception of a group that are in the area between eastern end of Lake Percival and Lake Tobin. Whilst we are in the area they will not return to Lake Percival or go south. Aircraft has not reported any sign south of Beadell Road.

In July 1963 Len Beadell completed the **Gary Junction Road**, grading from Well 35 along the southern side of Lake Percival and on to Callawa Station. PHOTO: ROBERT MACAULAY, 1964

Signal from WRE to MacDougall

You are authorised remain where you are until D+1 [The day after the firing of F1]. Advise if you are satisfied area clear, repeat answer to Gare [Frank Gare, the Commissioner of Native Welfare in Perth, to whom Long was answerable].

After sleeping for most of the day, Yuwali's group start walking south in the late afternoon. They go to Wilki, and then north to Wirninwirnin, where they stay the night. They cover a distance of 45 kilometres that night.

Yuwali

‘We were walking along, and we dug for some wild onion (*minyarra*). We ate some there.

We went south to Wilki. We climbed over the sandhill and had a drink of water. We met up all together at that big spring. Then we went back towards the south.

We couldn't go on so we thought, ‘Let's go north!’ We returned to Wirninwirnin in the north, and had a drink of water. We went to the west in the night.

Sunday **24 May** 1964

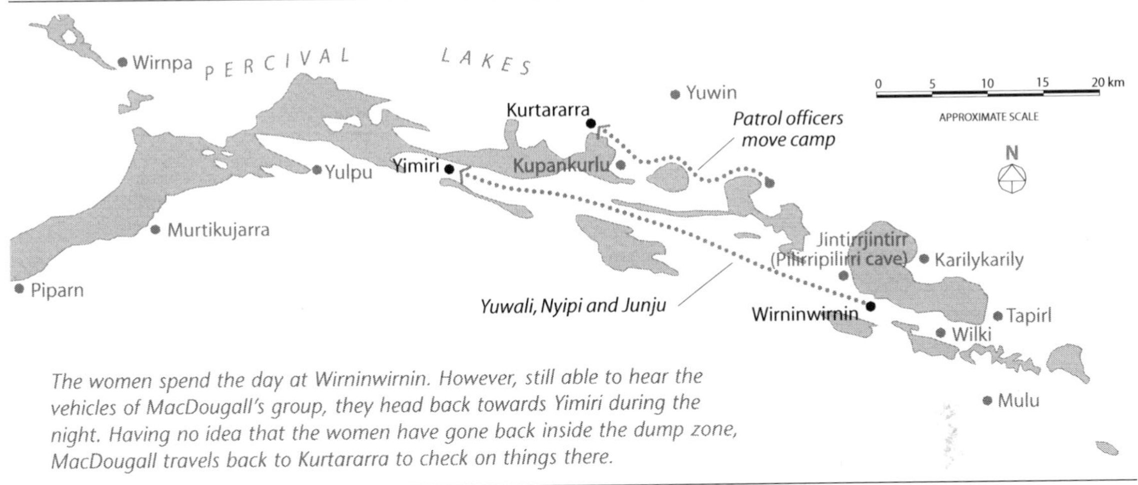

The women spend the day at Wirninwirnin. However, still able to hear the vehicles of MacDougall's group, they head back towards Yimiri during the night. Having no idea that the women have gone back inside the dump zone, MacDougall travels back to Kurtararra to check on things there.

Yuwali

We were eating *wilyki* [seeds] near our camp.

In the middle of the night we heard a noise: a motor car coming. We got up and ran and ran towards the west. They were searching for us in the east. The motor car was following us around.

They were following us in the distance, from the east. We began running away from them, heading north towards Wuputirltirl [Yimiri], the place of the water snake.

We went up till we got to Yimiri, but that car was close behind us, following us; but we ran. We ran in the middle of the lake till we got to Yimiri. We went right into Yimiri.

We had a drink. We went into the soak.

Long's journal

On the 24th it was decided that it might be profitable to examine the north shore of the Lake Percival in the vicinity of 2 soaks [Kurtararra] seen from the air by Mr. MacDougall. The soaks were off shore on 2 islands and well-worn pads ran to them from all points of the compass. These soaks were located at 1.00 pm. The area was an old and most extensive encampment with evidence of very recent occupation.

Terry Long's vehicle parked at Kurtararra. PHOTO: TERRY LONG, 1964

Monday **25 May** 1964

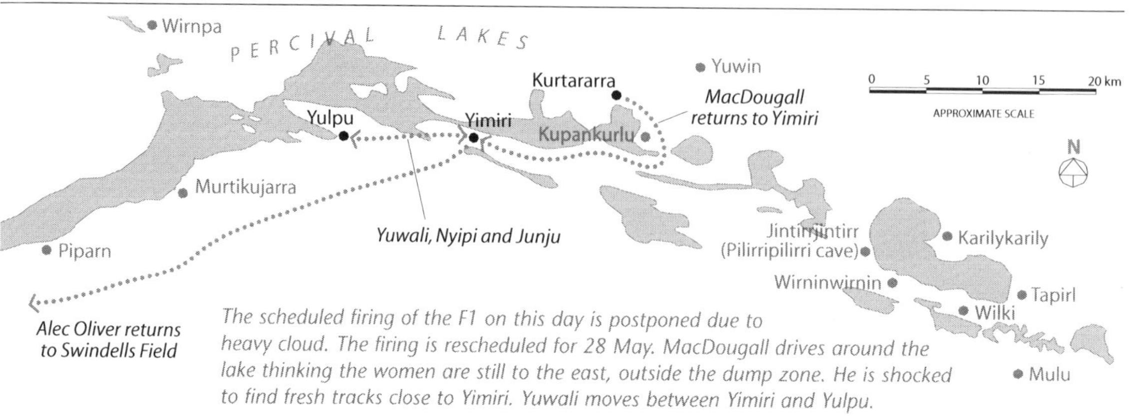

The scheduled firing of the F1 on this day is postponed due to heavy cloud. The firing is rescheduled for 28 May. MacDougall drives around the lake thinking the women are still to the east, outside the dump zone. He is shocked to find fresh tracks close to Yimiri. Yuwali moves between Yimiri and Yulpu.

Yuwali

In the morning, we saw that motor car coming back towards us. We went back and camped towards the west in Yulpu, and then they were coming for us. We saw them coming and we ran away from them.

Some of them were in the motor car, some were out of the motor car.

Yuwali and her group saw MacDougall coming around the lake and moved to Yulpu, after calling up the watersnake to protect them by drawing a **picture in the sand**. PHOTO: WALTER MACDOUGALL FILM STILL, ARA IRITITJA, 1964

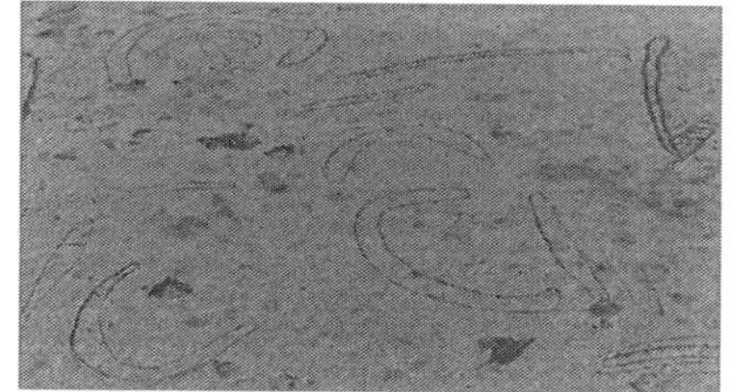

Drawing made in the lake's salt crust by **Kurtu**, Junju's ten-year-old son, close to Yimiri. The drawing, according to Long and Oliver, was very similar to paintings in Picture Hill Cave. Drawing a picture of the rainmaking snake was a way of warning 'Don't come!' or 'Look out!' and was part of an attempt to have the snake assist them to scare off the intruders. As it happened, heavy rains started around this time, which stymied the patrol officers for the next few days. PHOTO: TERRY LONG, 1964

MacDougall's journal

Whilst travelling east on the southern shore of the lake, I discovered I had pushed the group a bit too hard and that they had turned back from their last known position [north of Karilykarily]. They travelled west along the little lakes and crossed the lake [around Yimiri].

This fact complicated matters and I decided to remain on the lake to ensure that they did not move any further west.

Mr. Long decided to stay with me and this meant that Mr. Oliver and the native interpreter in my patrol vehicle returned to Swindells Field for petrol and water.

In the evening I caught up to a tame dingo completely exhausted, this emphasised the fact that I had been pushing the group too hard.

The women called up the spirit of **Yimiri**, the watersnake. MacDougall sent Alec Oliver back to Swindells Field. The women, seeing Oliver head west, assumed that the trucks had been chased away by the watersnake.

In 1999, a group of Martu — including Yuwali and Junju — returned to Yimiri, accompanied by Sue Davenport. While they were travelling along the lake 20 kilometres from Yimiri, a white spiral rose up in the far distance (possibly the wind lifting salt from the lake's surface). The wind moved the spiral so that it started to bend over to 'look at' the group. Yuwali described this as Yimiri the snake getting up from the waterhole and looking at the party. This manifestation of the snake was powerful and frightening for the Martu, who responded by warning him of their approach by lighting fires. When the group arrived on the shore of the lake close to Yimiri, Junju called loudly to Yimiri in Manyjilyjara — his language — to tell him who they were. The party then walked in single file to the spring, which is about 1 kilometre from the shore. As they walked, they scraped the lake's surface with branches and called out loudly.

As the party approached Yimiri, they shouted more loudly and finally ran to the mound, beating the mound with the branches. Yuwali then entered into the middle of the bulrushes. In the middle, she scooped up mud, which she then smeared on each person's face, arms, legs and hair. After this had been done, the party relaxed and entered the bulrushes to drink water from the spring. PHOTO: PETER KENDRICK, 1999

Yuwali

❝ Then we saw the cloud of the water snake, all spreading around. They kept on running away, the whitefellas in the motor car. We saw the water snake's tongue coming out from the spring.

That snake got out from his spring and he was way down looking at us. All the cloud was round that big spring of that water snake. It was dinner time. It was chasing these people westwards. They kept on running towards the west. We saw them go.

We were at our own camp, Yimiri. We ran in the middle of the lake till we got to Yimiri, then we went to the other side. We had to have a rest.

It started raining on us in the afternoon. We went and collected some wamurla. We returned to our camp for a drink from the spring.

It was late afternoon when we went back to Yimiri. We got the water in a wooden dish. We kept on running north climbing over some sandhills. We stopped and had a sleep.

Long's journal

❝ The weather now deteriorated rapidly and rain and wind lashed down during the ensuing 5 days while a patrol was maintained in a 60-mile [97 kilometres] length of the southern shore.

No more fires were seen again despite our attempts to attract the attention of any watchers by lighting large areas of spinifex.

It was learned that the firing was again postponed until the 28th May. It was now raining steadily.

We crossed fresh tracks on the southern shore at 2 pm, all heading across the narrow straits towards the north west.

Following the tracks on foot toward two rush islands in the lake [Yimiri] 1$^1/_2$ miles [2.5 kilometres] from shore, we counted 14 separate tracks and a number of dogs.

An artist in the group had drawn an extensive picture story in the salt close by the rush islands, which each contained a bubbling freshwater soak. The drawings were most interesting and several pictures were taken in the failing light. The legendary rock hole snake was the main feature, the same snake as drawn at Picture Hill.

Tuesday **26 May** 1964

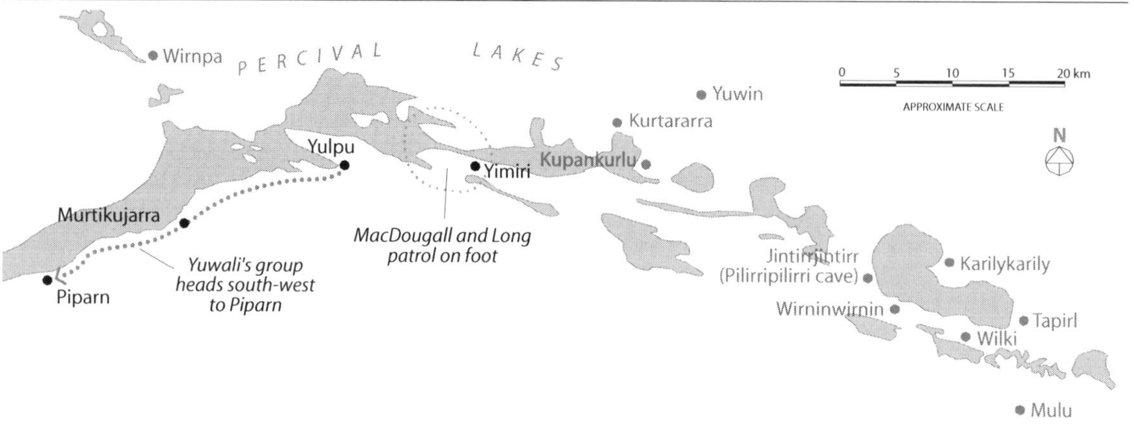

Yuwali

Then it rained all night, till morning. It stopped raining in the morning. Mum got up; she went looking for bush tucker. She went and got some *wamurla*, and brought it home. We all ate it.

Then we got up and walked to another place. We went to this place, Piparn. We went and stopped. We had to sleep, to spend a night there.

Following the rain, water settled on the usually dry lakes, impeding both parties' movements. PHOTO: ROBERT MACAULAY, 1964

Long's journal

MacDougall and I walked across the lakes and followed the tracks north-west for three miles but found that the rain and wind was obliterating the foot prints. It appeared likely the group had been heading for the three small lakes in the north-west.

Wednesday **27 May** to Friday **29 May** 1964

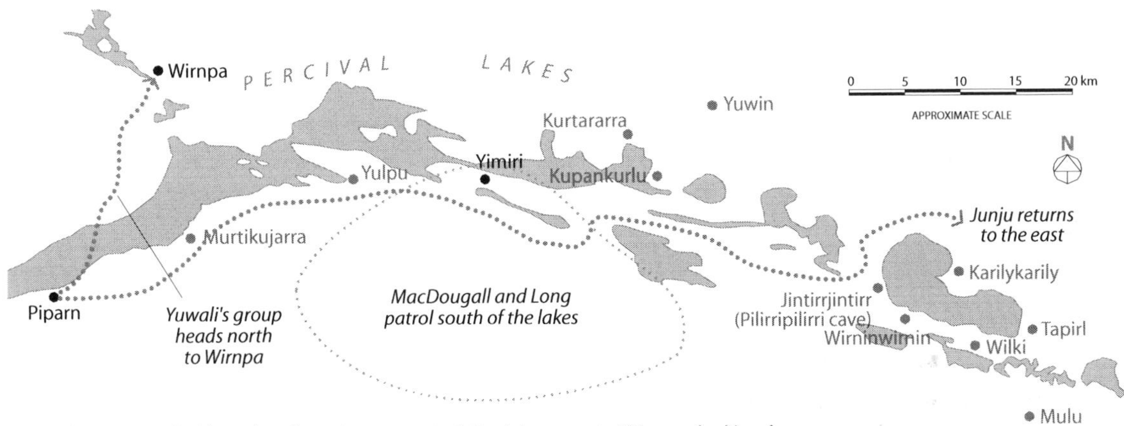

The women decide to head north-west, out of the lake area, to Wirnpa, looking for Yuwali's father. The group then have a discussion and decide to split up. Yuwali's group go in search of her father and Junju's group go east towards the country in which she was born. MacDougall and Long maintain their patrol along the south of the lake, trying to ensure that nobody comes into the dump zone.

Yuwali

Then we got up, walking again. Till those people that were looking for us stopped looking. Then we went back, because they couldn't find us.

Then we went back to our normal life.

We asked each other there, right there. We went back for this man [her father] to Wirnpa: north. We sent some people towards the east — the same four old ladies went towards the east: three grannies and Junju. I took the other four north.

Long's journal

On Friday 29th, news of the cancellation of the firing until 2nd June was received and I obtained instructions from Mr Gare to withdraw from the patrol.

It had now become evident that we could not contact the natives and it was only necessary to maintain a preventative patrol to prevent a return to the interior of the dump zone.

MacDougall's journal

Until the 29th May Mr Long and I maintained a daily patrol along the lake ensuring that the natives did not move either west or south.

As I had clearly stated before our departure, to effectively comb the area and evacuate any natives found within it was impossible without the necessary organisation and months of work. In view of the existing situation, I had decided that I could not make any further serious effort to make face-to-face contact unless ordered to do so.

In view of persistent enquiries [offering another vehicle and a helicopter], Mr Long and I, after several denials of further vehicle requirements together replied that if face-to-face contact was necessary, another Land Rover would help.

After the first patrol

On 29 May, Robert Macaulay arrived and was able to do several half-day trips independently. He was able to confirm MacDougall's belief that this group of natives was outside the prohibited area.

After being delayed twice F1 was finally fired on 5 June 1964. The test was not a success. The rocket veered off course, necessitating its destruction in mid-air by the WRE. Although most of the rocket burnt up, some debris landed in the Central Aboriginal Reserve not far from Giles weather station. None of the women heard or saw this rocket as it blew up many hundreds of kilometres south of the Percival Lakes.

On their way back to Woomera, MacDougall and Macaulay, 'Suffered a mild shock on the 6th June when we discovered that a party of at least four natives had camped at a point 5 or 6 miles [8 to 10 kilometres] west of Well 35 on the Canning Stock Route from 25th to 30th May'.[3] This group was therefore probably in the prohibited area during the firing of F1.

In a report that was highly critical of the preparation by WRE and the resources that had been made available to the patrol, Macaulay gave his assessment of its success:

> I patrolled the southern shore of the main Percival Lake over a length of fifty miles [80 kilometres] for a period of eight days. I visited several waters encountered by Mr MacDougall and I came to the same conclusion as he — that we were able to maintain a position between the aborigines and the impact area only because the aborigines agreed to this condition. At any time they could have by-passed us with comparative ease. Although this small group might be classed as Lake dwellers, there were obviously sufficient waters away from the lakes for them to move about in comfort.[4]

After the officers returned to Woomera, Yuwali's group continued with their lives. MacDougall and Long returned to their organisations to report on the patrol and its failings, and prepare for the second firing (F2) in October.

As described above, Yuwali's family split up from Junju's family before or during the firing, Junju heading east and Yuwali's family north to try and meet up with her father. Yuwali describes their journey, which took place over a period of months and through a series of water sources:

> We went back for this man [Daddy], northwards to Wirnpa. We sent some people towards the east, the same four old ladies: Karntipa, Junju, Yukurrpani and Kulata. I took the other four north. We went and had a drink at Lunkunku, kept on walking and had a drink in Ngarnin. From Ngarnin, we had a drink in Jitiri.

We had a drink in Lunkuran. We were digging for wild onion. We were still looking for the old man, in the north.

Then we went towards Jurlpananya. From Jurlpananya, we went to Ngarnin and kept on to Wuruwuru. From Wuruwuru to Jurlpananya, and on to Waparnukujirri. From Waparnukujirri we went to Wuyuta; from Wuyuta we went east to Purnti.

We were tracking the footprints. We saw Daddy's footprints, they were taking *warlpi* footsteps [i.e. travelling in single file with each person stepping in the previous person's footsteps so as to confuse anyone following them] around only one person — Jikartu [one of his wives] — and the old man Nyiwiljukurr.

We tracked their footprints to Martukura. We went back to Lunkurangu. It was the really hot time there. The lizards were getting up [i.e. breaking their hibernation]. There was no water there.

We kept on walking, still following the footsteps of Parnpakaka [Nyiwiljukurr]. We came back on our own tracks. We stayed around Wirnpa. We were homesick for another waterhole. There were four of us there and we were getting frightened. We didn't want to stay there. We got up and went towards [main camp].[5]

Yuwali's search for her father was unsuccessful and the group decided to return to the lake. They returned to Kurtararra on the northern side, where they were reunited with Junju's group, and life returned to normal. For a time.

The first patrol resulted in the family groups being scattered around the Percival Lakes. Junju's group headed east, while Yuwali's group travelled through the water sources north of the lakes in search of her father. The map below shows some, but not all, of the waterholes visited.

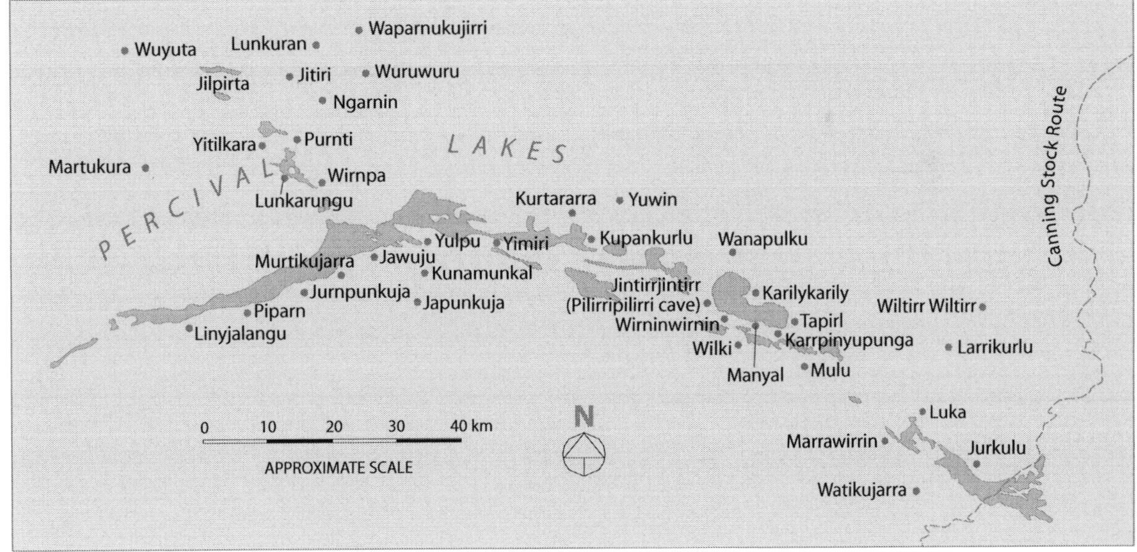

PART THREE

BETWEEN PATROLS

The fallout

> Already, nearly all good tribal land has been taken over for the fattening of sheep and cattle, or the extraction of minerals. This year — 1964 — the Northern Territory and Western Australian Governments are hurrying the last of our nomadic people from the poorer lands into civilisation.[1]

> Quite clearly, the Government wanted them out of the way of the rockets, into what appeared to be a crash programme of assimilation.[2]

The F1 firing was not entirely successful:

> Most of the powered flight went according to plan, but the last six seconds were curtailed. As the tanks emptied the remaining propellants began to slosh about, causing oscillations to build up which the sensitive steering system could not cope with. Slow motion film taken through telescopic lenses showed the rocket rolling and then cartwheeling spectacularly across the sky before the engines cut out.[3]

The rocket landed hundreds of kilometres short of its target, directly inside the Central Aboriginal Reser ve. Thankfully, nobody was injured. In the dump zone, MacDougall and Macaulay shepherded Y uwali's group away from any predictable danger, but failed to make contact.

By the time of the patrol for the F2 firing in October 1964, a series of controversies had created a far higher profile for the work of the patrol officers. The policy towards and treatment of desert Indigenous people by state and federal bodies was under the spotlight. Public debate, newspaper articles, parliamentar y questions, severe internal criticism and mutual distrust were creating a hot atmosphere. Any decisions about what should be done with Indigenous people found by the patrol officers was likely to be highly public and potentially controversial.

The adverse publicity began shortly after the F1 firing. In July 1964, a report by Macaulay to the superintendent in Woomera cited, 'an awareness of the immensely increased publicity, political and public interest in aborigines'.[4] What had happened?

Launch of a Blue Streak rocket.
PHOTO: FROM THE COLLECTION OF THE NATIONAL ARCHIVES OF AUSTRALIA

Three items of information combined to fan public debate: the decision by the joint patrol of April 1964 to bring forty-two Indigenous people in from the desert to Papunya; the conduct of the F1 patrol; and the misfiring of F1.

The disquiet actually began within the DNW and the WRE — the two agencies that had cooperated in the F1 patrol.

Terry Long wrote a full report, and his conclusions focused on the inadequate resources applied to the task:

> To carry out a really competent search of the target [area] would take six months, and would require two vehicles, plus a supply unit . . .
>
> It is obvious that a quite considerable number of aboriginals are living a full and free tribal life in the Great Sandy Desert . . .
>
> If contact is considered to be essential, it will require to be accomplished over an extended period . . . I feel it should be the prerogative of our Department to make the attempt to contact these people; but it will be time consuming and expensive. [5]

His most pointed criticisms dealt with the tactics employed in the chase:

> They [the Aboriginal people] should not, again, be subjected to the harrying tactics which were inevitably applied in view of the completely inadequate time at the disposal of the search party. Hardships resulted through the forced curtailment of hunting activities; long marches with children in company and probable exhaustion. The possibility of injury from an expended missile is so remote as to be almost non-existent and I would respectfully submit that we are doing them more harm in our attempts to ensure their safety than if we left them entirely alone. [6]

MacDougall's report concurred with Long's, saying that the objectives of the patrol required months of work. He expressed concern about the conduct of the patrol, saying that, 'considerable air activity and, to them, a very rapid approach . . . frightened the natives into retreat'.[7] He pointed out that limited planning and resources had directly compromised Aboriginal safety, citing the discovery of the small group of people camped on the Canning Stock Route, well within the 'dump zone' at the time of the firing.[8]

Immediately after the F1 patrol, MacDougall had continued with patrol activities and had made contact with several Indigenous people in the Central Aboriginal Reserve who had, 'heard the re-entry or break-up explosions . . . and one who claimed he had seen evidence of impact'.[9] From this he deduced that the debris had landed close to a mining camp at Mount Davies, an area frequented by Indigenous people.

In a post-mortem of the F1 failure, Macaulay highlighted the potential repercussions in relations with the DNW. He recalled a conversation with the commissioner in Perth on 21 May 1964, who, 'asked me the logical question of what would happen if natives were seen from the air in the impact area just prior to firing time'. Macaulay went on, 'From my experience it can be said that the W A Department has not always been confident in WRE activities in the Central Reserve . . . and any confidence engendered over the years by the NPOs could easily be jeopardised by a mismanaged programme such as the Blue Streak search programme'.[10]

Macaulay repeated the criticisms made by MacDougall and Long that the seach had been too rushed. The strength of feeling about how poorly the seach had gone was evident: 'It was quite ludicrous to send out one WRE vehicle to comb an unknown area of 120 miles [193 kilometres] x 90 miles [145 kilometres] in about one week'.[11]

That July the F1 patrol became the subject of public scrutiny . Kim Beazley (senior, a member of the Labor opposition in the House of Representatives, later to become a minister in the Whitlam government), had received a letter from 'a missionary' which raised questions about the conduct of the patrol:

> The target area for the recent firing is in territor y still inhabited by tribal nomadic Aborigines. When smoke and tracks were seen in the area attempts were made to locate these people by low-flying planes buzzing them and vehicles pursuing them. This naturally caused such fear that none could be located and contacted and the firing went on regardless. The effect of this buzzing and pursuit on future contacts with these people gives rise to concern. [12]

Dr Charles Duguid had also got wind of the firing, and was making himself a thorn in the sides of the various governments once again.

In a paper titled *Relentless Assimilation in Western Australia and Northern Territory — End of the Tribes*, Duguid charged that a new and cynical method was being used to find Indigenous desert people:

> When, fairly recently, smoke was seen from the air, low-flying aeroplanes buzzed forwards and backwards over the area frightening the Aborigines out of their wits. The terrified nomads went into hiding, and where they secreted themselves will not be known until in desperation they again have to light fires for warmth and cooking.[13]

Both Duguid and the missionary who had complained to Beazley had a remarkable knowledge in early July of the details of the F1 patrol and precise information on the crash. The Commissioner of Native W elfare in Western Australia did not have information about the location of the rocket's landing until after 17 July, the location of the debris was not notified to the Department of Supply by WRE until 24 July, and this information was not provided by WRE to the Minister for Territories until 15 August.[14] So where did the information come from?

The sour ce was an unhappy W alter MacDougall. Three weeks after the Blue Streak firing, MacDougall had called in at Ernabella to visit Bill Edwards, the mission superintendent. Edwards occasionally accompanied MacDougall on patrols.

> Mr Mac came in Sunday afternoon and spent the night with us. He had been waiting for the Blue Streak rocket for a couple of weeks. He was not ver y happy about the setup as they had tried to contact some Aborigines in the target area to clear them out but the buzzing by planes frightened them so much that they could

> not catch them. Then the rocket fell short in the middle of the Aboriginal reserve and close to a camp at Mount Davies.[15]

As in his battles with them in the 1950s, the WRE had once again let MacDougall down. He felt that he had neither been consulted about nor placed in control of the F1 search plans, which had led to 'buzzing' by the search planes. And while he was conscientiously trying to clear the dump zone, rocket fragments were lobbing in the central reserve, hundreds of kilometres down-range. Very upset, but knowing from bitter experience that he could not come out publicly, he had approached his friend to take action.[16]

If MacDougall wanted to create a fuss, he succeeded.

Woomera jumped at the controversy. This was exactly the type of profile they didn't want. The WRE controller in Salisbury, South Australia, provided a four-page signal to head office in Melbourne stating that, 'it is not considered that any persons in the area were endangered'. He acknowledged that the low-level air search, 'may have been construed as "buzzing" camps', but stated that, 'the action was not deliberate in this sense'.[17]

The same issues concerned the Western Australian government. Frank Gare wrote a pointed letter to Woomera about the failure of the F1 to land anywhere near the intended dump zone:

> The strenuous precautions taken were all based on the assumption that the fragments of the rocket would fall within the designated 'impact area'. It seems that this did not happen and advice would be appreciated as to just where it is assumed that the fragments did fall, please.[18]

Gare also demanded that a different approach be instituted for subsequent launchings to safeguard Aboriginal people. He suggested that the next meeting of the Central Reserves Committee was an appropriate forum to discuss the problem.[19]

Gare's suggestion was not received well at Woomera. A diary entry by EG Foreshew, the WRE chief safety officer who was largely responsible for the patrol planning, commented that discussion of safety measures for the firings by the committee was 'NOT on'.[20]

In July, Gare wrote to his minister about the relations between the DNW and WRE:

> It is beyond dispute that the activities of the WRE have interfered a great deal with the normal life of the desert Aboriginals and for this reason it has accepted responsibility so far as it is able . . . [T]here is no reason to doubt its sincerity or efficiency. In fact it has virtually unlimited resources at its disposal and appears to have little difficulty in providing whatever personnel or vehicles are required.[21]

Gare suggested that, given the WRE's resources, they should properly take the major responsibility for safeguarding any Indigenous people in the dump zone for the F2 firing, with the department only contributing the sevices of Terry Long, 'our most experienced officer in this field'.[22]

The minister concurred, but 'insisted' that a representative of the DNW travel with the next WRE patrol to safeguard the welfare of any Indigenous people found.[23]

As always, Gare's department had to juggle its responsibilities and its limited budget. After receiving the WRE's plans for the F2 firing, Gare outlined his requirement: that WRE take, 'full responsibility for safeguarding any Aborigines', that low-flying air craft not be used, and that ground parties have sufficient time to conduct a thorough search of the impact area.[24]

By early September, in the countdown to the F2 firing, a new controversy had hit the federal parliament and the papers.

The letter from Bill Edwards to Beazley had also targeted the April joint patrol, asking whether the transportation of Indigenous people to Papunya was evidence of a government policy of removal. After noting that the Indigenous people had been reportedly found in good condition, the letter questioned whether they should have been taken to Papunya. The missionary particularly queried whether, in view of language difficulties, the people had fully understood the implications of the choice offered to them, whether inducements (such as food) had been offered, why they had been taken to the over-crowded settlement at Papunya and whether they would be repatriated to their country if they wished it.[25]

Duguid also railed against what he saw as the hypocrisy and mindless expedience of government. He was particularly critical of what he saw as a new policy of removal inevitably following contact, particularly of people in apparently good health. Duguid asked: 'Why are they being enticed and impressed to leave their own homeland for a crowded settlement and to a life utterly foreign to them?'[26]

Beazley raised these issues in the House of Representatives, charging that the government was betraying its duties to Indigenous people. 'It looks like the old problem of dispossession because we want something,' he said.[27]

In reply to Beazley's questions, the Minister for Territories, CE Barnes, justified the removal of people to Papunya. He denied any use of, 'force or false persuasion' and stated that 'the patrol found that there was a severe shortage of food and water and that malnutrition existed amongst the Aboriginal children'.[28]

Beazley's reply, as reported in *The Australian* newspaper, summed up the scepticism of many critics in the community about the government's true agenda:

Kim Beazley senior, MHR. PHOTO: NATIONAL LIBRARY OF AUSTRALIA

> Mr Beazley . . . said he found it hard to accept that the Government had to wait for three years of drought before bringing the nomads out of their homelands.
>
> Quite clearly, the Government wanted them out of the way of the rockets, into what appeared to be a crash programme of assimilation.[29]

While Barnes assured the federal parliament that malnutrition and thirst justified a humanitarian act by patrol officers, the Western Australian government was caught in a no-win situation. On the one hand, it could be accused of participating in the

Commonwealth's forced removal of people, on the other it could be charged with neglecting its duties to people starving and dying of thirst in the desert.

Beazley played both cards. The Labor opposition in the Western Australian parliament, aided by a telegram from Beazley to his state Labor colleagues [30], took the opportunity to put the boot into the state government. The Minister for Native Welfare was asked to comment on Barnes's statement, and particularly on his assertions that the joint patrol had found people suffering from malnutrition and a desperate water situation. The Labor shadow minister further asked why it had taken three years of drought before it was left to a Commonwealth patrol to discover such a dire situation (on Western Australian land) and whether the DNW denied responsibility for assisting these people. [31]

The state minister denied coercion and further denied that any of the people were suffering from malnutrition or from a shortage of water, citing information supplied by Dr Elphinstone, the patrol's medical officer, and other state representatives on the joint patrol. [32]

In fact, Dr Elphinstone's draft report had gone quite a bit further than this, contradicting the federal minister's suggestions of malnutrition. In several paragraphs that the DNW unsuccessfully attempted to have removed, Elphinstone stated:

> The main purpose [of the patrol] with which I was not officially concerned, was to offer the natives in the Desert the opportunity of being transported to Papunya Native Settlement in the Northern Territory. The natives were to have a free choice in the matter.
>
> Although a few natives did elect to remain in the Desert for the present, it was a well-chosen time to suggest to them that life could be pleasanter elsewhere. There had been three unusually dry years in succession and game was very scarce.
>
> The decision to encourage the natives to move into a Settlement had already been taken and was not dependent on the Medical Officer's assessment of their health. [33]

On the question of the health of the people met by the patrol, the medical report was clear that there was no suggestion of vitamin deficiency or malnutrition. [34]

Bob Tonkinson, a young anthropologist whose research base was Jigalong, had accompanied the April joint patrol. He tried to defuse the party-political controversy about forced clearance on the joint patrol. In a letter to the *West Australian*, Tonkinson expressed amazement at the statements being made by people, 'who obviously know nothing of the true circumstances'. He denied that there had been any coercion, emphasising that people who wished to stay in the desert had stayed, while others made a decision to move to Papunya:

> The reasons they gave were (a) that too few of them now remained in the area to enable them to carry on essential ceremonial activities and (b) that they wanted to join relatives who were already at Papunya. [35]

Tonkinson then took the politicians and commentators to task:

> Both parties were at fault in their debate on this matter .
>
> Mr Beazley, seeking to make a political issue of it, based his whole invalid argument on statements made by Dr Duguid, whose erroneous outbursts, especially his allegations of bribery, proved that he was quite ignorant of the cir cumstances.
>
> The T erritories Minister Barnes, attempting to justify the shifting of the Aborigines, wrongly blamed poor health and drought conditions.
>
> The simple truth is that the Aborigines exer cised freedom of choice in deciding to join their relatives.[36]

Bob Tonkinson, Jigalong. PHOTO: TREVOR LEVIEN, DATE UNKNOWN

With the conflicting information, concerned members of the public could feel justified in their suspicions about the various governments' actions and designs.

This atmosphere of internal criticism, public scrutiny and greatly heightened sensitivity formed the backdrop to the planning and conduct of the F2 firing. The patrol had to be effective, and any actions that it took in relation to Indigenous people that it found had to withstand scrutiny. In particular, the patrol couldn't be seen to be taking unjustified steps to clear Indigenous people from their land.

PART FOUR

THE SECOND PATROL

PART FIVE

THE CONFINES OF CIVILISATION

Bringing them in

Yuwali's group now found themselves at Jigalong, a mission of the Apostolic Church. It was a situation they could not previously have begun to imagine. How had this happened, and was it right?

Just prior to joining the patrol for the F1 firing, Macaulay had visited Frank Gare, the Commissioner of Native Welfare, in Perth. In discussing the chance that people might be found in the dump area around the Percival Lakes, Gare had made his wishes clear:

> Mr Gare was concerned that no plans had been proposed for the welfare of any evacuees. This was ultimately a matter for the officers on the spot, but Mr Gare naturally insisted that any persons moved away should be returned to their point of evacuation.[1]

Why was this 'insistent' instruction not followed? Despite the atmosphere in parliament, government and the media, Yuwali and her group were taken to Jigalong with no thought of repatriation. What was the department's policy, on this or any of the questions that this patrol raised?

Immediately after the women were found by Sailor and Nyani, MacDougall had signalled WRE, requesting that they contact the commissioner in Perth:

> Now have a total of twenty . No men. Women state there are no men in the area. But there are babies. Suggest you ring Commissioner and suggest that he send welfare officer to care for these, whilst I look for others. [2]

The following day, MacDougall reported that he suspected one woman had leprosy Despite these reports, the DNW took no action, holding to their plan to delay Terry Long's involvement in the patrol for four more weeks.

Once the women and children had been found the sensitivities of the situation were immediately apparent to both the DNW and the WRE. An internal WRE signal, sent the day after MacDougall had contacted Yuwali's group, reflects this:

> Discussed MacDougall situation with Deputy Commissioner WA in absence of Gare at Kalgoorlie. Anderson is reluctant to take any action in absence Commissioner and in any case said that staff situation is such that he could not spare an officer for a period likely to run into 3 weeks or more. Considers also that the alternative of taking natives to a mission would not be politic at present. [3]

Macaulay voiced similar concerns:

> MacDougall has reported that Nyani, a guide, has married Yuwali, approx. 16 years of age. MacDougall would like Gare advised and for Gare to notify Jigalong Mission.

> I believe that the significance is that Nyani will want to take her back to Jigalong and this may lead to her parents, relatives etc. all moving in — similarities with publicity over aborigines moving to Papunya.[4]

Gare's and Anderson's concerns about resourcing may well have justified withholding an officer from the search. But once the women were found, it is surprising that Terry Long was not sent to the Percival Lakes for almost four weeks. Instead, the group — including a leprous woman — was left alone with MacDougall for three of those weeks in a situation that he clearly found difficult.[5]

Once Terry Long did finally join the group, how did he make the decision to bring the group out of the desert to a mission? On what basis did the department resolve the dilemma of appearing either heartless or coercive?

Years later, Terry Long summarised his memory of the extent of any policy on the issue:

> General feelings in those days, particularly through the press, were that Aboriginal people should be allowed to remain in the desert and not be brought into missions and that was the policy of our department at that stage. We were never ever encouraged to bring people in simply for the sake of bringing them in from the desert with the hope of giving them a better life in the mission or in any other place where they might like to settle.[6]

The department's annual report for 1964 included the following discussion of the issue:

> No pressure of any sort is used to persuade them to leave their tribal territory, but should they express a wish to do so, they are given any assistance they may need to put this intention into effect. In practice, most of the Aborigines so contacted do ultimately elect to join their kinsmen in one or other of the settlements or missions which border the desert.
>
> Whether this is to be regretted or not depends largely on the point of view.[7]

In light of the debate in federal parliament immediately prior to the firing of F2, Gare had written a briefing note for his minister outlining the department's policy on desert patrols and forced removal: 'Our field officers are empowered to offer transport facilities to any people they encounter, but they are instructed not to use any persuasion to influence the natives' decision'.[8]

All this, the only real evidence of departmental policy, appears to be at odds with what happened: removal to Jigalong, despite Yuwali's consistent claim of reluctance to leave.

Perhaps the fact that this group consisted solely of women and children was decisive in the eyes of the white men. MacDougall hints at chivalrous concern when — in the knowledge that there was abundant food and water in the area, and that all but one of the group appeared to be in good health — he signalled that, 'I suggest that the problem of Eves without Adams be left for Mr Long. Personally I cannot see how these women can be left on their own'. [9]

Macaulay echoed this emphasis, saying, 'We gave our support to the relocation by the West Australian government of [Yuwali's] group to Jigalong Mission because of the unique structure of the remnant group'. [10]

Terry Long later recalled the controversial situation for the department, and defended his decision to bring Yuwali's group from the Percival Lakes to Jigalong:

> We really had no option. I think we were talking by radio to Perth, and it was at this stage that Kim Beazley Sr was getting very angry in Parliament about us pulling people out of the desert. I am sure that Frank [Gare] had some trouble down there in Perth.
>
> We said there was no option: they wanted to go, and they had no men with them. They were entirely women and children. They could neither teach the boys the law, nor could they feel safe wandering around as they were. If there were other groups, they might take exception to them.
>
> They were more than pleased to come with us. And of course Sailor and Nyani explained to them what the mission was all about. So, they came quite willingly. [11]

In fact, the policy of the department was to leave Long to exercise his judgement, based on limited options and common sense:

> [N]o one had been out there. The desert, as far as the Department was concerned . . . was an unknown, as it was to the whole of Western Australia. The Warburton Ranges [were] as far as anybody got.
>
> People in those days knew absolutely nothing about Aborigines living in the desert. [I knew] nothing, other than what you would read in novels, nothing whatever; it was a [mystery] as far as I was concerned. We were not taught the language; in fact what language would you have been taught? It was never part of the training — in fact there was no training to be a native welfare officer in those days. You just picked it up as you went along. [12]

Long was in a difficult position, acting in a policy void despite the state government having had almost a century of responsibility for the welfare of Indigenous people. The department had only recently accompanied patrols into the desert. Patrol officers, with virtually no experience, or knowledge of language or culture, had to play it by ear.

As it happens, deft political management in Perth avoided any controversy for the department. On 24 October, as the convoy of patrol officers and Martu left Swindells Field, an article appeared in the *West Australian* under the headline 'Native Women, Children Found Alone in Desert'. With all the information being provided by the DNW, it painted a picture of helpless women and children, lacking the protection and support of their menfolk, being helped out of 'bleak sandhill country'. The article noted the earlier furore over the removals to Papunya, but stated that, 'The natives will be asked [at Swindells Field] whether they want to stay in the desert or go to a mission — either Jigalong or La Grange . . . The Minister said it was the policy of the department to meet the wishes of the natives'.[13] Thus, after the novelty of their discovery had been recorded, Yuwali's party disappeared from public view.

So was the removal of the women and children consensual or coercive? Was it essential or expedient, prudent or unfortunate? Was the decision based on knowledge or ignorant assumption? Was it justified? Who made the decision, and why? And what was the real effect of the decision?

These are not simple questions. To explore them adequately requires some understanding of the history of desert contact prior to Yuwali's story and of the Martu perspective on this contact.

To judge the effects of the whitefellas' actions, we need to see what happened next.

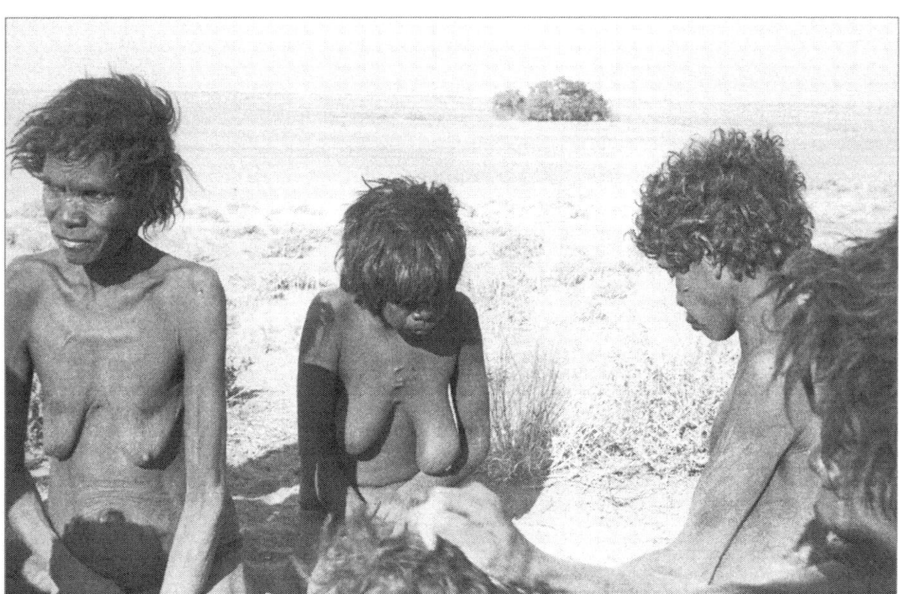

Some of Yuwali's group at Kurtararra. PHOTO: WALTER MACDOUGALL, 1964

We've got to take you mob

> Wirnpa went east until he became tired and lay down at Wirnpa, where he went inside the water as a big snake. And big clouds rose up from the waterhole. Wirnpa was the last man, the last one to lie down and die. Physically, they all died, but spiritually they are all there and living on forever in the ground, in the sky, in things, all over the place.[14]

Until the 1950s, the European history of Western Australia's deserts was thin: a few explorers and the two heroic failures of the Rabbit-Proof Fence and the Canning Stock Route. Several parties had crossed the Western Desert in the late nineteenth and early twentieth centuries, and the first direct contact that the Martu had with Europeans was with these explorers. These interactions were, sadly, often brutal, and contributed to a general sense of wariness about or outright fear of white people.

Warburton and, later, Wells (of the Calvert Scientific Exploring Expedition) both record imprisonment of Aboriginal people as a way of forcing them to lead the explorers to water. Assaults, retaliatory spearing and so-called 'punitive expeditions' by the police typify and characterise this period.[15] The use of neck-chains was a standard (and sanctioned) means of securing the cooperation of Indigenous suspects and witnesses by the police, a practice defended by Middleton as late as 1958.[16]

While a handful of Europeans had entered the Western Desert by 1910, there were no real settlements. Towns and pastoral properties loosely ringed the vast, arid region, which was considered too marginal for exploitation.

Between 1910 and 1950 there was a steady but growing trickle of European activity in the desert: prospectors sought the next big lode, doggers sought dingo scalps, the Rabbit-Proof Fence supported a number of maintenance depots strung along its length, and a very small number of drovers actually used the stock route.

A group of reserves (referred to variously as the Central Reserves, the Central Aboriginal Reserves and the Central Australian Aboriginal Reserves) were created between 1918 and 1938, ostensibly to provide protection for the Indigenous desert inhabitants. These reserves spanned millions of acres of the Northern Territory, South Australia and Western Australia. Intended as sanctuaries, these were initially seen as a means of preserving the integrity of a dying race, but later as a means of preserving traditional culture.

The 1950s heralded the first real European exploitation of the desert: the defence work of the WRE; survey and mapping activities; mining; tourism; and new scientific investigations. While the WRE's activities did not really encroach into the

Western Desert until the establishment of Giles weather station in 1956, their effect accelerated over the next seven years. Its roads opened vast desert areas to an increasingly large number of visitors (see Part One, pages 50–6).

All of this foreshadowed the mineral-led boom in Western Australia from the late 1960s which saw the establishment of mining towns such as Tom Price, Newman, Paraburdoo and Telfer in remote areas.

Between 1900 and 1965, a parallel history was taking shape. Over this period — and particularly from 1940 to 1965 — the Indigenous inhabitants of Western Australia's deserts 'cleared out'. In an extraordinary migration, Aboriginal people moved from their nomadic existence in traditional territories to settlements around the desert, often in quite new territories. This migration, which mirrored the movement of Central Desert people to the east and south, was unquestionably a response to the presence and actions of white Australians.

The migration was influenced by several different factors. In the beginning the dominant factors were probably curiosity, trade and access to food in harsh times.[17] As a relationship developed between the desert people and pastoral stations or other communities, however, the attractions changed: the relative ease of a settled life, proximity to family members who had already settled and ready access to a wider social and community life. As Bob Tonkinson noted:

> The initial contact pattern was of periodic brief sojourns, followed by a return to the old nomadic life; but it was eventually reversed to a more settled existence punctuated by brief returns to the desert heartlands. This major transition was caused by a subtle process whose implications could never have been sensed by the Mardu: the link between increasing involvement with, and a growing dependence on, an alien economy. They rapidly acquired a strong desire for tea, flour, twist tobacco and sugar — as several Mardu have described it, 'We were captured by flour and sugar'.[18]

The basic trio of flour, sugar and tea provided easy and alternative staple foods. Europeans also created stable water sources and introduced new types of meat and tobacco as well as readily useful implements such as knives, axes, cans and a variety of steel items that could easily be converted to their needs.

Encampments on stations, close to ration depots (such as the Jigalong maintenance depot on the Rabbit-Proof Fence) provided the Martu with supplements to their traditional food and water sources.

> When we were collecting seed one time we saw a whitefella on a camel and a Martu man, an old father.[19] We ran up the hill away from them. When we came down again, my mother said, 'That was your father'. Our father said, 'Go to this whitefella and get some food and flour'. We formed a line — they made us kids line up. The whitefella gave out damper and tinned meat. We followed the whitefella. The whitefella tried to take the kids into Jigalong. The whitefella had all his things on the camel. We wanted to follow the tucker.[20]

Before the second patrol

The second Blue Streak rocket firing (F2) was scheduled for 20 October 1964. Once again, it was planned to drop in the Percival Lakes area.

MacDougall had noted the fact that the range of Yuwali's group appeared to be limited to the area around the lakes, 'and a total of nine water supplies, consisting of eight soaks and one rockhole, were seen. All were either on or close to the lake'.[1]

This second time around, the WRE had prepared a detailed plan, the *Specification for the Clearance of the Talgarno Impact Area*. The plan provided for six weeks of coordinated air and ground searches, covering the area from the Percival Lakes through to the Canning Stock Route.

Walter MacDougall was again in charge of the ground search. The plan was for him to arrive in the Talgarno area on 2 September, make a preliminary ground search of the area from 6 to 19 September, with more substantial searches taking place over the following month. In the final week before the firing, Robert Macaulay would arrive to help him.

The only specific instructions about treatment of any Indigenous people encountered were that:

> Every care shall be taken to observe the fundamental requirements of native welfare.
>
> In order that there be minimum disturbance to natives from aircraft movements, air searches shall be conducted at the highest altitude consistent with the search task.[2]

MacDougall's report on the first trip had been critical of their guide, Gordon McKay, an elderly man who had not been able to travel far on foot, and certainly not quickly. Terry Long later commented that McKay had been uncomfortable and reluctant to chase the group, being in unfamiliar country. MacDougall's report commented:

> Avoidable difficulties were experienced from the lack of pre-patrol organisation in several aspects, the most serious being no suitable native guide. It is imperative that in such an exercise a native guide, who is closely related to the area and its people, is employed, especially when quick contacts are desired. It is a comparatively simple matter to transport such a person to a point close to the people desired to contact. Then, on foot, he can make face to face contact, dispel their fears and arrange contact with a white patrol officer.[3]

The DNW consulted with Bob Tonkinson about guides who would be suitable for searching for a group in the Percival Lakes and the relevant part of the Canning

Punuma Sailor. PHOTO: BOB TONKINSON, 1964

Nyani. PHOTO: VIC SURMAN, 1964

Stock Route. It was important to have guides who knew the country, and could speak to any people found in it.

Tonkinson recommended two men, Punuma Sailor and Nyani, both of whom were mature but fit and healthy. Each was to be paid the state's basic wage of £15 per week for their work.

Punuma Sailor was a Kartujarra man who spoke a language that would have been understood by Yuwali's group. Aged about forty-five at the time, he had been in from the desert for several years and had never been as far north as the Percival Lakes area.

Nyani was about thirty-five years old and had come in from the desert in 1963, from the McKay Ranges, to the east of Jigalong. He was a close relative of a group which MacDougall came across in the Well 35 area while on patrol earlier in 1964, and on whom MacDougall intended to check in this patrol. Nyani was a Manyjilyjarra man and could be understood by Yuwali's group, but — unlike Punuma Sailor — 'had very little English'.[4]

Concerned about the cost of the first patrol, the DNW asked that Terry Long observe the search only during the final week leading up to the firing. However, the detailed plan that the WRE had prepared and forwarded to the department was barely followed. MacDougall made a long sweep to the east, through Papunya and Jupiter Well, before heading towards the supply base at Swindells Field, with two WRE vehicle maintenance staff, Vic Surman and Eddie Meakins. He then picked up the two guides from Jigalong on 21 September and started the real search of the dump area on 22 September, a month before the firing. A preliminary air search had identified that two of the many pathways over Lake Percival seemed to have been used recently.[5]

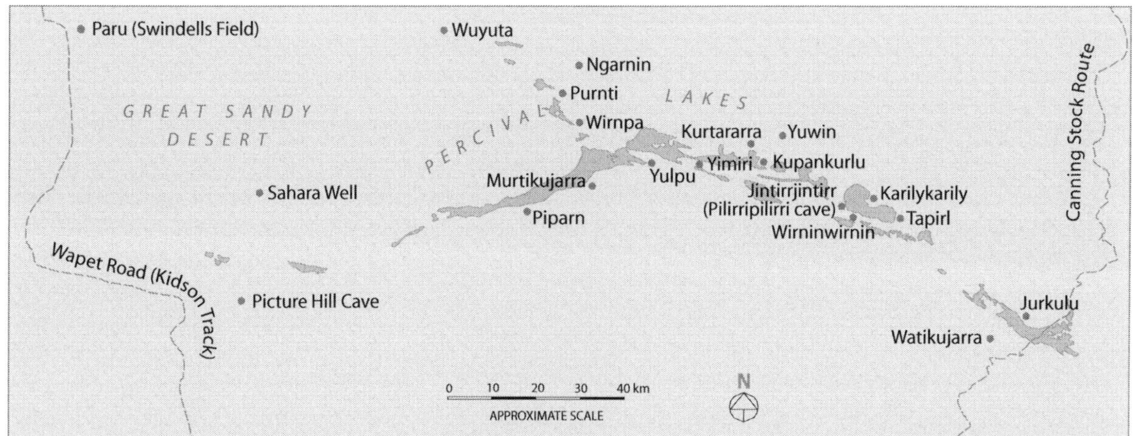

In the following section, Yuwali's story is aligned with extracts from the original patrol diaries kept by Walter MacDougall and Terry Long in 1964, and with an interview with Long in 1999. The map above shows the area in which the action takes place.

Tuesday 22 September 1964

As MacDougall approaches Lake Percival from the south-west, Yuwali and her group are in one of their main camps, Kurtararra, on the north-east of the lake. MacDougall camps at Yulpu, Yuwali's birthplace.

Yuwali

We kept on walking. We were walking in the night time and got up in the morning. We walked during the morning and then sat under the shade. The four old people in Junju's mob were already there at Kurtararra. We all stayed together.

It was the very hot time, it was the time for *wamurla* to be cooked. They left us there in Junulanya [Kurtararra]: Karntipa, Yukurrpani, Pinkirri and myself. The others went to the east, collecting *wamurla*. They took some little kids with them. We stayed there and we had one night there, then we all walked around together.

Two old grannies dug a hole, and we slept there.

An image (taken at a later date) of **Yuwali and her group at Kurtararra**. Interviewed in 2000, Yuwali said: '[We] would dig a hole in which to sleep, scoop out the moist sand to make it cool. [We] would put four pieces of wood at each corner and cover it with spinifex. The cool sand and covering would keep the sleeping place cool, and then you sleep underneath.' PHOTO: WALTER MACDOUGALL FILM STILL, ARA IRITITJA, 1964

MacDougall's journal

Travelled to Lake Percival via Picture Cave Hill with Sailor and Nyani as guides. Sighted smoke on arrival at the lake. Travelled 20 miles [32 kilometres] north-east and saw two-day old tracks at Yulpu, Pam's Soak. Camped.

MacDougall's International driving through the spinifex on the side of Lake Percival. PHOTO: WALTER MACDOUGALL FILM STILL, ARA IRITITJA, 1964

Wednesday **23 September** 1964

Yuwali is out alone, collecting ant sugar, when her dingo warns her of strangers. She sees MacDougall driving along the southern edge of the lake, about 20 metres from her, and hides in a ring of spinifex.
MacDougall is heading from Yulpu, past Yimiri, along the southern and eastern edges of the lake, moving to where he saw the group's fire the previous night, at Kurtararra on the north-eastern edge of the lake. It is slow driving.

Yuwali

It was morning. We went towards [the] *kurtikurti* [ant 'sugar'].

Only three of us — me, Karntipa and Yukurrpani, and Pinkirri — stayed back. [Yuwali does not count the child, Pinkirri, in 'three of us'.] The others went on their own towards the north and I went on my own to the east. I went further southwards and went over towards the lake. I crossed over towards Yimiri.

I went on my own and stayed, collecting *kurtikurti*. I was collecting them and had a bit of a feed and went on. I took one dog with me — it was my dog, a dingo.

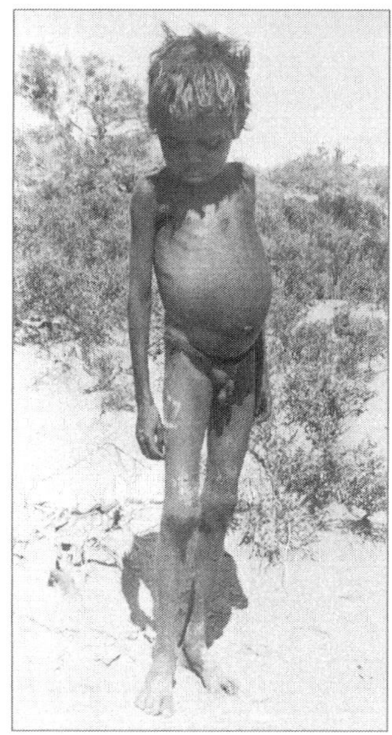

Pinkirri, Yuwali's classificatory brother. PHOTO: VIC SURMAN, 1964

I was sleeping in the shade. My dog saw the motor car coming along the side of the lake. It was coming towards me.

The dingo came and jumped on me. He told me to get up. I got up and saw this motor car coming. The glass in the motor car was shining. I quickly went inside a spinifex bush. I went right underneath. I was inside the spinifex, and the dog was with me. The motor car went by. The people in the motor car didn't see me hiding. When the car had passed I went in the opposite direction.

MacDougall's journal

Moved along the eastern aspect of the lake. Fresh tracks seen at Yimiri (bulrush soak).

MacDougall's International skirted the outside of the lake. PHOTO: WALTER MACDOUGALL FILM STILL, ARA IRITITJA, 1964

Yuwali

I got up; I ran off, back to the camp. I ran north and went over the sandhill and ran for my two grannies, Karntipa and Yukurrpani. I had left them both there at Yimiri spring.

I kept on running to our camp and had a drink and saw they weren't there. When I got there I saw that no people were there. I was frightened, because they ran away, without me.

I looked around and I kept running. I went east looking for them.

One of my old grannies [Yukurrpani] was running to me from the west on her own. They had Karntipa and Pinkirri and took them to the east in the motor car.

Junju

Some of them saw on the south side a motor car going along very fast. That's Punuma. He ran along and stopped at Kupankurlu and then came around from the east towards us. Then, when we saw them, we ran west.

We saw a black motor car going south. All the kids were running away from the whitefellas' motor car. I carried one little boy on my back. And other old people took [Kurtu] away, and I was carrying [Tajaka].

Nyani contacted **Karntipa** and her grandson, Pinkirri, at Yimiri. Karntipa hid in the bulrushes of the spring on the lake and the Martu guides brought her out, terrified, as MacDougall recorded on film. PHOTO: WALTER MACDOUGALL FILM STILL, ARA IRITITJA, 1964

MacDougall may then have taken Karntipa to Kupankurlu, on the north-east corner of the lake, where she was released before he returned to collect the others who were with her. From the east, Junju's mob saw MacDougall's truck. PHOTO: WALTER MACDOUGALL FILM STILL, ARA IRITITJA, 1964

The group ran from MacDougall. They sent Karntipa and Pinkirri back to Kurtararra with Yukurrpani. MacDougall found the two women and children at Kurtararra. Sailor and Nyani followed the full group on foot. PHOTO: WALTER MACDOUGALL FILM STILL, ARA IRITITJA, 1964

MacDougall's journal

Sent Sailor and Nyani to follow tracks on feet, and they returned with a woman and child.

Sent the woman and child to collect the group. They are to meet me at Kurtararra (Rita's soak) tonight.

Signal from MacDougall to WRE

Have contacted a woman and small boy . . . Have sent her to collect others. She states there are many men, women and children on the lake.

Yuwali

The motor car took Karntipa and Pinkirri and dropped them halfway on the road. (They went with the Land Rover to Kupankurlu. I ran back to Yimiri — ran back to Kurtararra [to warn the others][6].) Those other old ladies [Junju and the others, to the east of Kurtararra] saw them from the east while picking *pura* [bush tomatoes], and they also ran away along the eastern side of the lake. The car was going along the north side. The motor car drove past in the gully on the north side of the sandhill.

Junju

When the kids in Kurtararra saw the motor car coming they ran over the sandhills towards Yimiri and met Yuwali and two grandmothers. It was a very hot day and the woman with leprosy [Nganja] had sores on her legs and arms and body. When they ran from Kurtararra they just dropped everything where it was.

Yuwali

I looked around and I kept running [towards Kurtararra, about 10 kilometres]. I went east looking for them [Junju's group]. As I went running, I saw the people and I was frightened; they were rushing back to me, running. We were all frightened. I was so frightened to see a white person. He was coming.

The old ladies were running from the east. I ran to meet them, west of Kurtararra, on the sand dune. I ran back till we met up with my mum.

We looked back and saw Karntipa and Pinkirri with billycans in their hands. They came around and gave us the billycans, and we said, 'No, you eat that. You two go back to them, because they've got you two.'

We told them we were going west. We went towards the west. The rain was coming. We ran back to our main spring, Yimiri, that same spring as before. We stayed there and were lying there under the trees, having a rest from the heat and the sun.

Nyani and Punuma followed the women's tracks, while MacDougall stayed with the vehicle. MacDougall knew that the only way he could gain the women's confidence and cooperation was through the Martu men. PHOTO: WALTER MACDOUGALL FILM STILL, ARA IRITITJA, 1964

Martu are excellent **trackers**. They can read a great deal of information from the types of tracks in the sand, across rocky ground or saltlake and from broken spinifex, twigs or bushes. PHOTO: WALTER MACDOUGALL FILM STILL, ARA IRITITJA, 1964

MacDougall's journal

Skirted the north-eastern end of the lake and found two women and two children waiting. They insist that there are no men. Gave them meat and billy of tea and sent them off [to contact the larger group].

Sailor checked their tracks and found that they hid them when out of sight. Nyani followed.

Junju

We went back west, and we drank [at] Yimiri again. We drank the water from Yimiri, where the water snake smelt us.

Yuwali

Then we went back southwards. We said, 'No water. Let's go back. We might die'. The people in the motor car went east and back around again. They came to [Yimiri]. That *marlu* [kangaroo] was down there — that *marlu* from the dreamtime.

That white man stopped his car and they [Punuma and Nyani] started walking. He followed our tracks until he came close to us. They were all walking behind us.

Old man Punuma kept on following us, kept on walking. It was night time now. We kept running away from them, we kept on running. We drank the water then kept on running, going towards the west. We couldn't stop.

So we tried to hide. We ran, looking for thick bushes. We went inside. We hid till sunset — night time.

Then we started running again. We stopped to have a rest, drank some water then kept on running, going towards the west.

Then we stopped and had a rest again. We finally got to our camp. We camped overnight. We were sleeping under the moonlight.

Thursday 24 September 1964

Yuwali

We started running [straight away] — got up and started running. We couldn't stop, we were still running.

It was midday and the sun was so hot and our feet were so cooked from the sun and sand. It was so hot for us, we couldn't run any more. But that man was still following. He went back and got the Toyota [i.e. four-wheel drive]. He was coming after us.

Our feet were so sore, we couldn't run any more. So we tried to hide. It was burning us, the lake was so hot. We stopped to have a rest.

When we stopped, we saw this Martu [Aboriginal person] coming for us. He came close. His name was Punuma Sailor. We couldn't run any more. We had to stop.

We saw two men standing up. They had these huge hats on their heads. We thought they were carrying dishes, but they were only hats.

Then the old man Sailor yelled out to us. He was waving his hat. He was waving to us, telling us to come back to him.

We went back, and they got us there.

We were sitting under the tree when Punuma came close, and told everybody, 'Don't run any more. We are your families, stop!' We were all sitting down, we couldn't run.

They said to Junju, 'Stop! Don't run. We're your families — we're here to take you away to Jigalong, to see other families there. We have other families out there. You can see them. They're worried about you mob.' Punuma was telling them all the names of people living in Jigalong.

Then we got up. We followed this old man back to Kurtararra. We got up and followed this old man. We walked and were walking slowly.

We didn't want to go with them. We wanted to stay in our camp, Yimiri.

Nyani with the boys. The fact that Punuma and Nyani spoke in a known language must have been reassuring to the group. However, it may have been the information about relatives in Jigalong that convinced the group that these Martu meant no harm. PHOTO: WALTER MACDOUGALL, 1964

Long's journal

MacDougall told me that Nyani and Sailor had first contacted the main groups of women and had run after them and after a great deal of discussion between them explained what was happening, not that they could understand about rockets. The women were carrying bundles of bush tomatoes round with them speared on sticks and dehydrated. The young boys were using slings to knock down galahs and pigeons.

The frightened women accompanied Sailor and Nyani back to Kurtararra, where MacDougall was waiting. For the first time, MacDougall realised that the group comprised only women and children. He offered food, but the women were too scared to eat.

Punuma with women and children. PHOTO: WALTER MACDOUGALL, 1964

Junju

He took us with him and we went towards the east to where the motor car was. We kept on going and finally got to our camp, Kurtararra. Punuma was already there, cooking a damper for us. They took a photo of us as we were coming towards them.

The women and children walk into Kurtararra. Junju recalled that '**they took a photo of us** as we were coming towards them'. MacDougall took a great deal of photographs and film during his many patrols, but only one of MacDougall's films has been found. This film is of Yuwali's group. Junju also remembered MacDougall filming the women as they approached him. PHOTO: WALTER MACDOUGALL FILM STILL, AR̲A IRITITJA, 1964

Yuwali

There were a lot of other people back in camp. They were waiting, even that white man that we had never seen before. It was *pina* [demanding attention to authority] and we were frightened and ashamed. [When a relationship between people demands restraint, deference or respect, it is often translated into English as 'shame'.]

We walked inside the bush and were sitting under the tree. We were frightened, still frightened.

Those white people got food. They were giving it to us to eat, but we were ashamed to take it and frightened to eat. We were still sitting under the tree.

The women and children are given **damper**. For some time they refused to eat any food offered by the patrol officers, believing it to be poisoned; a recurring theme in Martu contact stories. This fear possibly originated from baits used on cattle stations to control dingoes. The Western Australian Vermin Control Board was still dropping poison baits from planes in areas in which Martu camped in 1965. PHOTO: WALTER MACDOUGALL FILM STILL, AR̲A IRITITJA, 1964

MacDougall's journal

Nyani returned late afternoon with a total of 20. (7 women, 2 teenage girls, 6 boys, 5 girls, youngest about 6 months.) Suspect one women woman has leprosy.

Signal from MacDougall to WRE

Now have a total of twenty. No men. Women state there are no men in the area. But there are babies. Suggest you ring Commissioner and suggest that he send welfare officer to care for these while I look for others. Please wire Jigalong Mission that guides are well and successful.

Junju

He cooked everything — potato, onion, meat — for everybody.

Yuwali

The white man was telling us to eat. 'Take it — it's food you can eat.' But we still couldn't take it. He was putting it in our hands, giving potatoes to us, and we were burying them in the ground. We thought he was going to give us poison to eat — we thought maybe it was poison. We couldn't eat so we went to sleep with no food.

We stayed all night and had a sleep with them. We were still frightened of them.

Long's journal

The group told him [MacDougall] the story that there were no men with the group at all. This was astonishing to him.

F2 minus 25

Friday **25 September** 1964

Yuwali

We got up the next day. We still couldn't eat. We stayed all day. Then he [Sailor] told us that he's going to take us.

He told us to get into the motor car. We were sitting inside the motor car and we were staring at the whitefella. We didn't know what that whitefella was. He told us, 'I'm going to take you to Jigalong. There are some other people up there'.

We left from Kurtararra through the lake, on the side of the lake.

Signal from MacDougall to WRE

One woman has very lumpy face, elongated ear lobe, small lump upon upper arm. Suspect leprosy.

Total nine women, two teenage girls, five little boys, four little girls.

Walter MacDougall and the women. The women are told that they must leave Kurtararra. MacDougall suspects one woman is suffering from leprosy. This photo is a copy (belonging to Vic Surman), one of the few surviving from MacDougall's collection, and was taken by Nyani. PHOTO: NYANI, 1964

Yuwali

They put us in the back of a Toyota and it was our first day to ride. It was frightening to see all the trees, grass — they were running.

As we were in the back of the truck, I thought we were going to fall out. Everything was running — trees, grass, and the ground was moving round. This was our first ride in something moving really fast.

And it was really funny: we all got sick, we were all bringing up something that was in our guts. We had nothing to eat but we were all sicking up.

Then we went and we stopped, we were so sick. We sicked up all night and all day. We were frightened.

We stopped at Yimiri to rest because all of us were sick. We were so sick; everything was aching: our feet, and our guts were sore from vomiting.

'**They were running**.' This is a very common description in Martu stories of a person's first ride in a vehicle. Having never travelled in any form of vehicle it was difficult to grasp that they, rather than the ground, were moving. Bob Tonkinson remembers that, weeks later, the women were still very frightened of vehicles, even after they had ridden in them a number of times. PHOTO: SUE DAVENPORT, 2002

MacDougall's journal

Returned to Yimiri (bulrush soak). Native group cut across the lake and were waiting for me. Fed them all. The story as I understand it is that the young men and boys ran away. The men went after them, leaving 4 men, one of them blind, to look after the women. Three of them died, and the blind man [Nyiwiljukurr, Yuwali's father], taking two wives, left the lake. He is supposed to be living north-west of the lake. The mother of the 6 [actually nine] month old baby says he was alive when she visited him approximately 18 months ago.

Walter MacDougall on the **radio to Woomera**. Having found the women, the authorities now had to decide what to do with them. PHOTO: TERRY LONG, 1964

Internal WRE signal from Director of Safety to WRE Superintendent

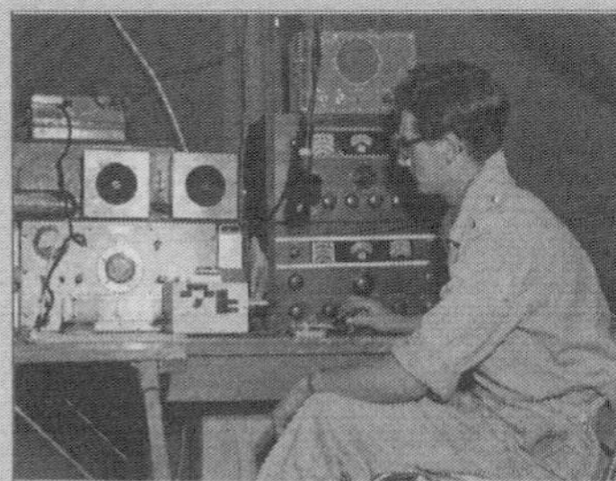

A radio operator at Woomera. This patrol took place in the shadow of considerable press and parliamentary debate about alleged forced removal of Indigenous people from the desert to Papunya in April 1964, and about the actions of WRE in the first patrol in the Percival Lakes in May and June. PHOTO: FROM THE COLLECTION OF THE NATIONAL ARCHIVES OF AUSTRALIA

Discussed MacDougall situation with Deputy Commissioner WA in absence of [Commissioner] Gare at Kalgoorlie. Anderson [Deputy Commissioner of the DNW] is reluctant to take any action in absence Commissioner and in any case said that staff situation is such that he could not spare an officer for a period likely to run into 3 weeks or more. Considers also that the alternative of taking natives to a mission would not be politic at present. He will take up whole question with Gare on return.

In view of proximity of location to northern limit of impact area consider best course of action would be to encourage natives to remain present position. If need be more food from Port Hedland should be obtained. Further check on their position could be made nearer the date when Macaulay is available to help.

Signal from Superintendent WRE to MacDougall

Your messages have been passed to Deputy Commissioner Western Australia in absence of Gare in Kalgoorlie. Anderson is going to discuss question fully with Gare on return. Suggest you encourage natives to remain present position. Obtain more food from Port Hedland if required.

Signal from MacDougall to Superintendent WRE

Sorry my message [from the previous day, suggesting that a welfare officer should be sent] misunderstood. Do not require help but thought good chance for welfare officer to get practical experience whilst I am in the area.

Saturday 26 September 1964

Yuwali

We got up the next day but we still couldn't eat; we stayed all day then he told us that he was going to take us. They kept us there and took us west to Yulpu.

MacDougall's journal

Back to Yulpu (Pam's soak) followed by natives. Left the guides with instructions to give the group a piece of damper and a drink of tea. Continued search eastwards. No sign of native occupation.

MacDougall was not certain the women would stay if he left them. Thus, he left Punuma and Nyani with them at Yulpu while he went to search along the lake for other Aboriginal people who may have been in the prescribed area. PHOTO: VIC SURMAN, 1964

F2 minus 23

Sunday 27 September 1964

MacDougall's journal

Met Meakins and Surman. Filled petrol and water tanks, and sent International to Port Hedland. Returned to the lake. Back differential smashed whilst skidding on the lake 2 miles [3 kilometres] short of Yulpu. Still mobile with front wheels only.

Vic Surman with two of the children. Surman and Eddie Meakins were mechanics from WRE providing MacDougall with technical support. MacDougall's International broke its differential and could not be driven, forcing him and his group to wait at Yulpu for a new one. PHOTO: VIC SURMAN, 1964

F2 minus 22–F2 minus 17

Monday 28 September to Saturday 3 October 1964

In a signal from Punuma Sailor to Jigalong, he stated, 'I have found your sister'. Punuma claimed that Nyipi (Yuwali's mother) was the sister of his wife, Yipijalu Peterson, having the same mother. Nyipi later told Bob Tonkinson that they had separate mothers, but were classificatory sisters in the Martu social system. Macaulay recorded in his journal notes, 'Sailor's wife at Jigalong is a first cousin of Kulata and Nyipi, placing these women in a "kiri" or wife relationship to Sailor'. Sailor later claimed Kulata as a wife.

Signal from Macaulay to Foreshew (WRE Safety Officer)

MacDougall has reported that Nyani, a guide, has married Yuwali, approx. 16 years of age. MacDougall would like Gare advised and for Gare to notify Jigalong Mission. I believe that the significance is that Nyani will want to take her back to Jigalong and this may lead to her parents, relatives etc. all moving in — similarities with publicity over aborigines moving to Papunya.

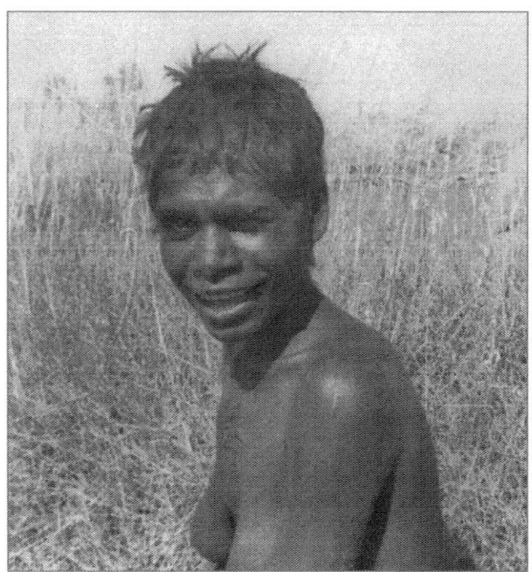

Yuwali. While awaiting the delivery of the International's new differential, MacDougall camped at Yulpu for six days with the women. Nothing is known of this period as neither MacDougall nor the women relate any memories of this time. F2 was still to be fired on schedule.
PHOTO: VIC SURMAN, 1964

Kulata and Pilumpa. Nyani claimed Yuwali as a wife, and Punuma Sailor later claimed Kulata. Macaulay's concerns of wholesale removal to Jigalong were well-founded.
PHOTO: BOB TONKINSON, 1964

Sunday **4 October** 1964

Once MacDougall's truck was fixed he left the women and children at Kurtararra and headed east, to where the smoke of another group had been sighted.

Yuwali

We were staying there and we saw another motor car coming from the direction of Warburton [from the south]. The truck arrived and they drove it towards us. It was close to us.

We had a little bit of a talk there. He was telling us that he was going to get Pukina and the rest [i.e. the group located at Well 35 after the firing of F1]. That old truck was standing there with us. They stayed and rang up [radio].

He took my younger brother — took him in the truck towards the south. We were staying in our camp Kurtararra, we just stayed there. It was cold, like winter time.

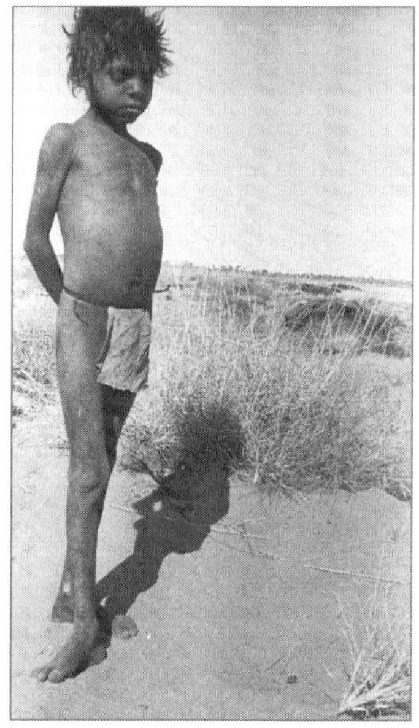

Yuwali's younger brother, **Yaji**. MacDougall may have been unsure that the group would still be there when he returned from patrolling the Well 35 area. Therefore, he took both Martu guides with him and took Yuwali's younger brother, possibly to ensure the women waited for him. PHOTO: VIC SURMAN, 1964

MacDougall's journal

Meakins and Surman arrived last night with new differential. Both guides and both vehicles left the lake for Well 35.

No sign of native occupation.

The International, with its new differential, struggling over a sand dune. PHOTO: TERRY LONG, 1964

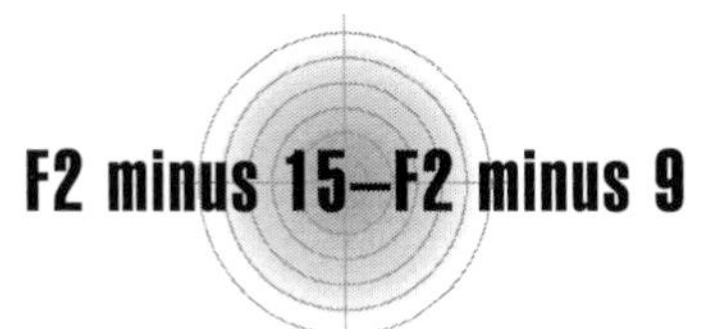

Monday 5 to Sunday 11 October 1964

MacDougall left the women alone for seven days while he patrolled the Canning Stock Route between Well 35 and Well 40.

After the firing of the F1, MacDougall had discovered signs that Martu had camped around Well 35, well within the impact area. MacDougall had a duty to make sure that this group was clear of the prohibited area for the firing of F2.

He did not come across signs of this group, or any other, during this patrol of Well 35 to Well 40.

During this time, it appears that the women stayed in the area of Lake Percival.

Signal from Macaulay to MacDougall, 5 October

Re marriage Nyani. If bride returns Jigalong with him, how many if any relatives likely to go in as well? Can you send approximate answer to Supt?

Signal from MacDougall to Superintendent WRE, 8 October

I have not taken an interest Nyani's marriage. Suggest there should be no dependants. I suggest the problem of Eves without Adams be left for Mr Long. [Terry Long, from the Port Hedland office of the DNW, was scheduled to join MacDougall later in October.] Personally I cannot see how these women can be left on their own.

Monday 12 October 1964

MacDougall returned from his patrol alone, having left Meakins and Surman with Macaulay at Well 35 to assist with the patrol of the Canning Stock Route.

Joint signal from MacDougall and Macaulay to superintendent, Woomera

Our plans for 12th to 18th are MacDougall returns to group at Percival and proceeds with them to NE of lake returning to Swindells at about 15th to meet Long and transport him to Percival group for him to decide on any long-term welfare requirements.

MacDougall's journal

❛ Left for Lake Percival. Refuelled at Picture Hill Cave. Meakins, Surman and both guides to accompany Mr Macaulay. Smoke seen on arrival at the lake. Camped at Yulpu (Pam's Soak).

Tuesday **13 October** 1964

MacDougall's journal

Inspection of vehicle showed tearing chassis. Suspect there is a possibility of breakdown in steering mechanism. Learnt that Mr Macaulay's vehicle had broken down. This will delay Meakins and Surman. Although mobile I will not risk a complete breakdown between the lake and Picture Hill Cave until the workshop vehicle is available. Notified L.M.F [the aircraft] that I cannot meet Mr Long at Swindells Field. Macaulay, Meakins and Surman are to move to Swindells Field later. Will stay here in case Meakins and Surman will not be delayed as long as anticipated.

F2 minus 6

Wednesday **14 October** 1964

MacDougall's journal

Remained at Yulpu. Will move to Kupankurlu soak tomorrow.

F2 minus 5–F2 minus 3

Thursday **15** to Saturday **17 October** 1964

MacDougall rejoined the women at Kurtararra. They stayed there for the next four days until Terry Long arrived on 19 October.

Yuwali

We went towards the west, back to Kurtararra.

MacDougall's journal

Water in soak at Kupankurlu inadequate. Moved to Kurtararra. Established camp all the group present.

Signal from Director Safety to Superintendent WRE

Consider it important that mobile workshop be available to MacDougall . . . in order to shepherd him back to Lake Percival with Mr Long in order to ascertain state of part [sic: party] there. MacDougall should remain north side of Lake Percival until launch completed.

Sunday **18 October** 1964

Yuwali

We saw an aeroplane bringing some tucker. They threw a couple of bags down from the air. We thought those white people were throwing some poison, so we got up and ran.

When we came back, they gave us a biscuit and a cool drink. But we didn't take that — we were frightened. We buried it in the ground, covered it up with the sand. We didn't want to eat it. We thought it was poison.

But the other lot was telling us to eat. They were saying, 'Eat, it's okay'. We said, 'No, we're not going to eat it because it's poison. You eat it because you know it. We're not going to eat it'.

Then we went looking for our own tucker. We went hunting. Went looking for lizard, goanna and blue-tongue. We wanted our own bush tucker. We didn't want to eat biscuits and cool drink.

So, we went and got bush tucker and took it back to our camp and cooked it and were eating what we caught: goanna, lizard and a blue-tongue.

The rocket was due to be fired on 20 October and, although Kurtararra was inside the prescribed zone, the WRE instructed MacDougall to continue patrolling on the south side of the lake to keep the group out of the impact area. Here, the women and children look at the **storpedo** dropped by the plane. The clothes they are wearing were brought out by Sailor and Nyani; the group didn't like them and took them on and off repeatedly. They finally continued to wear them after arriving at Swindells Field. PHOTO: VIC SURMAN, 1964

Junju

Then the aeroplane came. From the aeroplane, they dropped a plastic container and food into the lake.

They brought some cool drink — dropping it down. They dropped some cool drink into the lake, and water was there, so that cool drink dropped down. The kids were drinking the cool drink. They were all collecting cool drinks — the whitefella was delivering it.

Long's journal

Shortly after the plane landed at 8.30 am Mr. Macaulay arrived by vehicle from Well 35. Earlier, both Macaulay and MacDougall had intimated that a final air search was unnecessary and could frighten the natives already gathered together for the firing. However, as it was imperative that a member of this Department also be satisfied as to the situation in the area, I insisted that a final air sweep take place.

The plane took off at 9.30 am and I was accompanied by Mr. Macaulay. The area appeared to be without any form of human habitation; even the vicinity of Well 31 was empty of life, despite the fact that we expected a party to be making their way in this direction — that is the 3 guides Sailor, Tjakamarra [a guide picked up by Macaulay in Warburton on his way to meet MacDougall] and Nyani.

The International parked at Kurtararra, as seen from the air. Macaulay and Long dropped supplies to MacDougall and the group from their RAAF reconnaissance plane, before driving to the lake. PHOTO: ROBERT MACAULAY, 1964.

MacDougall's journal

Airdrop of bread, fruit juice, tinned meat and potatoes.

Macaulay's journal

Flew in aircraft to Mr. MacDougall at [Kurtararra] on Lake Percival and successfully dropped fresh supplies, flour, potatoes, tea and stores. Plastic jerry can of water burst on impact.

Long's journal

When the plane landed at 12.30 pm Macaulay and I left for Lake Percival and camped that night at Picture Hill Cave. The Commissioner [Gare] was wired as follows: 'Concur with combined signals by WRE officers concerning clearing of area. Personal and radio contact made and final air sweep conducted today indicates area clear.'

Monday **19 October** 1964

Yuwali

We were waiting for the truck to come and pick us up.

Junju

Then another motor car was coming from towards Warburton. One came towards us. There were a lot of whitefellas.

They came and they gave us everything, like tins of meat or whatever. They had plenty. We stayed there, stayed the night there.

Macaulay and Long arrive from Port Hedland. After discussion with the women, via the interpreters, Long became convinced of the need to evacuate the women and children.
PHOTO: ROBERT MACAULAY, 1964.

Long's journal

When I got out to the group, it was a very relieved MacDougall that saw me there, because he was on his own. We laid on the meat for a couple of nights and fed them.

After considerable discussion and conversation with the native woman in charge of the group a telegram was forwarded to Mr. Gare worded as follows:

'Have contacted Mr. MacDougall and 20 native women and children. Evacuation absolutely necessary for tribal, physical welfare and medical reasons, plus women's own request for evacuation. Mr. MacDougall and Macaulay agreed to give their assistance for transport to Swindells. Anticipate arrival there Thursday for Elphinstone to examine woman leprosy suspect. Suggest Jigalong as destination and please contact Roberts for early arrangement of truck to mission and RAAF for transport of Doctor to Swindells.'

The women were desperate to quit the area. [This is at odds with Yuwali's account.] They had seen no men for years and were frightened that if they did run into a group containing men, that some of them may have been killed if they were considered unsuitable as wives. Also, the boys in the group were growing up and, apart from having no choice of women for themselves, they were arriving at adulthood without being instructed in the law.

Any attempt to drive a vehicle for any purpose at this stage resulted in an avalanche of women and children piling themselves aboard. There was no question as to their wish to leave Lake Percival at the earliest possible moment.

On our previous search in May, the women had watched our every movements, every day, and were delighted to tell us of how we behaved on that occasion.

They had never seen a whitefella before.

The women and children at Kurtararra. Long described MacDougall's reaction as 'very relieved' upon his arrival. Because of MacDougall's seniority and provision of food, several of the women had felt they needed to reciprocate and offered him sexual favours. PHOTO: TERRY LONG, 1964

Long observed that several of the boys were 'arriving at adulthood'. Martu boys commence their initiation into the Law around puberty. This continues throughout their lives, but with an important milestone in their late twenties, when they may take wives. Yuwali's group included one boy aged twelve and two aged ten. PHOTO: TERRY LONG, 1964.

Long speaking in 1999

‘When we got there, we were on the edge of the dump area and no one had the skills to properly describe about the rocket being fired and to get out of the way — it would have meant nothing to anybody. The chances of them ever landing where we were were very remote indeed. So, we decided to take what little risk there was, and say 'Fire!' and we would remain with the group on the edge of this dump area and see what happened.

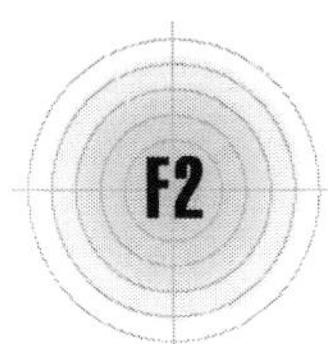

Tuesday **20 October** 1964

Long speaking in 1999

We laid on the lake itself on our backs in the sunlight and watched the sky and first of all we saw a white streak of condensation going through the sky, then a sparkle, then after the sparkle there was a dull boom which we counted. It appeared to be about 40 or 50 miles away. That rocket wasn't found for years, where it landed. A big search went out, but no one ever found it. It think it was the last of the rockets found. They didn't find it for a long time.

The [women's] reaction to the re entry was extraordinary — they watched what we were doing, when they saw the sparkle and then the boom, they just buried their heads in the sand, absolutely terrified.

The flight of the **Blue Streak rocket F2** is successful and uneventful. The impact is close to the aiming point, about 50 kilometres south of the Percival Lakes. Although the women and children witnessed the re-entry of the rocket at Kurtararra, it is not mentioned by Yuwali in either of her stories. PHOTO: ROBERT MACAULAY, 1964

MacDougall's journal

Good view of re-entry.

Junju

We stayed there, and then the two motor cars with the [white] mob went back east. But our mob, we went west, down the lake country.

We Martu went walking back to Yimiri. They told us to go out to Yimiri. We went and drank the water at Yimiri.

After that, the motor car came and picked us up. We were climbing on the motor car, getting into the motor car. We climbed on the truck at Yimiri.

Yuwali

We slept and got up the next day and started another trip, and then stopped and had a rest.

People told us that they were going to take us. They were saying, 'We're going to take you people to see another lot of families up there. We're going into town. You've got family up there'.

They said, 'There's no one here to look after you. There are no people here. All the people that were out in the bush are in the mission. We're taking you mob'.

We didn't want to go but it was getting hard, and the white man came and picked us up. He was putting us in that truck telling us, 'We've got to take you, don't stay here'. But we wanted to stay, we were struggling to stay but the white man kept coming around. We were struggling to stay but they kept telling us, 'You've got to go, you've got to go, we've got to take you mob'.

Junju

Then we went west to Kanjumaka, and drank the water in Yulpu. We came round to Murtikujarra and had dinner there. We went to Wirnkurra, another place again, and we had a night there. We camped there.

Long's journal

Afterwards, photographs of the women and children were taken and relationship particulars noted. The following telegram was sent: 'Acknowledgement and confirmation of yesterday's telegram concerning transport and other arrangements for native women is requested. Recommend presence Welfare Officer Winderlich [Heather Winderlich, DNW welfare officer] on journey Swindells to mission. Women travelling with MacDougall in damaged vehicle and expected Swindells Friday. Macaulay and self proceeding Well 35 tonight to contact guides and possible other group.'

Long and MacDougall took photos of the women and children and recorded their relationships to one another. Clockwise from top left: Yukurrpani; Karntipa (left) and Yapaji; and (left to right) Yukurrpani, Nyipi and Yuwali. PHOTOS: TOP LEFT: TERRY LONG, 1964; TOP RIGHT: WALTER MACDOUGALL, 1964; BOTTOM: TERRY LONG, 1964

MacDougall's journal

Long decided to move the group to Jigalong Mission. Sent girls on [International truck] 070. Four boys on 075.

Long's journal

It was a sad moment, leaving it forever. And of course, they had to leave their dingoes behind. We didn't shoot them; we left them there. They were like pet dogs, really.

MacDougall's journal

Camped at south-western end of lake. Macaulay, Long, Meakins and Surman continued towards Well 35.

Wednesday 21 October 1964

Yuwali

The whitefella was still with us, he was in Linyjalangu waiting. We stayed there and cooked wild onion and ate it. Then we went towards the east of Linyjalangu and on to Junpunku and we stayed there for a day. We went towards the west and came to Kirriwirri and camped for the night.

Then we went north to Kalany and then came back and went around. We got up and went on; we kept on going through Paru [Swindells Field] eastwards. We stopped at Paru for quite a long time.

Kirriwirri waterhole. PHOTO: VIC SURMAN, 1964

Junju

We came round to . . . Linyjalangu, Mutiputu and Tawuju, and through Piparn and Wirnkurra and then were walking down to Kirriwirri. We were going along westwards towards another rockhole in the west. We went along and camped half way and got into Kirriwirri. Then we went south, on the south side of Kirriwirri.

Then we went westward. We went and sat down on *junturukuru* [a type of tree]. Then we went around on the north side, where the lake is, north of Punmu [a community established in the early 1980s, to the north of Lake Dora]. We went down from where the road goes to Wirnpa and Mulyakirri. We stayed and camped. We arrived in Papija [Swindells Field].

MacDougall's journal

Sent women on foot into Piparn soak for water. They came back without water but lots of onion grass. Moved on slowly and arrived Swindells Field.

Thursday 22 October 1964

MacDougall and the women arrive at Swindells Field, which has an airstrip and had been used as the resource base for both patrols.

Yuwali

We were still in the desert waiting for them [the group from Well 35].

MacDougall's journal

Waiting at Swindells Field for Long, Surman and Meakins.

Swindells Field, an airfield and depot used by WAPET, was known to the Martu as Paru or Papija. In the 1970s it was used by an Aboriginal group based at Strelley Station as a 'drying out' camp for Aboriginal drinkers. PHOTO: BOB TONKINSON, 1964

The women and children waiting at Swindells Field. PHOTO: BOB TONKINSON, 1964

Friday **23 October** 1964

Yuwali

Another lot of people arrived in that truck, coming from the direction of Warburton. Uncle Nyarinyari, and Pukina Morgan were all coming in the truck. Those people asked us to go to Warburton, but we didn't want to go there.

The white man asked us, 'Where do you people want to go, do you want to go to Warburton or Jigalong?' and we said, 'Yes, we want to go to Jigalong.'

Some of us became weak and sick because we weren't eating any of the stuff the white man brought. We were frightened to eat, and some of us got sick.

They had everything: flour, oranges and apples, bananas. They were asking us to take it and eat.

When we took the fruit, like banana, oranges and apples, we used to cook them in coals. Sugar was the only thing we took. We were eating it like sugar from the tree — we thought it was *yakurlakarta* [a desert source of sugar, made by an insect (lerp) on the leaves]. It almost tastes like that. But the rest of the fruit that we cooked on the ground was gone. It went soft, and we couldn't eat it.

So we went and had a rest because we were so sick. They were waiting for us to get better.

MacDougall's journal

Long, Meakins and Surman arrived [from Well 35] with another 8 natives. Three Land Rovers from Port Hedland arrived.

The group of men contacted by Macaulay at Well 35 and brought to Swindells Field. This group preferred to go to the mission at Warburton, as they had relatives there. The women in Yuwali's group new little about Jigalong, other than the information supplied by Sailor and Nyani. ABOVE: Cyril Morgan, Walpiri Carnegie and Pukina Morgan. RIGHT: Nyari and Walpiri Carnegie. FAR RIGHT: Nyari with spear and spearthrower. PHOTOS: TERRY LONG, 1964

Long speaking in 1999

Sailor and Nyani were self interested in the women going to Jigalong as they were wishing to take Kulata and Yuwali (respectively) as wives.

MacDougall's journal

Aircraft arrived with Dr. Elphinstone, Mr Tonkinson and Sister Winderlich about 2 pm.

The plane from Derby. On it were Dr Elphinstone (medical doctor), Heather Winderlich (a DNW welfare officer) and Bob Tonkinson (anthropologist). Interviewed in 1999, Long remembered: 'When they saw the aeroplane, they didn't look at it, they looked away [in fear]. They had no idea what it was really, when it was on the ground'. PHOTO: VIC SURMAN, 1964

Yuwali

Then we heard another plane coming. It was the doctor coming to check on us for sores or any sickness that we might have. So the white man told us, 'We've got visitors coming — the doctor. He's going to check on your eyes and your whole body for any sickness'.

But we were so frightened we were throwing dirt at the doctor, we didn't want him to touch our bodies. We were frightened. He was looking at our eyes. That doctor checked every one of us and found one person was sick and that person was flown out to Derby.

The group at Swindells Field. Back (left to right): Heather Winderlich, David Kininmonth (obscured), Eddie Meakins, David Webster (with baby), Walter MacDougall, Vic Surman, Punuma Sailor, Terry Long, Yaji. Front (left to right): Yuwali, Nyipi and Yapaji. This photo was taken by Bob Tonkinson, who translated for Elphinstone during the medical examinations. PHOTO: BOB TONKINSON, 1964

Junju

We saw lots and lots of planes. Plus the motor car as well — we had never seen a motor car before. They were giving us injections, checking out who was sick — who had that *bangarang* sickness [leprosy].

Long's journal

Dr Elphinstone examined the group and confirmed that the woman Nganja was to be taken to Derby Leprosarium. The doctor was determined to leave the child behind, but it was obvious that the effect on this unfortunate woman would have been disastrous, and he was persuaded to take her with him to Derby. The plane left at 4 pm.

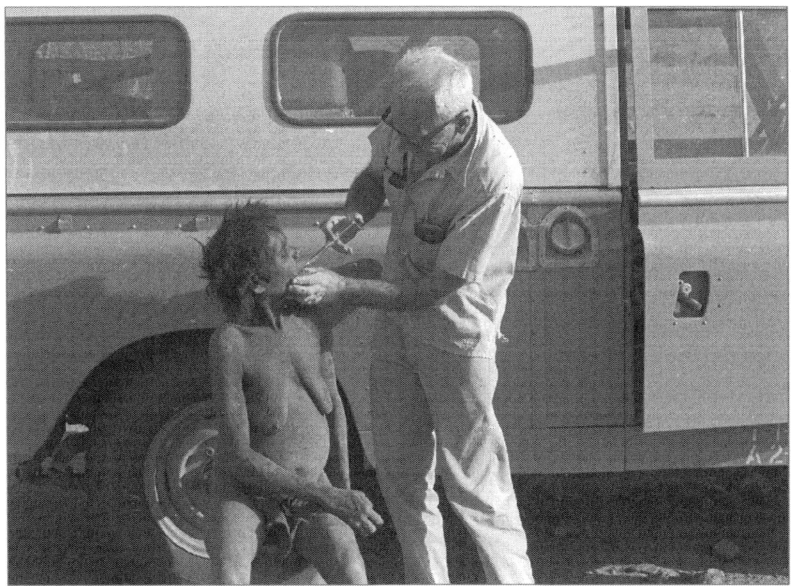

Dr J Elphinstone was the senior doctor at the Derby Leprosarium. He had been on desert patrols in 1957 and 1964 to document the health of desert Aborigines. Soon after he found the women, MacDougall had notified the Department of Native Welfare that he suspected one woman of having leprosy. Elphinstone was asked to check the women in order to confirm this and any other cases. This photo was taken at Papunya in April 1964.
PHOTO: IAN DUNLOP, AIATSIS

Long speaking in 1999

❛The air force were worried by the fact that we had a woman with us who had leprosy, and she was to be taken to Derby, so they had the whole aircraft covered in white sheets. What worried me then was the fact that we had a woman, who had just come out of the desert, knew absolutely nothing about Western civilisation, who was going to be put on an aeroplane. I didn't know how she would react. The doctor didn't want to take the daughter with him. He was going to the leprosarium, and he wasn't having anyone else with him. But I said, 'Well, you're not going to leave her behind, because it is absolutely essential that she doesn't have to go through that trauma'. We had a bit of an altercation there, but I was backed up by the pilot, and she went.

Tonkinson speaking in 1999

❛We got going fairly quickly on the examinations of the women and kids. I assisted the doctor by interpreting things — 'Open your mouth', 'cough' — whatever it was he was wanting, and trying to reassure people . . . 'He's just looking, he's like a *maparn*, like a healer and it's okay.'

Junju

Late in the afternoon, they gave us a shower, in the water, where the women were. We had a bath there.

Yuwali

They gave us some clothes for us to put on. When we put the clothes on we took them off again, because we wanted our own things made from animal fur. Mother made these for us. When we took the clothes off we said, 'We don't like this. We don't know what it is called, but we want our own things'.

We had our own things called *marrapunti* [traditional Martu clothing; the women and boys wore hair belts around their waist and sometimes around their heads and as pubic coverings].

They were killing some turkey and they gave it to us. We said, 'No, we don't want that. We want to eat our own things, like [feral] pussycat. Catch some for us'.

We told them to eat [their food], but we wanted our own things, like lizard, goanna and pussycat. 'Kill them for us.' They used to give us other kinds of meat, but we didn't take those.

Heather Winderlich organised a bath for the women at Swindells Field. Sailor and Nyani had taken clothes out for the women, which they gave to them at Kurtararra. However, the women put them on the spinifex, choosing not to wear them. They finally put them on at Swindells Field. The group had difficulty working out how to put the clothes on. Yuwali said in 1999: 'One boy put the trousers on backwards, the zip was to the back. Punuma had to tell him how to put it on the right way round.' PHOTOS: BOB TONKINSON, 1964

Junju

We had potato. I had plenty of potato for myself. The white lady put rations on the motor car for me, to take them to Jigalong.

Long speaking in 1999

Our party with Heather Winderlich decided that we would have to do something about making the women more presentable for their short visit through civilisation. We were going through Marble Bar, and Heather thought it was essential that they get a wash, have a bath.

I had reservations about that, but really I suppose that there was nothing else that could be done; they were really in a very bad state.

There was a handy little small, plastic-lined dam there with a windmill, and they were persuaded to wash in this with the help of Heather. It was an extraordinary performance, really. They washed, and some had their hair cut a bit, and cleaned themselves up.

Sailor and Nyani had decided that they wanted to take clothes out to them, so they took mission clothes out to clothe the women with. They had absolutely nothing. It looked pretty grotesque, really, when they got these on.

Saturday **24 October** 1964

Yuwali

Then we started another trip. We left Paru. We went northwards. We were all together in one big truck.

We came to a roadhouse and bought some cool drinks. We went towards the west and camped at Callawa [station].

The convoy leaves Swindells Field and heads towards Jigalong. PHOTO: BOB TONKINSON, 1964

The Callawa road. The group camped in the Oakover River close to Callawa Station, approximately 80 kilometres north-north-west of Marble Bar. PHOTO: BOB TONKINSON, 1964

Long's journal

And then very helpfully, MacDougall decided that he would come with us, and make an extra 750 miles [1200 kilometres] detour, because we didn't have enough vehicles to transport them in comfort.

MacDougall's journal

Made preparations to transport 28 natives to Jigalong mission (26 bush people and 2 guides).

Repairs to my vehicle. Port Hedland vehicles took 15 of the natives leaving 13 for me. Late start. Refuelled at 21 miles [33 kilometres]. Camped in the Oakover River.

F2 plus 5

Sunday 25 October 1964

Yuwali

We left and had a cup of tea in Coongan River then kept going to Marble Bar. We had to stop and eat dinner there. They told us, 'Don't walk round too much because they'll see you. There's another lot of people here'.

So we stayed and camped in one place. We couldn't walk around. The white man went to Marble Bar and got some dinner and some government blankets. He came back and gave them to us. We were all at Julunya Creek.

We kept on going towards the east. In the afternoon we went to Nullagine. We didn't stop in Nullagine. We saw a lot of people there, but we just drove past. When we were looking around we were looking at the people. They were all blackfellas.

We climbed on the truck and went south. We went to Roy Hill camp. There were some Jigalong people on a truck coming towards us. They were going on the mail truck to Nullagine. We were going south on the highway. We didn't know what was happening.

The mail truck to Nullagine. PHOTO: JIM PLUMB, DATE UNKNOWN

Long's journal

Mr. Kininmonth and Mr. Tonkinson were detached from the party at Marble Bar and sent on to Port Hedland.

Mr. Tonkinson's assistance was invaluable and he did much to keep the natives contented and free from fear.

It was strange to see them react to houses for the first time, a bit like the old story of Captain Cook and aborigines turning away from them, wouldn't look at them. It was exactly what they did, they wouldn't look at the houses. They looked inwards to each other and the trucks. [When Martu meet strangers and when in the presence of elders or those in authority, they will often look away, down, or sideways as a sign of deference.]

The party camped near Roy Hill that night.

Monday 26 October 1964

Yuwali

Next day we started and the white man told us, 'We're getting close to your people now. You can see them. You'll meet all the other families there'.

We got up and started another trip. Then around dinner time we got into Jigalong.

When we got to Jigalong, everybody came around, all looking at us. They were all looking at us. We were all very shy. We were frightened and feeling ashamed. We were frightened of all the people we didn't know. We were frightened. They were all staring at us.

Long's journal

The mission was reached on the morning of the 26th and the natives left in the care of the guide Sailor and the Superintendent and staff. Mr. MacDougall's two trucks left us on the morning of the 27th bound for Woomera. Miss Winderlich and myself returned then to Port Hedland via Wittenoom and arrived at 2.00 pm on the 28th having completed a trip of 1038 miles [1670 kilometres] from Swindells Field.

Jigalong residents gathered around the new arrivals. PHOTO: VIC SURMAN, 1964

Long speaking in 1999

When we arrived at Jigalong, when the group was taken to the spot they were going to live, we left them there. I suppose it is embarrassing to say, but in the Department, we did lack the sort of training that perhaps we should have had. We just went on our way.

The women and children at Jigalong. PHOTO: BOB TONKINSON, 1964

> They brought lots and lots of rations for the old people. Rations — they were all bringing them. All the missionaries were bringing all the food for the people from the bush. They brought lots and lots of food for the Martu. [21]

In gravitating towards stable food sources, these people were making decisions that were readily intelligible within their own culture:

> The twin principles which kept Aboriginal society functioning were the need to find food and the desire to limit effort in doing so — vital elements in a hunting and gathering economy. Put in ecological terms, it was a question of maintaining an energy input/output balance favourable to human survival. When the news came that the whites had abundant, if strange, food, more than they could possibly eat, this was like news of Eden — or the super waterhole, in Aboriginal terms. Hence, just as they had always moved to the sources of food — the ripening of the figs, the run of witchitties — so they moved to the whites, not in order to take part in white society, not in order to experience social change, but in order to eat the food.[22]

The early movement of people towards settlements in the north, west and south — and the new water sources provided by the Canning Stock Route — also changed the inland desert people's traditional ranges. They moved further into land that had previously been occupied and worked by other groups that had moved to settlements. In time this resulted in a gradual shift of people in a westerly direction, into increasingly less marginal country. The Martu also ranged north and south along the Canning Stock Route's wells, which provided reliable and generally good quality water at convenient distances.

Giving out rations at Jigalong. PHOTO: JIM PLUMB, DATE UNKNOWN

The migration attracted the missionaries. In the 1930s there were missions at Warburton and Mount Margaret. Between the mid 1940s and 1950s missions sprang up all around the desert; first at Balgo, then replacing government stations at Jigalong, Wiluna, Karalundi, La Grange and Cosmo Newberry.[23] The missionaries dispensed food, clothes, medical aid and religion.

When the Apostolic Church set up a mission at Jigalong in 1947 it immediately took responsibility for over 100 people who were camping there.[24] Some missionaries actively went into desert areas to bring people in. The conflict of interest for the missionaries, whose mission budgets were determined by the size of their Aboriginal clientele, was not lost on the WRE patrol officers.

In 1960, Macaulay refused to transport thirty-one Indigenous people from the Great Victoria Desert to Cundeelee Mission. The superintendent, after threatening Macaulay with retribution, took out a truck and trailer and collected them himself. Macaulay's detailed report of the incident raised questions about an active policy of desert clearance by missionaries. Based on figures supplied to him by the missionaries at Cundeelee, he determined that 122 people had been brought out of the desert to Cundeelee by the missionaries, and a further two (for health reasons) by Walter MacDougall. Macaulay commented:

> [These] form sixty per cent of the native population at the mission.
>
> The policy of the Australian Evangelical Mission Incorporated is for the Cundeelee missioners to contact as many 'bush' natives as possible and pull them into the mission for evangelising — to quote Mr . Stewart [Mission Superintendent], 'first and foremost is that their relation with the Lord Jesus Christ is right'. Mr. Stewart is also training native preachers to spread the Gospel.
>
> The policy of the W estern Australian Native W elfare Department is to discourage the movement of the Interior natives as it is obvious that Cundeelee has no facilities for accommodating natives in their initial contact . . .
>
> It is not for me to comment on the need for a mission at Cundeelee although I have heard that grave doubts have been expressed as to its necessity . Certainly, there would not be a mission except for the 120 natives brought from the Interior.[25]

Missions were paid subsidies from the DNW based on the number of Aboriginal people in their care. As Macaulay suggested, while some missionaries were coaxing or coercing people in from the desert, their motivation may sometimes have been more self-serving than evangelical.

The response to Macaulay' s report illustrated the ambiguity of Middleton' s policy on desert clearance. While generally espousing a non-interventionist position at the time (1959–60) he now explicitly renounced that policy , condoned the action taken by the mission and chastised the NPO. 'For Mr Macaulay's information,' he wrote to to the WRE, 'there has been a change of policy for that area in that this Mission has been given permission to bring in any natives found in that area.'[26]

In fact, the DNW actively fostered contact by missionaries, contact which frequently led to settlement. In the department' s 1955 annual report the mission at Jigalong was described as a 'contact mission', a feature of which was 'a policy of contacting, and maintaining contact with, desert natives'. [27] This role of missions created further ambiguity in the department's vague continuum of policy from formally strict 'hands-off' segregation of nomadic desert inhabitants on reserves, through to interventionist assimilation and absorption.

By 1960, through a combination of migration, active contact, persuasion and occasional pressure, most areas in the deserts were ver y sparsely inhabited. In that year, Macaulay presented a paper to the Australian and New Zealand Association for the Advancement of Science conference, in which he stated that, 'the pattern of deserted Reserves is fixed firmly'.[28]

The missions and government stations to which people congregated had by this stage grown to support large populations: Warburton had 450, Jigalong 140, Balgo 180 and La Grange over 100. To the east, there were severe problems with overcrowding in settlements and missions: Areyonga had 230 people, Papunya and Haasts Bluff had over 600 and Ernabella 350.[29]

Yuwali's group was one of the last to come in from the desert[30], and the second last to come in from the Percival Lakes: her father and his three wives were brought into La Grange from Joanna Spring (north of the Percival Lakes) in 1967. One group of four was taken by MacDougall from a remote area east of Lake Disappointment to Warburton in 1965, having requested transport 'on the grounds of extreme loneliness'.[31] The last reported Martu were brought in to Wiluna in 1977[32], and what appears to have been the last group of nine Pintupi came in to an outstation in 1984.[33]

The desert had effectively emptied by the time Yuwali's group was located by Sailor and Nyani. Most of their relatives were living in missions, either at Jigalong or La Grange, although it appears that the group (or at least Yuwali) knew little about this.

Why did Yuwali's group decide to come in?

It wasn't for the food: they had adequate food and water at the time, were mostly in very good health and had survived perfectly well without men for the last two years. In any case, they had no idea that there was an endless supply of food on offer; they simply saw MacDougall giving them food, then leaving them on the lakes and returning some time later with more food.[34] They had no conception of what lay outside their immediate, known world.[35]

They weren't seeking to come in: they chose to evade the patrols for an extended period, obviously not wanting to be 'caught' by them. Even having been found by Sailor, they were reluctant. As Yuwali said, 'We didn't want to go with them. We wanted to stay in our camp'.[36]

While MacDougall was required to move people out of the Blue Streak rocket dump area he did not have a record of forcing people to come in with him, and appeared perplexed about what to do. Terry Long is adamant that he had no agenda to remove people, and that he did not exert any pressure on the group to come in. This is hardly surprising: the patrol took place immediately after significant adverse publicity and parliamentary debate about removal of Indigenous people from the desert.

The pressure to come in did not, in fact, come from the white men, who were largely incidental to the decision.[37] Charles Duguid suggested an alternative source of pressure: the Indigenous guides and interpreters who accompanied patrols and promised abundant food and goods, on condition that people return to the settlement with the patrol.[38]

In 1965, Bob Tonkinson wrote the first set of guidelines for DNW patrols on how contact situations should be handled. In these, he included the following:

> When you are attempting to find out whether or not the group wants to go in to a settlement, make use of as many interpreters as are available, but use each one separately, to question the group. Invariably, most interpreters 'feel sorry for' the group and want it to be taken in to a settlement so they 'interpret' accordingly. Even with cross-checking such as that suggested, it is difficult to ascertain the true feelings of the group without communicating directly with them yourself, so you are very much at the mercy of your interpreters.[39]

Yuwali recalled that 'the old man' talked forcefully to them when he eventually found them:

> They said to Junju, 'Stop! Don't run, we're your families. We're here to take you to Jigalong, to see the other families there. We've got the other families out there. You can see them. They're worried about you mob'. Punuma was telling them all the names of people living in Jigalong.[40]

Whatever the patrol officers may have thought, Punuma Sailor knew what was going to happen to the group; he immediately made it clear that he intended to take them to Jigalong. The people from Well 35 who were later brought to Swindells Field by Macaulay clearly wanted to go to Warburton Mission.[41] The patrol officers were willing to go to either mission, but it appears that the guides informed the officers that the party wished to go to Jigalong, where Sailor and Nyani were living.

MacDougall and Long were almost completely reliant on the Martu men to communicate with the women.[42] No matter what the policy or intentions of the patrol officers and the DNW were, it appears to have been the intent of the Martu guides to take the women back to Jigalong, as soon as they found them.[43]

Right up to the time that they left the lake, Yuwali claims that she was reluctant to go, but was pressured by the Martu guides: 'We were struggling to stay, but they kept telling us, 'You've got to go, you've got to go, we've got to take you mob'.[44]

Punuma Sailor was the older of the two guides who made contact with Yuwali's group. Years later, his daughter recalled him saying that he'd had to talk hard to convince the group that they had to come in.[45] A later, third-party record of the patrol made the comment, 'It does seem that relatives on the patrols often put pressure on their kinsfolk to come in and that in the case of [Yuwali's group] pressure was clearly put on the people'.[46]

What factors would have weighed in the discussion between Sailor and the women?

According to Yuwali, the appeal to family was forcefully made. Prior to leaving Jigalong, Punuma had received instructions from relatives of the group telling him to convey a message to them, asking them to come in.[47]

This would have resonated strongly with the women. Martu society and life is based around extensive social networks and obligations of social reproduction. Without a sufficient population, with a proper spread of relatives, it would have been difficult to satisfy some cultural obligations. The desire to see family would have been likely to be ver y powerful, and based on far more than sentiment.[48]

One potential pressure was a need for marriageable men. The group included two young women of marriageable age (Y uwali and Y apaji) without husbands. Marriages created enduring alliances, loyalties and an extended range of familiarity and safety for a family group.[49]

Men could not marry until they had been through the Law — a process of initiation and learning that started when they reached puberty and ended some fifteen or so years later . A boy entering initiation would have a marriage arranged with a baby girl, so that by the time he had attained marriageable age, the girl was ready to join her promised husband. Men could acquire multiple wives over their lives, including widows, for whom remarriage was traditionally obligator y since neither 'spinsterhood' nor 'bachelorhood' was an accepted status.

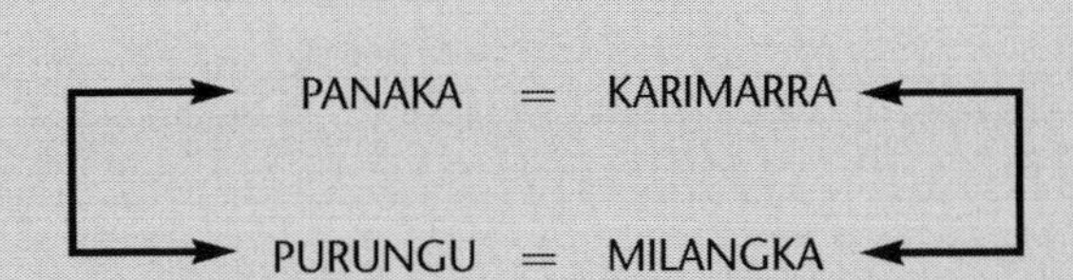

A Panaka man will marry one or more women of the Karimarra section. Their children will be Milangka. Any Milangka children will take a spouse of the Purungu section. A Karimarra man will marry one or more women from the Panaka section, and their children will be Purungu. When they grow up, these Purungu will marry a spouse of the Milangka section.[50]

'Almost all Aboriginal societies are divided into two, four or eight categories . . . Because membership is ascribed by birth, it is impossible for individuals to change categories . . . The categories provide individuals with rough guides to the kind of patterned behaviour expected of them.'[51]

Marriage was strictly regulated, and both the family and the alliances formed between intermarr ying groups were vital to the integration of Martu society . Correct marriage partly depended upon what is commonly translated as 'skin groups'. Among the Martu every person is born into one of four 'sections' (see box above), and one's section is different from — but determined by — those of one' s parents. For example, Purungu women' s children will belong to the Panaka section. Karimarra women have Milangka children, and vice versa. A Purungu person's spouse will come from the Milangka section. A Karimarra can only marry someone from the Panaka section.

The section system and the marriage rules that are part of the kinship system are central elements in the workings of Martu society .[52] The kinship system provides the blueprint for all social relationships, giving each person a clear , detailed sense of their relationship to each other person, their obligations and responsibilities, their legitimate expectations, their mode of behaviour in the presence of each other person, and the people whose direct presence they must avoid. The system allows strangers to be placed instantly into a relationship with every member of a group, once the stranger's section is known.

Even if Yuwali's group had been in contact with the few other groups remaining in the desert, the chance that any such group would contain men who could lawfully marry these young women was minimal. Because of the complex considerations that bore on marriage, it has been estimated that in a community of even 100 people each person of marriageable age had only three eligible spouses.[53]

The requirements of the Law also make it essential for young men to be in contact with a broader society at certain ages. The initiation of young men is a long process which can only be guided by older, initiated men. Yuwali's group included two boys who were growing towards the age when initiation commenced.

Other ritual and social activities required the full span of society in order to fulfil obligations.

> You need 'mother's brothers' and 'father's sisters' and 'spouses'. You need a whole range of people for certain cultural activities and purposes. And when the number drops below that critical level, then you simply have to break the rules, which a few of the last groups had done by having marriages that were not 'straight' [correct] or by having uncircumcised men, who did not have the correct categories of men there to circumcise them, take wives (one man had three of them) . . . this kind of breaking of the Law is very unsettling and totally unacceptable to these people.
>
> It's a source of concern because they know that is not what they're supposed to be doing. And that's another very important incentive for them to move, to go to the settlements, where there are of course large numbers of people.[54]

As it happened, Nyani and Sailor were of the proper sections and sufficiently remote to marry the two young, available women, and took the opportunity to do so: Nyani claimed Yuwali and Yapaji as second wives. Sailor claimed Kulata (although he was quickly — and, by all accounts, violently — disabused of this idea by his first wife on his return to Jigalong).

Terry Long recounted that, 'Nyani was a bit of a nuisance. He should never have been with us. I think he was obsessional about one of the young women there, and had to be curbed. But Sailor was very, very good'.[55] Long described Nyani as, 'a very disturbed young fellow' who later on got into trouble at Jigalong. 'He was paying a great deal of attention to Yuwali, the sixteen-year-old girl in the group. We had trouble keeping him separated from her'.[56]

Bob Tonkinson concurred:

> I certainly remember that one of the guides, Punuma, was very keenly interested immediately in one of the young women [Kulata], and certainly tried to take her as a second wife . . . So there's no doubt that Punuma and Nyani both would have perhaps self-interestedly wanted the group to go down to Jigalong because there

> were young women at that stage unattached . . . and it could have been personally advantageous to those men.[57]

It may also be that social obligations prescribed or influenced the women's 'cooperation' with the whitefellas and the Martu guides. In a society regulated as thoroughly as Martu society, are white perceptions of voluntary cooperation likely to be reliable?

There were many sources for these obligations. A host of avoidance, respect and authority relations would have attended the entire, month-long interaction at the lakes. While MacDougall may have had some general knowledge of them, Long probably did not.

Sailor and Nyani, for example, each had avoidance or respect relationships with women classified as their mothers-in-law or daughters. When camping at the lakes, Sailor and Nyani settled into separate groups. Sailor — the older of the two, and thus holding greater authority and status — camped with Nyipi and Kulata, his 'wife's sisters'. He may, therefore, have been in an avoidance relationship with Yuwali (his skin daughter); Nyani had similarly defined relationships in a separate camp.

The fact that MacDougall, Sailor and Nyani fed the women may also have given them some authority. The women may have felt obliged to offer hospitality, particularly to an older man (*jirlpi*) such as MacDougall. This was illustrated by the fact that the women felt obliged to offer what Macdougall understood to be 'sexual services' during the weeks when he was alone with them on the lake.[58]

The provision of food may have had some more substantial effect as well. The reciprocal obligations that arise in a similar Western Desert society (the Pintupi) when one person 'looks after' another, are captured in the concept of *kanyininpa*.[59] (The Martu use the same word and concept.) Fred Myers described *kanyininpa* as authority resulting from nurturance:

> Some people assumed authority by looking after others, and they in turn had legitimate expectation of being looked after by others who wielded power over them. The notion of *kanyininpa* not only enabled the Pintupi to make sense of relations between adults and children and between ritual leaders and novices, but between the Pintupi and the structures of welfare colonialism with which they had come into contact since the 1930s:
>
> On the whole the Pintupi understand the Australian government and its representatives as largely autonomous 'bosses', to whom deference and obedience is owed. In turn, the government is obliged to 'help' and 'look after' [them]. Their interpretation of past government behaviour convinces Pintupi that their view is appropriate.[60]

Tim Rowse, reading Myers, interpreted this concept further: 'Following Fred Myers' account of the Pintupi, we can imagine a kind of reciprocity in frontier transactions

MacDougall gives Yuwali's group food at Kurtararra. PHOTO: ROBERT MACAULAY, 1964

. . . Typically, missions and welfare officials rationed as an instrument of command'.[61]

Whatever the actual forces operating on the minds of the women, the politics of the situation on the lake were hardly simple. However, these subtleties would have been lost on the non-Martu participants, who had their own perceptions of the women's wishes and of their own responsibility and obligations.

They also had their own political concerns to worry them. Terry Long described the difficulty of his decision to take the group to Jigalong:

> MacDougall had reported to the WRE establishment that Nyani had 'married' Yuwali, aged 16 years, and he felt that as a result of this, Nyani would return to Jigalong and most of the party, most of the relatives of the girl, would want to go to live in Jigalong. That was very much the case. Apart from that, Sailor, the older of the two guides, had found that one of the women was his [classificatory] sister-in-law, and he too had relatives at Jigalong.
>
> I had no hesitation in saying this is where we should take the women, if they really insisted on leaving the lake area.
>
> The decision to take them away from Lake Percival wasn't made lightly. It took a great deal of soul searching before we agreed to comply with the women's arrangements to take them with us, because we felt that we would be criticised, whatever we did. But they certainly did not want to stop, and you could see why not: they were totally isolated, had no family or tribal life, and it would have been impossible to leave them in that sort of situation.[62]

Desert people in previous decades had come in for a variety of disparate and sometimes complicated motivations: the attraction of reliable water and food; the exigencies of drought; a desire to take up a life easier than the harsh life in the desert; the desire to see relatives; loneliness, fear or curiosity; a sense of adventure; intimidation; the need for medical help; social obligations. All played a part at different times in the minds of different people.

By the time that Yuwali's group was contacted it was likely that new considerations were becoming compelling. Martu life finds meaning in a complex society, but the desert no longer sustained that society. If people's obligations to Law were to be satisfied, they had little choice but to move to where the society had relocated.

The women were reluctant to come in, even when they knew that they were being chased by a Martu man, right up until the moment that they were loaded into the truck to leave the lake. It is unclear from Yuwali's story exactly what arguments were put by Sailor, but it appears that it was Sailor who convinced the women that they had little choice but to come in, or virtually forced them to come in.[63] A transaction, replete with social and political considerations and invested with Martu meaning, took place at the lake. This was entirely distinct from the relatively straightforward administrative event that the patrol officers could otherwise be seen as directing.

Even when people freely decided to come in, it was impossible for them to understand the full content and long-term implications of their choices. Most viewed it as a temporary move: the idea that they might never see their country again was unlikely to have been contemplated. As it was, Yuwali and Junju would not go back to their country, to the lakes and Yimiri and Kurtararra for thirty-five years.

Over two or three generations, the people of the Central and Western deserts chose to adapt their lives and their society to a new set of opportunities, a new resource base and undoubtedly a new set of challenges, demands and problems. For Yuwali and her group, the new world they would have to negotiate would be a mission.

Asylums for refugees

> One still hears much criticism of Missions but, quite apart from their inestimable value in the humanitarian and welfare field of their endeavour, there is no doubt about the fact that they are of ver y great administrative aid to any Government concerned with natives.
>
> Even an atheist, if he were sincere in his appreciation of the work of missionaries, would have to admit that Christianity was of tremendous value and importance as a civilising influence and an aid to the assimilation of natives into the framework of a white community.
>
> I [Commissioner Middleton] regard Missions as being valuable and important administrative adjuncts of this Department, and missionaries as being vitally essential to the welfare of the native race. [64]

Many people who came out of the desert in the 1950s and 1960s made first contact with local pastoral stations such as T alawana or Balfour Downs, on the western fringe of the desert, or with missions. [65] Institutions such as the Aborigines Rescue Mission at Jigalong provided concentrated points of settlement, with most people gravitating at some time to these centres. [66]

From the missions, most men of working age (and some women) then moved to work on the pastoral stations in the surrounding area, leaving a core of older people, mothers and school-age or younger children.

First contact on these pastoral stations meant that the prototypical 'whitefella' from whom they developed initial perceptions of white culture was a station bachelor. Missions often provided their second substantial (and confusingly different) contact with Europeans. Between 1940 and 1970, the missions in Western Australia were instrumental in shaping a new world for the people from the desert and their children. The missions defined the structures and expectations according to which they would forge their longer-term relationship with the European world.

Middleton embraced the missions, in contrast to the far more antagonistic position that his predecessors had taken. Early in his tenure, he provided a lengthy justification for the increased role that missions would play under his administration:

> The natives of W estern Australia, with ver y few exceptions, have lost or are fast losing what little religion they had, in the face of an advancing civilisation . . .
>
> Christianity has ser ved our own people faithfully and well for two thousand years — can any of us argue, with any conviction, that it is likely to be harmful in any way to our aborigines?

> Missionaries are invaluable, also, as advocates for the native. The Government can hardly do this because it has to be impartial, and even the Department of Native Affairs, largely because of strong political pressure that is frequently brought to bear upon it, is impotent to help the native in some circumstances when he needs friends to stand up for him and express his point of view . . . the danger of the native side of the question being lost altogether is a very real one. Unless the native has someone to act as his advocate and speak up for him, he is in a position of very great disadvantage. The missionaries can and do act in this way.
>
> The educational, medical and welfare work of the missionary demands of him or her a full working day seven days a week, and the value of this work and their quiet influence on the lives of natives, the young ones especially, which comes from the examples of clean and honourable lives, cannot be estimated in terms that are readily understood by the general public.
>
> The life of a missionary is not an easy one and those who go out to the mission field are not going to an easy life. It is a life that takes all their pluck and all their endurance and all their courage. There can be no doubt whatever in the mind of any man who seriously thinks about the question, that missions exert a most important influence for good and by their noble, educational and spiritual teaching and training contribute in a very material way towards the economy of this State.[67]

A typical dwelling at the Martu Camp, Jigalong. PHOTO: JIM PLUMB, DATE UNKNOWN

Middleton's views on the role and conduct of missions were shaped by his commitment to assimilation — or 'absorption' — as the proper goal for his department and aspiration for Indigenous people. The missions' activities were to be judged in accordance with this goal: preparation for life as a productive and assimilated member of the Western Australian mainstream community:

> The native girl or youth whose character has been stabilised by lengthy Mission influence is usually found to have a sense of responsibility and duty, provided that their education and training is recognised and appreciated by their employer, and consequently is a more reliable and efficient worker than the average native of the camp environment; thus they should, and undoubtedly will, become an economic asset to the State.[68]

The missions certainly expanded and prospered under Middleton. The number of missions grew from sixteen in 1948, shortly after Middleton took office, to thirty-four by the time he retired fifteen years later.[69] He invited churches and mission societies to take over government settlements, ration depots, children's homes and hostels. In 1949, one year after his appointment, government subsidies to missions doubled from £6,835 to £13,670.[70] Subsidies for Aboriginal children in missions rose 1000 per cent in the first six years of his administration, and by 1954 subsidies for Aboriginal children had reached parity with those for white children in institutions.[71]

By 1956, 48 per cent of the departmental budget was spent on missions, which accommodated 10 per cent of the state's Indigenous population.[72]

Missions were an indispensable part of the department's front-line service structure because, in spite of the state's contribution, their staff and costs were largely subsidised by churches and philanthropic organisations. The churches, orders and societies that founded the missions provided a reasonable supply of idealistic people who were willing to move to and withstand a harsh life, often in very remote areas. The missionaries provided a relatively stable workforce, working for what little pay their employers could afford. The inherent idealism of their undertaking also deflected criticism.[73]

Hence, the missions provided a convenient resource that appeared at the time to be cost-effective, reasonably appropriate, and largely above public scrutiny.[74] This public–private partnership would stretch far further than pure government funding was likely to stretch.

However, the government — having no direct responsibility for the living conditions on missions — allowed quite deplorable conditions in many places to continue while ostensibly fulfilling its responsibilities through small grants-in-aid. In the department's mind, it would have been practically and financially impossi-

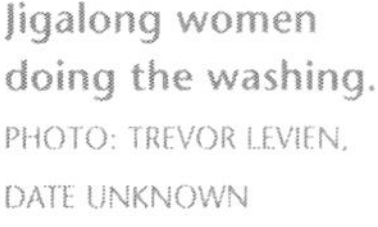

Jigalong women doing the washing.
PHOTO: TREVOR LEVIEN, DATE UNKNOWN

ble to carry out the work of the department in any remote parts of the state without the missions.

While the missions provided this adjunct to his administration, Middleton greatly expanded the number of departmental field officers and devolved responsibility to the district offices from which they operated.[75] The role of the field officers was to patrol townships, missions, settlements and stations, while the missions provided the vast bulk of settled services. The two groups were complementary:

> The essence of the Department's work lies, of course, in the activities of its officers in the field and, in another sphere, the missionaries who work under departmental administrative supervision and benevolent control.[76]

This 'administrative supervision and benevolent control' exercised by the department was often illusory or highly compromised. Because they were indispensable, the missions had Middleton over a barrel.

Berndt highlighted the mission's central, and often unaccountable, role in the state's administration when commenting on the Grayden committee's highly critical report on Aboriginal welfare in the Laverton and Warburton regions:

> One of the most important features of contact between Aborigines and Europeans in this particular region, as in so many others, is the continuing presence of the Missions. The extent to which they influence native policy generally is rarely, if ever, appreciated. In some cases they are to all intents and purposes autonomous. In others, and in the area under review, they are expected to shoulder nearly all practical responsibility as far as native welfare is concerned, in their immediate neighbourhood. Yet during the controversy the missions in the Laverton–Warburton region were referred to as if they had no such responsibility, and received virtually no share of the criticism. I do not want to discuss the reasons for this here: but since the missions represent a dominant factor in the situation, their influence on the whole question of social and cultural change and adjustment of these Aborigines should be given more attention.[77]

In this alliance of convenience the department's relationship with the missions was dominated by the existence and needs of the Indigenous population. While its district officers occasionally visited the missions to try to ensure that certain minimum standards were being maintained, they had little real capacity to effect change. Even Middleton, the missionaries' champion, became exasperated in private by the relationship:

> This Department disagrees with the recommendation that more assistance should be given to the Warburton Ranges Mission until it can be assured that the management of the Mission is in more capable hands; the present superintendent is a hopeless incompetent and his first assistant a well-meaning, religious moron. Very few U.A.M. missionaries have any practical knowledge or business ability; they

> themselves frequently remark that they are there for one purpose only, the preaching of the Gospel. They are the most improvident, incapable missionaries I have encountered in thirty years.[78]

His frustration was shared by the NPOs:

> Although I was at the mission for only four days it struck me forcedly that Mr Green was not suitable to be Superintendent of a mission. He lacks information of native life, knows almost no native language, appears extremely poor at administration and shows an amazing lack of knowledge of conditions on the mission.[79]

The missionaries were formally answerable only to their employers, the various churches. Apart from the most egregious misbehaviour, in which case the department would secure the dismissal of a mission employee, the state government effectively abrogated responsibility for the conduct of missions to the churches, just as they had abrogated any responsibility for securing knowledge about the situation and needs of desert people to the WRE native patrol officers.

The foundation of Jigalong mission is a case in point. It was set up after the secretary of the Apostolic Church in Sydney wrote to the commissioner for Native Affairs in 1944, proposing the siting of a mission, 'somewhere between Beagle Bay and New Norcia'. Having never heard of the Apostolic Church, the commissioner requested, 'details about the tenets of the Church and the extent of its ability to finance the mission'. Within six weeks the church's application was approved, thus placing, 'the destiny of Western Desert Aborigines into the hands of a group of people in Sydney, who knew absolutely nothing about Western Desert Aborigines, who had never been to the Western Desert, and who he had never met'.[80]

Western Australian missions were run by a disparate array of groups across the spectrum of churches. A minority were operated by the mainstream churches (various Catholic orders or the Methodist church), but the majority, such as Jigalong, were run by more fundamentalist churches.[81]

These institutions not only differed in their theology and the aggressiveness of their evangelism, but also in the quality and knowledge of their staff, the extent of their resources and the opportunities provided by their local environments.

The missionaries themselves were also diverse. Some became authorities on the language and culture of Indigenous groups, seeking a deep understanding of the people with whom they worked. Others had no interest in seeking such an understanding. Some were authoritarian, insensitive and even cruel and were not viewed well by the Aboriginal people. On the whole, those who were sensitive, gentle and respectful are remembered fondly. Virtually all were directly motivated by a sincerely held sense of mission, within whatever social, cultural and theological framework that 'mission' was manifested. By European standards their lives were difficult, particularly in remote missions.

The 2 Ways, designed by Wilf Douglas, Warburton Mission, 1959. PHOTO: RONALD BERNDT, UNIVERSITY OF WESTERN AUSTRALIA, BERNDT MUSEUM OF ANTHROPOLOGY

These missions were not necessarily sited on ideal ground, often simply taking over former government ration depots or other facilities in locations that had a water source. Jigalong was neither planned nor sited, having replaced a maintenance depot for the Rabbit-Proof Fence [82], which had long been authorised to distribute rations. By 1947, the settlement was well known to people from the desert.

However, facilities for supporting the mission population were often basic or non-existent, principally restricted by the shortage of potable water. Ten years after its foundation the local DNW district office reported that the mission was, 'little more than a dustbowl, caused by denudation of natural herbages over the years'. [83]

When Yuwali and her family arrived in 1964, Jigalong was still a harsh environment:

> It was a terrible place. Conditions were hard . . . It was very tough living out there for the whites and the Aborigines. The housing was very primitive. The Jigalong site, I don't think it had been well chosen. It was absolutely isolated and bare. No redeeming features round it at all. Treeless and hot.[84]

When the Percival Lakes group arrived the mission buildings included six houses for the mission staff and one for the schoolteacher, two hospital buildings, the school, three separate dormitories (boys, senior girls and junior girls) and a combined church/dining hall. The Martu adults lived across Jigalong Creek in another world, known simply as The Camp.

The Camp was mostly open, lean-to structures made of corrugated iron and canvas plus a number of small, one-room iron huts for old people. By 1964, it also included a water tap. The nearest DNW office was over 300 kilometres away in Marble Bar, and the nearest police were 225 kilometres away in Nullagine.

Jigalong lies not far from the edge of the desert in the territory of the Nyiyaparli people, but by the time it was established most of them had already drifted westwards, and the Aborigines living there were immigrants from the Western Desert. A well-known string of waterholes running west from the Canning Stock Route became the most popular route in to the outlying pastoral stations, and thence to Jigalong.

At a rhetorical level, the missions on the desert fringes were seen by government administrators as the first port of call for Western Desert people on their journey to assimilation.[85] However, Berndt noted the many questions that the official assimilation policy raised, particularly in these fringe desert settlements:

Jigalong: houses and hospital in the background, with the Martu Camp in the foreground.
PHOTO: TREVOR LEVIEN, DATE UNKNOWN

> In recent years Government administration of Aborigines in Australia has been preoccupied with the problem of *assimilation* . . . Whether or not this is a good or desirable aim is beside the point. In most cases the process is taking place more or less inevitably , even apart from any Administration help. It is the situation as we find it.
>
> But there is not enough awareness of what assimilation actually involves. Nor is it realised fully that if people of Aboriginal stock are to be adjusted and eventually absorbed into Australian social and cultural life, more attention must be paid to means, as well as to possible ends.
>
> We need to be quite clear about what this concept of assimilation involves. Further, we need to decide what kind of people we expect or would like them to be, as a result of the process which is going on today . We need to realise further that the current policy means, in effect, unequivocal opposition to all traditional Aboriginal cultural and social aspects.
>
> We also need to ask ourselves, and the Aborigines themselves should be articulate on this point, whether we want all of the Aboriginal traditional life to be irretrievably eradicated . . .
>
> [T]hese Aboriginal people are becoming more and more Europeanised. But what kind of Europeanisation is this? They are mostly in contact with (a) missionaries; (b) Government officials (of various kinds, including police); (c) pastoral station employers etc.; (d) restricted population in small countr y towns; (e) prospectors, doggers, and so on. Their knowledge of 'white' Australians is thus restricted to only a small section of our culture and society, and consequently their view of European (Australian) life generally is quite narrow.
>
> This question of 'assimilation to what?' is quite vital to them, as it is for us. [86]

The Berndts' questions were real and practical, and highlighted the naivety of the policy in these remote communities. There were economic, social and spiritual dimensions to the missions' assimilative responsibility but, for different reasons, each was substantially doomed.

The immediate employment opportunities available for Aboriginal people on missions were limited to menial work on the mission or more skilled and substantial work on local pastoral stations. Receipt of rations usually involved a reciprocal obligation to work. This basic economic relationship between European work and European goods was a cornerstone of the idea of assimilation.

Other than that, there was an ill-defined sense that education would provide the young with individual opportunities for economic and social advancement in the wider world. Taking up those opportunities would generally require them to leave their society and move to towns. Almost no desert Aborigines were in a position to do this, and most of the few who did soon returned to their people and culture. Others preferred to stay at the missions, where there was little or no immediate employment.[87]

MacDougall had repeatedly railed at Middleton against the failure by government to actively provide Indigenous people in the deserts with a viable, local, economic base. He saw missions that lacked 'useful work' as places that encouraged destructive idleness. He charged that the missions' existence distracted government attention from the need to invest in such opportunities for Indigenous people:

> Missions are not the answers. The best of them, apart from the fine work they do in regards to spiritual instruction, are little more than asylums for refugees. They have not the necessary finance or capable staff for anything other than evangelical work which they state is their main and, in many cases, their only concern. Besides, you get what you pay for nowadays.[88]

The need for properly funded enterprises that provided Indigenous people with both training and a viable economic base was repeatedly suggested by WRE patrol officers, anthropologists and critics of government policy. It was regularly rejected by Middleton as financially impossible. In the case of Jigalong, such a policy was not really contemplated until after the end of the mission era.

The broader goal of assimilation was that Indigenous people would learn the ways of European society, as a prelude to their inevitable entry to that society. But, on the whole, the Indigenous experience on the missions was one of 'assimilation' to a unique and highly contrived environment.

In Jigalong, a fairly strict separation grew between The Camp and camp life, and the buildings and work of the mission itself.[89] Missionaries and Indigenous adults chiefly interacted in the provision of material services: at the clinic, mission store or dining room. The missionaries also organised employment, either on the mission or on surrounding pastoral stations, where men worked as stockmen and women as domestic servants. On the whole, adults were seen as being beyond redemption, both socially and spiritually.

The Indigenous population of the mission took advantage of the new material resources, but maintained their society and law, with a strong ritual life. Jigalong residents continued their traditional ways in initiation, marriage and ritual life, and organised life in the camp in accordance with the Law.

> The Mission staff insist that the adult inmates of their institution are a gentle people, but do agree that certain injurious tribal practices are carried out. So far, they have not intervened, apparently for fear of antagonising the natives. There is

Martu men at Jigalong dressed for ceremony. PHOTO: JIM PLUMB, DATE UNKNOWN

> no doubt that aborigines for hundreds of miles around regard Jigalong as a centre of very strong tribal influence — not all of it good. [90]

The traditional social and cultural life were regularly reinforced and enriched by the arrival of new people from the desert. Over time, Jigalong became recognised as one of the major centres of traditional Law in the desert region.[91] At the same time, the society was adapting to the new communal, settled environment and to the 'benevolent authority' which the missionaries appropriated, and which the Indigenous people generally accommodated.

On some missions the missionaries' power over the adults was exercised in extreme ways, ways which were not always accepted by the Indigenous people. For example, a schoolteacher, De Graaf, writes of Warburton:

> It is much easier for these people to get a ride with the truck *to* the mission than *from* it. On many occasions I have witnessed the verbal battle between missionary and aborigines which ensued when the latter were not allowed to leave the Mission. Serious incidents have taken place, during which mission personnel were stoned (1962–63).[92]

The control of resources by missionaries also extended to direct receipt of the residents' social security payments. This provided another means whereby missionaries could prevent the movement of people — particularly after 1960, when the major pensions became available to Indigenous people. To receive any reliable benefit from their payments, in the form of rations or pocket money, the older people had to stay on the mission.

This physical 'containment' was a metaphor for the missions' effective role in government policy, particularly in relation to Indigenous adults. Missions provided the government with a readily administered, relatively cheap set of buffer settlements, which prevented or delayed Indigenous people from moving to the politically embarrassing camps on the fringes of towns.

Martu girls outside the girls' dormitory at Jigalong. PHOTO: TREVOR LEVIEN, DATE UNKNOWN

This may not have been the primary intent of official policy, and Indigenous preferences undoubtedly played a part in the formation and maintenance of these settlements. Nevertheless, the isolated and largely invisible 'holding pattern' provided by remote mission settlements saved the administration a world of problems in negotiating just what 'assimilation' actually meant for traditional Indigenous adults.

Forsaking the adults, the missionaries targeted the children as the primary medium of 'advancement', and — through the often rigid separation of children in dormitories, strict education and religious indoctrination — sought to train them for an assimilated future.

Writing about Jigalong in the early years after the missionaries arrived in 1947, Tonkinson describes their strategy:

> The missionaries placed all school-age children in dormitories. This policy had a two-fold purpose: it provided the missionaries with a captive audience, and it partially separated the children from their parents and what the missionaries considered to be the pernicious influences of Camp life. [93]

The assumption was that, once educated, the children would not be capable of returning to their traditional life. The traditional life would break down, and, by default, the children would move into mainstream European society.

The strategy of separation was often enhanced by the fact that the children's parents were required to be away, working as station hands or domestic help on pastoral stations, often for months at a time. This meant that, for much of the time, the Camp was largely populated by children and older people. The missionaries sought to keep the older people at the mission because they, along with the children, formed the primary source for the missions' recurrent funding. By 1960, child endowment and age and invalid pensions dwarfed the state funding, and were paid direct into the mission coffers.

Ubiquitous mission pictures of scrubbed, smiling Aboriginal children, lined up for school or playing in a dusty yard, suggest that mission life was characterised by grateful acceptance of the missionaries' authority, charity and 'civilising influence'.

A group of boys at Jigalong. PHOTO: JIM PLUMB, DATE UNKNOWN

In reality, the missions constituted a new frontier, in which contact between Aboriginal and European Australia was negotiated in an ideologically charged symbiosis: the Aboriginal people wanted food and supplies and the missionaries sought their souls.

The missionaries' desire to save and shape the children was sometimes manifested in highly intrusive but ultimately counterproductive ways. They sought to 'protect' the virtue of older girls by locking them in dormitories at night, but the girls 'periodically rebelled by breaking out of their dormitory and fleeing into the bush or into Camp or, as on one memorable occasion, by breaking into the boys' dormitory.'[94]

The remoteness and day-to-day autonomy of the missions allowed autocratic and quite high-handed behaviour by the missionaries, within the sphere of their authority. They controlled government money and rations, were able to threaten parents with the removal of their children, banned the use of Martu languages in the school and dormitories, assisted some young women to avoid marriages to older men, and dispensed corporal punishment.[95]

At Jigalong, the frontier politics led in 1962 to a complete breakdown in this strained relationship. The Martu walked out of the mission, taking their children with them. They decamped to Nullagine, where they enrolled their children in the school, and claimed rations. They only returned when the department threatened them with the loss of their rations.

The missions became a political battleground in which often mutually uncomprehending parties pursued their interests and agendas. This battleground was shaped by the fact that relatively few missionaries — at Jigalong or at any of the state's other missions — spoke any Indigenous language or had any significant understanding of Aboriginal culture.

The Berndts highlighted their unhappiness with missions generally, and particularly those in which the missionaries had little knowledge of Indigenous society or language:

> Of course, it is difficult for many people to acknowledge that the Aborigines have or have had a well-developed religion of their own; and we are all cynical enough to understand that 'freedom of religion' applies only to that which we hold ourselves.[96]

Equally, the Indigenous people had no substantial knowledge of European language or culture. This created a contact environment that could be shaped by mutual incomprehension. Bob Tonkinson believed that, at Jigalong, both parties, 'deliberately perpetuate this poor communication as part of their respective adaptive strategies':

> As long as the messages remain confused and ambiguous, the Aborigines can exploit misunderstandings by extracting maximum concessions from the missionaries for a minimum physical output, while retaining the freedom to manage their own internal affairs. Faulty communication enables the missionaries to sustain untarnished their negative stereotype of the Aborigines and continue to rationalise their evangelical failures by laying the blame squarely on the Aborigines . . . [T]he Jigalong Aborigines' successful maintenance of cultural identity in the contact environment is best accounted for in terms of such strategies. [97]

A church service at Jigalong. PHOTO: JIM PLUMB, DATE UNKNOWN

The Indigenous inhabitants of missions had to negotiate a complex dual world made up, on the one hand, of the 'whitefella business' that was the inevitable corollary of the new abundance and, on the other, an unfamiliar, settled form of their traditional society. They largely ceded control of the alien 'whitefella business' to the mission authorities, who in any case assumed that control. But the traditional life, particularly on a mission such as Jigalong, continued as a parallel set of social institutions, largely unaffected by the white co-residents.

The interplay of these dual worlds defined the mission inhabitants' new society; it was to this society that they were 'assimilated'. The missionaries' adopted and accepted role was to provide material goods and services (such as health care), and that provision justified a measure of coercive authority in certain material realms. But the Martu at Jigalong had not signed up to the missionaries' other evangelistic agenda, to remake them and their society, and were hostile to interference that contravened the Law. They maintained their identity, their languages, their Law and their society.

In 1988, Bob Tonkinson reflected on the mission that he had studied throughout the 1960s, and the fairly harsh criticism he had made at that time of the missionaries, revisiting his views on the dialectic in this meeting of cultures:

> [O]utcomes transformative of the Aborigines' culture would have been much the same, regardless of the status of the resident whites, as fundamentalists, atheists or whatever. Poor communication, mutual distrust, inadequate understanding of each side by the other, and so on, are best comprehended in terms of the conjunction of Indigenous people and carriers of a powerful alien culture . . . [In retrospect] I paid insufficient attention to the systemic nature of the colonising culture for . . . the colonial world, in terms of its thought, values and mode of organisation, was a system. An adequate analysis therefore requires a perspective which sees the colonisers as acted upon by those they attempt to rule . . . the missionaries seemed to be in a state of protracted culture shock. [98]

The problematic meeting of two cultures, largely ignorant of each others' language, values and social systems, was often exacerbated by the lack of any real desire to see the world through the other's eyes, and the consequent distrust and polarisation. Missions such as Jigalong did not promote effective cultural dialogue so much as a wary negotiation of reciprocal exploitation, fulfilling each group's reasons for being there.

By late 1964, when Yuwali's group arrived, Jigalong had 250 Martu residents.[99] For the majority of people like Yuwali and her group, who had walked (or were brought) out of the Western Desert, missions were the place in which their new lives were forged. The missions provided the context in which these people participated in the reshaping of their society, learned about the European world and developed strategies for dealing with it.

Mission life therefore largely shaped the relationship between the people of the Western Desert and the rest of Australia in almost complete isolation from mainstream European society and policy makers. The government of Western Australia not only acquiesced in this but advocated and supported it. After the reserves, the missions provided the next 'holding pattern' for an administration with no real policy for the desert peoples. But that 'holding pattern' was not a static, benign state, at least for the mission residents.

Like the Department of Native Welfare's own staff, the majority of missionaries had no training, no knowledge, no practical policy, no plan and no effective means or intention of negotiating with the Martu about what kind of future they wanted. The government knew this, and also often knew of the problems in the missions. The missions provided a source of dedicated, salaried staff prepared to endure extremely harsh conditions in remote locations, while providing basic services to Indigenous populations who were happy to gravitate around these sources of food and goods.

For a department with relatively few resources, and which already devoted a vast proportion of its budget — in relative terms — to people on the missions, it was arguable that there was little else it could do. As Middleton acknowledged, 'I know Missions are not the complete answer, but they are the only people who are at present prepared to remain and work in remote areas for the benefit of the natives'.[100]

Terry Long echoed this sentiment, and provided some insight into the department's view of available options:

> The missions were a rescue operation. Although we had views, and so did Middleton, that the religious emphasis was too grotesque for Aborigines, they at least were doing something that nobody else was doing, and they did care for the people.
>
> They dealt with it as best they could. There was no real policy in those days. They at least did a rescuing job — I might not have agreed with their religious per-

> spective, but they did their best in trying circumstances. There were aspects of it that the Department didn't like of course, but in lieu of the fact that we couldnt do anything much ourselves, it had to be put up with. Essentially, they were good people.[101]

With the indulgence of hindsight it is inviting to suggest that the people and government of Western Australian were happy for Indigenous people to remain invisible while in the desert. Once some contact brought them to public attention, as happened with Yuwali's group, they were equally happy for them to be quickly moved to another site and situation where the cloak of invisibility could once again descend. This effectively fulfilled their sense of responsibility in the negotiation of an uncomfortable problem for which they had no real answer, at least on any terms they were prepared to contemplate.

By the end of the 1960s, the days of the missions were numbered and the era of 'assimilation' had passed. At Jigalong, as elsewhere, children raised in the mission had neither rejected their traditional life nor 'progressed' to mainstream white society.

From 1 January 1970, Jigalong Mission was replaced by the Jigalong Aborigines Project, for which the Department of Native Welfare became directly responsible. Under the principles of self-determination, Jigalong was handed over in 1973 to the community for self-management by an elected eight-member community council.

But, with self-determination, the Jigalong community stayed (more or less) where the fence maintenance depot, the ration depot and then the mission had been located; on remote and economically marginal land, outside Martu country, with few communal resources, and with limited local opportunities for an economic base. The community had taken shape within a culture of distributed rations, coercive European authority over whitefella business, a jaundiced relationship with a small, unrepresentative group of Europeans and an attempt to combine donated European resources with a new, settled form of traditional life.

What is most notable about the era of mission-based 'assimilation' is what it created: a bizarrely mixed world unrecognisable as either wholly traditional Martu or remotely mainstream European. This world was neither what the European players had predicted nor what they had intended.

Detribalisation is inevitable

> Between defence projects . . . and commer cial enterprise, the tribal life of the aborigines in their home country is in process of being destroyed. They are losing cohesion and in a generation will have ceased to exist, except as oddments here and there, without any hold on life, unless something is done at once. No Government has yet made any suggestion as to how the tribal aborigines of the Reser ve are to be helped to meet the new situation.[102]

> De-tribalisation of the aborigine is inevitable, and, provided the contacts brought about by the construction and use of the range are controlled and of a wholesome nature, their only effect would be putting for ward the clock regarding de-tribalisation by possibly a generation.[103]

The story told here of first contact between Europeans and Martu involved a range of different European perspectives: federal and state governments, WRE patrol officers, anthropologists, and opponents of the rocket range. In their different ways, each of these interested parties helped to shape either policy or its practical implementation, and hence the future lives of Y uwali and her companions.

Despite the Europeans' differences in politics and motivation, what is interesting is the extent to which their attitudes and positions shared themes and characteristics. Because of these shared foundations, their views illuminated more about the culture from which they arose than they did of the culture they discussed.

First, Dr Duguid, in opposing the rocket range, voiced the opinions of many advocates of Indigenous interests. Their essential concern about cultural genocide remained constant, and their per ceptions of government hypocrisy became more entrenched as the histor y of contact unfolded.

> No plans have been made to offset the impact on the black nomadic people of the 'civilised white men' who will be brought into the area . . . Always such contact has proved disastrous to the dark people, demoralising them, destroying self-respect and building a new half-caste population.[104]

Next, Professor Elkin and the Australian Committee on Guided Projectiles were sanguine and confident in their views of the future course of Indigenous society , the dangers to it, and the safeguards that would protect Indigenous interests.

The committee's statement that 'de-tribalisation of the aborigine is inevitable' provided the foundation for their reassurance — and that of the federal government — to concerned citizens. The uncontested notion of 'inevitability' dissolved questions of responsibility.

Yet nobody explored or explained at the time just what 'de-tribalisation' meant. It was unquestionably a negative term, evoking some wholesale and irreversible cultural disintegration. It appealed to a general sense of 'loss of traditional society' that reflected the continuing migration from the desert, and the concerns of opponents to the range. Y et in retrospect, it was more misleading than helpful in its conjuring of a simple and wholesale abandonment of tradition and culture, despite the truth of the physical migration. In fact, even the reference to the idea of 'tribe' — and white Australia' s understanding of what was meant by that word — was soon challenged by anthropologists as being inappropriate to describe the structures of Aboriginal society.[105]

Elkin had documented what he saw as a pattern or process following initial contact between European and Indigenous societies: a first 'tentative approach' followed by 'clash', leading finally to 'intelligent parasitism'![106] This last stage was a form of equilibrium in mutual adaptation, worked out in pragmatic terms by the two communities. In this last stage, the Indigenous people make use of intelligent and selective use of the dual worlds they inhabit. However, this could lead, over time, to 'pauperism', as the strength of the traditional society was undermined by increasing loss of respect for the old ways among young Indigenous people.

Unlike Elkin, W alter MacDougall was no academic, but he was recognised throughout the WRE as having far more practical knowledge of the situation and needs of the Indigenous people than any of the other European staff. His views represented a fair consensus of 'informed opinion', both in their description of rapid personal and social disintegration, and in their lurid, value laden, negative words. Descriptions of the time, from advocates and opponents of Indigenous interests and from anthropologists, are liberally sprinkled with colourful terms: helplessness, indignity, low moral standing, annihilation, parasitism, craving, despair , demoralisation, degeneration, begging, paupers, perish, disintegrate, destruction, outcasts. This is language used to make the moral rectitude of certain political positions and actions self-evident.

MacDougall identified two stages in the moral and social disintegration that characterised de-tribalisation. The first stage was the personal fall towards depravity as a result of idle hands:

> Contact with white men has so far resulted in degeneration of the aborigines. It is only necessary to patrol areas where detribalisation has started to see this process in full operation and to realise how many natives now exist without working or hunting. Because of their own socialistic way of life, the generosity of their friends and friends' employers, and government rations, they inevitably adopt the routine of moving from Station to Station for free food. The result is laziness, uselessness and loss of self-respect. They neither hunt nor work for food and the evils of unemployment of able-bodied men are never brought home to them. [107]

The second stage was a process of social collapse. 'The breakdown commences immediately contacts are made', he charged, citing as successive causes a lack of consciousness of personal ownership, the assertion of European over traditional law, the failure of traditional sanctions that relied on 'the supernatural' to affect Europeans, the consequent 'breakdown of secret life', and the change in food gathering to a substantial reliance on rations: 'By this time, all those things that tend towards a strong, dignified, vigorous although primitive, people have, or are well on the way to being discredited, disbelieved and discontinued and the people well on the way to refugism'.[108]

MacDougall also saw the imposition of European habits of life, revolving around scheduled work, as a further pressure on tribal structures. 'Besides breaking down his law and social structure without giving any effective return, we expect to change his way and habit of life overnight.'[109]

In spite of their differing backgrounds, both Elkin and MacDougall drew the same conclusion regarding intergenerational breakdown, with younger people losing respect for the old people, and a resultant tearing of the fabric of Aboriginal society. MacDougall saw this younger generation defying their elders as 'outcasts' with, 'no pride of race, no faith in their secret life, no law , no ambition except to exist with as little effort as humanly possible'![110] The result, he was certain, was, 'degeneration from self-respecting tribal communities to pathetic and useless parasites'.[111]

For his part, Robert Macaulay married the anthropological perspective that he'd learned under Professor Elkin with first-hand experience at Giles and on desert patrols. He had the unenviable task of regulating contact at the Giles station in accordance with policy to ensure that the dangers identified by MacDougall did not occur. While segregation from the weather station stopped 'physical parasitism', the 'parasitism of the mind' was more difficult to control:

> The Native Patrol Officers work to this end, minimising contact and continually bolstering the sociological mechanisms holding the old life together . The machinery of social life contains its own powers of preser vation and a certain amount of flexibility, but it is felt that this machiner y would be over strained if the contact position was not controlled rather rigorously.[112]

Stanley Middleton saw his department as being charged with the guidance of a weaker people through the turmoil of their full absorption into a dominant society:

> They are a host moving along the highroad of histor y. The white race as the dominant race is morally bound to make that road as free from obstacles and hardship as it can . . .
>
> They have now reached a point beyond which without our guidance and assistance they cannot readily progress . . . The question . . . is how are these people to be lifted to what we consider to be a normal living standard?[113]

The Berndts saw the assimilation policy as eradicating Indigenous society largely leading to 'pauperism':

> Traditional economic life has been upset, and a consequence of this is a desire to take up new ways — to become absorbed in the European–Australian economic system. This cannot always be fulfilled, and the great majority we might class as paupers — or 'indigents' as the official term has it. [114]

Several themes emerge from these comments. The first is that Indigenous people were considered to be rendered helpless by a craving for free European food and goods, and would quickly abandon their traditional life to satisfy these new cravings. The second is that Aboriginal society was fragile, its rapid disintegration inevitable in the face of this seductive wealth and the unquestionable dominance of European society. The third is that the only path that would protect the dignity and value of individual Indigenous people, once they had been introduced to European goods, was to become full and productive participants in European society. This last theme highlights a normative focus on individual assimilation — communal salvation flows from the creation of enlightened, assimilated individuals.

These themes and their expression disclose some characteristics of the European culture from which they arose: a conviction of the adequacy, objectivity and truth of its perspective, a belief in the superiority of its culture and values, and certainty as to cause and effect. [115]

In retrospect, all of the themes of the European perspective failed to contemplate the negotiation of a relationship with Indigenous people on any but the terms, perceptions and assumptions of the Europeans. The interpretations and predictions proved to be incomplete and awry, despite some apparent foundation, and can now be seen as dangerous bases for policy or action.

At Jigalong, the flaws in the European perspective and expectations became manifest. The Martu made choices about how the new resources and opportunities would be used, and preserved what was essential or preferable about other aspects of their life.

European food and material goods were incorporated into Martu society On the whole, those that were useful were valued and those that lacked utility were not. Their constant availability at points of settlement led to changes in the organisation of Martu material economy . The formation of large settlements, such as Jigalong, led to changes in social interaction and organisation — adaptation to meet the new circumstances.

Martu society did not disintegrate. Rather, Jigalong became one of the strongest traditional Law centres of the Western Desert. On the whole, Martu people did not leave Jigalong to join the wider, dominant society. At one level, this can be attributed to difficulties of transport, lack of effective English and lack of opportunity . However, their sense of community was a key factor in the effectiveness of their adaptation to the new, external forces.[116] They valued this community. The mission gave them the resources, time and autonomy to pursue what they enjoyed the most: their social, cultural and religious life.[117]

The Martu stayed at Jigalong, moved to other similar settlements such as Bidyadanga (La Grange) or participated in the movement through the 1980s and 1990s to homeland communities: communities that were essentially similar to Jigalong but within their own country. Those children born at Jigalong saw it as their home and the only territory they knew.[118] Although some people moved into towns such as Port Hedland and Newman, they continued to see themselves as part of the Martu communities. They did not want to assimilate, but wanted to assimilate Europeans and their resources in convenient ways into their Martu society.[119]

In fact, their history is remarkable more in its demonstration of the resilience, complexity and pragmatic flexibility of their culture than of the fragility, moral weakness or unsophisticated simplicity that Europeans projected onto it. On the whole, theirs has been a story of intelligent adaptation, not annihilation.[120]

Of course, there are great difficulties in this process of adaptation. The Martu could not completely control the process, and the adoption of some aspects of European life has had unforeseen ramifications. The Martu must now deal with new health and social problems, the repeated failure of government policies to achieve intended benefits, and the impact of alcohol and its calamitous consequences for some individuals and families.

While the Martu communities of Jigalong, Punmu, Parnngurr and Kunawarritji are 'dry' communities (that is, they prohibit the importation and consumption of liquor within their boundaries), liquor bought or consumed hundreds of kilometres away has resulted in numerous deaths, 'as a result of alcohol-related violence, motor car accidents and illness. The community has tried many different strategies, none of them successful, to deal with this most serious of their problems'.[121]

There is widespread concern — almost a loss of hope — in the Australian population about Aboriginal communities. Few have an effective economic base. In many the standards of education, health and housing, relative to the wider population, are viewed as a disgrace. There is well-founded concern about violence, family trauma and substance abuse. Using almost any conventional indicator of social wellbeing, the communities are in trouble. The old summations using words like parasitism, annihilation and destruction have been replaced by headlines of malaise, tragedy and despair, with the need for action supported by appalling comparative statistics. There is still a large measure of bewilderment about what should be done, about what will work.

Meanwhile, the Martu continue to deal with new challenges that they cannot avoid, the inevitable consequences of their contact with European society. While they have not yet found answers to many of these challenges, they will unavoidably continue to adapt, drawing on what is familiar and strong.

Everything changed, nothing changed

The worst imperialisms are those of preconception.[122]

Two fundamental characteristics of Aboriginal religion and society are a sense of constancy and yet the accommodation of change. WEH Stanner saw the ethos and principles of Aboriginal life as, 'variations on a single theme — continuity, constancy, balance, symmetry, regularity, system or some such quality as these words convey'.[123]

Similarly Bob Tonkinson believes that, 'Nowhere does their ideology admit structural change [to the Law, or the Dreaming] as a possibility. On the contrary, the emphasis . . . is on continuity of present and future with past, and the notion of progress does not exist'.[124]

The Dreaming provides an unchanging reference point for an understanding of the world, for the continuity of life and for the correct ordering of society. The Martu concept which is translated into English as 'Law', *yulupirti*, literally means 'everlasting'.[125]

Yet the life of the Martu is also characterised by an extraordinary flexibility: an ability to adapt and to refashion their circumstances, their behaviour, their ritual life and even their myths.[126] In these ways, they accommodate change.

Yuwali's group came to their contact with MacDougall with a sophisticated understanding of the world and the immutable nature of reality, and yet also with an ability to incorporate new elements into that understanding. This new presence in the desert, with its unexpected powers and with all its material bounty, would need to be negotiated through this worldview.

The significance of this episode and the expectations and relations created by it cannot be understood without some understanding of how it was interpreted and given meaning within a Martu world view. In conversation, Yuwali has repeatedly emphasised that they only viewed what was happening from the perspective of their culture and experience. 'We didn't know anything about white society,' she said, 'We were *pujiman* [bush people] — we didn't know anything but our country.'[127]

Each of the participants operated from within their culture. The actions of Yuwali's group were shaped by their knowledge and loyalties, their assumptions and interpretation about what was happening, their fears and concerns, their pressures and political considerations. Similarly, when MacDougall and Long made decisions, their concerns and actions were inevitably shaped by their knowledge, loyalties, assumptions and political constraints. Neither had any significant comprehension of the other's perspective.

It is naturally easiest for non-Martu Australians to understand the views of the non-Martu participants. Their attitudes reflect the world view, values and concerns of a familiar society. While some of the language and views of the 1950s may grate on a twenty-first century reader, it is dangerous to feel too righteous. In today's negotiation of the relationship with the same people — many of whom are still living in desert communities — is anything really different?

White Australia doesn't speak the Martu language in either a literal or a metaphoric sense. We have never been equipped to make decisions that affect Martu lives, nor to create environments that are conducive to a healthy Martu society. Yet we still purport to.

Our responsibility to act is seen as a consequence of the sovereignty that we have appropriated over land in which many living Martu like Yuwali were born, oblivious to our existence. Whatever the merits of our assumption of sovereignty, its legal effect is unlikely to be foregone. But our manner of engagement continues to disclose a silent assumption of cultural sovereignty, which simply fails to accord with Martu reality; it is a denial of reality.

A consistent thread has run through Australia's treatment of the Martu, despite the apparent shifts in policy that occur every generation. This thread, evident in this story from the assimilation era, is a general failure to acknowledge that the Martu have a distinct and resilient society, flexible in some respects and tenaciously rigid in others, with which we must genuinely interact if we wish our actions to have remotely predictable effects.

This failure persists in practice, despite several decades of rhetoric about 'self-determination' and 'self-management', responses to some of the failed or unsavoury aspects of the assimilation years. The European community largely continued to set the parameters of the social and political relationship while purporting to disengage from management of that relationship and day-to-day life, asserting the dignity of Indigenous culture.

The existence of such a constant, underlying thread is illustrated by the consistent failure of the different policy positions to achieve their outcomes (as defined by white society), and the attendant and continuing Australian bewilderment at those failures.

The gulf in understanding that flows from a lack of true engagement now feeds an increasing lack of trust.

> Whitefellas don't understand Martu. They put everything upside down and mix it up. Government people come in but don't really learn from the Martu. They don't talk in the right way; they don't respect Martu law; they don't hear the Martu. The Government is in front and they put the Martu behind. The Martu are always behind — they're always leaving Martu behind. It's getting tougher every day. The Government is shutting the door on us, leaving us behind.[128]

> When your father left me[129], he said, 'You have to be careful, because these white-fellas will come around and hurt the Martu. They're tricky buggers — they'll keep coming around, coming around. They'll give you stories all the time and money to keep you quiet, and then they'll come back and keep on taking.' [130]

We are locked in an endless re-enactment of the story of Yuwali, MacDougall and Middleton. The broader Australian community continues to chase about, seeking to improve Martu lives, driven by a mix of politics, guilt, good intentions and concern about public perceptions, without fully recognising the need for policy and actions that have the right resonance within Martu reality.

The Martu cannot be viewed as an unfortunate projection of wider society. They have a distinct society. That society, grounded in the Law, provides meaning, richness and aspiration. It sets priorities; people's decisions and actions are founded upon it. It influences the forms of social groupings and transactions and requires that people fulfil obligations. It allows creative accommodation of new resources and situations, but is essentially constant, unchangeable. To the Martu, its prescriptions are paramount.

There is a need for an honourable dialogue, in which the dominant society fully discards its sense of social and cultural sovereignty. Otherwise, the same old assumptions continue to silently inform new policy positions and their implementation.

The non-Martu Australian community can only engage properly if it is within Martu society: within Martu language, and within the concepts, structures and modes created by the Law. Otherwise, we are not engaging with reality.

The future of the Martu can go in many directions. It is unlikely to move along paths that are completely predictable. The environment that is provided for their creative use will ground any new dynamic equilibrium which will inevitably emerge. Whether this balance is as a structural underclass in material terms, or as a materially healthy community, depends on the environment from which the future takes shape and the relative priorities of the Martu.

These communities have already appropriated aspects of European economic and material resources, some effectively and some disastrously. However, they seek to accommodate these resources within a Martu religious, social and cultural life. What we can learn from the past is that this life is resilient, confounding predictions either of disintegration or movement towards the mainstream.

European Australia must work in partnership with the Martu, but will only do this effectively when it acknowledges and truly engages with Martu society. It will only be respectful when it respects Martu society. It will only be informed when, from a Martu perspective, it incorporates some conception of its own responsibilities and obligations. Its initiatives will only work if they accept both the new social environment of the Martu and the persistent forms and values of Martu life. No path will be likely to be embraced and taken unless it is conceived, assessed and processed within a Martu world view.

When Yuwali's group walked out of the desert, and was transplanted to Jigalong by staff of the Commonwealth and state governments, those governments acquired a responsibility to them. The cornerstone of their responsibility has always been a need for respectful, inquisitive and ultimately informed engagement. Outside the compromised field of native title, where such a disposition at least has credence, fulfilment of the Australian responsibility to the Martu has scar cely begun.

In our new policy era, seeking understanding is a mutual obligation.

Kartiyakajalu-la mirta kulirni Martukaja. Mirta-la nyakuni warrarnpa. Mirta-la wangkani Martu Wangka. Mirta-la kulirni jukurrpa. Parnpa-la. Ngakumpa-la. Kulilkura-la.

EPILOGUE

The whitefellas

Woomera and the range

The long and extraordinary history of the rocket project and activities at Woomera is beyond the scope of this book. Nevertheless, it was integral to this story and its subsequent history is worth noting briefly.

The joint British and Australian government rocket project started to wind down from 1967.[1] The British government was becoming increasingly reluctant to continue to fund an enterprise in Australia, and began to make gentle suggestions that their partners should take over more of the facility's business and costs.

The project and the establishment at Woomera had gone through many phases, from weapons research and testing to the contracted launch of civilian rockets and satellites. It had repeatedly overcome the withdrawal of primary programs, each time finding new reasons for existence. But the substantial withdrawal of the British — from the status of partner to paying customer — spelt the end of the range.

The negotiated run-down was announced by the Whitlam government in 1974. It was gradual, as trials were scheduled for some years ahead. However, on 30 June 1980, the joint project was formally dissolved and, despite some minor continuing use by the Australian Defence Force, the range was effectively finished.

In 1989, an assessment was made of the total cost — in contemporary terms — of the thirty-three-year joint project. It was estimated that the two governments spent 3.25 billion dollars.[2]

The town of Woomera continued to exist thanks to the construction of nearby Nurrungar, one of three communications facilities established with the US government (along with Pine Gap and North-West Cape). But it, too, gradually ran down and deteriorated. Writing the official history of Woomera and the joint project in 1989, Morton commented:

> By the mid-1980s much of the physical evidence of the early and middle years of the joint project had been expunged from the Woomera village. Nearly all the brick houses had vanished or were slated for demolition. The 'Silver City' . . . had been sold in two big auctions, the battered prefabs carted away to start new careers as holiday shacks somewhere along the coast. All the messes have gone except for the large comfortably ugly building which is now the combined restaurant, pub, hotel and disco for the village. To the residents this place is just 'ELDO' [European Launcher Development Organisation, the international consortium behind the Blue Streak rockets]. Most of its habitués have forgotten, if they ever knew, that its name was originally the acronym of a space enterprise of a boldness unimaginable in Australia today.[3]

After initial use as an accommodation facility for the staff of Nurrungar, Woomera lay quietly for several years before being revived — once more to controversy — as a detention centre for refugees seeking asylum.

WRE's native patrols

There were only ever three native patrol officers: Walter MacDougall, Robert Macaulay and — after Macaulay resigned in 1965 — Bob Verburgt.

By 1969, the Commonwealth Department of Supply was under pressure to reduce costs, and the continued need for patrol officers at Woomera was questioned.

A set of draft notes on the political considerations surrounding a decision to terminate the patrol program was prepared for the secretary. After summarising the source and history of the NPO program, the notes eloquently restated the Commonwealth's principal concerns. The patrol officers' 'local knowledge and the good relations' were acknowledged to have prevented, 'a number of situations from developing into major issues of friction between the various State Government Departments and the Commonwealth'. Further:

> I see this matter as a political issue . . . The need for native patrol officers is much the same now as it was twenty-odd years ago. The patrol officers are an 'insurance policy' ensuring the Commonwealth Government has a relatively uninterrupted use of the Range. I feel sure that any reduction in [their] activities . . . would bring an immediate reaction from the States.
>
> I believe that the continued operation of Giles, for instance, would be well nigh impossible if the rules and regulations were applied in accordance with the letter of the Law.
>
> In short, I believe that we get value for our money both directly and indirectly, and that it would be also politically impossible to operate the Range without the Native Patrol Officers. I therefore recommend no change to the current situation. [4]

By 1970, though, the situation had changed. The secretary of the Commonwealth Department of Supply wrote to the commissioner of the Western Australian Department of Native Welfare, proposing that NPO activities be 'tapered off' over the following two years, a period which (not merely fortuitously) would coincide with MacDougall's retirement:

> [O]ur Patrol Officers were appointed to meet specific needs with the setting up of the Woomera Range which in many cases no longer exist, and the passage of time has inevitably resulted in environmental changes which in turn vary the scope of action required to fulfil the Government's policy.
>
> Although in fact many of the environmental changes are well established, it is not considered desirable or reasonable to restrict immediately our activities, but rather to allow them to taper off over a period of two years. Such a course will allow time for all concerned to re-adjust to any new arrangements. [5]

The reply from the commissioner , Frank Gare — while agreeing to the suggested taper — was forthright about the the impact of the WRE' s activities on Aboriginal people:

> While the nature of the duties carried out by your Patrol Officers have changed to some degree over the years, they continue to operate, at least so far as this State is concerned, in areas where the lives of Aborigines have been irrevocably changed by the operations of the Weapons Research Establishment.
>
> Apart from other contributing causes, the grading of a network of roads was instrumental in bringing desert Aborigines into contact with civilisation far earlier than would otherwise have been the case.
>
> These roads also resulted in the movement of substantial numbers of Aborigines away from their traditional lands into settlements and missions with a consequent aggravation of local health, economic and cultural problems. [6]

But by 1970 the deserts were effectively clear . Missions, too, were about to disappear, replaced in time by independent Aboriginal communities as the policy of assimilation made way for one of self-determination. The migration from the desert to the fringes was virtually complete.

But the migration back to new, more scattered communities deep in the desert — the 'homelands movement' — was about to start, ironically often making use of WRE roads.

The NPO program was terminated in 1972, when W alter MacDougall retired.

The native patrol officers

Robert Macaulay resigned from the WRE in 1965 and moved to a career in the Commonwealth public ser vice. After having worked as a patrol officer for nine years, he initially worked for the Department of Territories and then moved to the Department of Immigration until his retirement.

In 2001 he reflected on his patrol work with the WRE:

> I believe that over the period of my involvement, 1956–65, both MacDougall and I shared something of a small sense of histor y. The groups of Aborigines with whom we were in contact across the W estern Desert language grouping were small remnants choosing to remain in their 'countr y' after the bulk of the population had moved, over decades, to missions and settlements. They were at serious risk from a range of 'push' factors to end their isolation. We gave our support to the relocation by the W est Australian government of the Martu [Y uwali's] group to Jigalong Mission because of the unique structure of the remnant group. This was a particular set of cir cumstances in a brief period of time. There were numerous other episodes across the vast desert areas over a number of years, and looking back, I feel somewhat privileged to have been involved in such a fascinating period of Australian history.[7]

Macaulay also emphasised the need for actions to be interpreted in the light of the society of the time:

> Although in comparative terms, the 1950s and 1960s are quite recent, in real terms, such was the pace of change in desert Australia they appear to be ages ago. Many , writing of the period, were, and still are, unable or unwilling to place the thinking, planning and action of the times in their context. [8]

Recommendations that Macaulay and MacDougall put to state and Commonwealth authorities, in vain, through the 1950s and early 1960s anticipated the later moves to self-determination, land rights legislation and recognition of native title. Robert Macaulay now lives in retirement in Canberra.

Walter MacDougall continued to work as a patrol officer until his retirement in 1972. He moved quite quickly to a church-run nursing home in Melbourne, where he died in 1976. He was cremated, and his ashes buried at Ernabella.

At the time of the patrol, MacDougall had remarked on his shock at finding the large group of women and children walking the Per cival Lakes without men for so long. But, other than on this point, the 1964 patrols were 'business as usual' for the NPOs, simply two patrols among many in which they made first contact with Indigenous families.

MacDougall had an extraordinar y life, spending 40 years working with Indigenous people. He was a key witness to the emptying of the Western Desert. He took vast numbers of slides, photographs and film, virtually all now unable to be traced.[9]

Frank Gare recalled MacDougall fondly: 'W e had faith in MacDougall,' said Gare, 'he was so transparently pro-Aboriginal. He was a ver y kind man. Y ou couldn't fault him in any way at all. [10]

Bill Edwards, the former superintendent of Ernabella, knew MacDougall well and wrote his entry in the *Australian Dictionary of Biography*. His entry ended with the following:

> MacDougall's task at Woomera had been a difficult one. Prickly and pertinacious, he dealt with Aboriginal welfare departments from two States and the Northern Territory, as well as with superiors whose priorities were scientific and militar y. His concern for the welfare of Aboriginal people often led to conflict. One chief scientist wrote that, while MacDougall was sincere in protecting the interests of Aborigines, he lacked balance and 'placed the affairs of a handful of natives above those of the British Commonwealth of Nations'. No epitaph could be more fitting. [11]

The Western Australian Department of Native Welfare

Frank Gare was the commissioner of the department in 1964. He retired in 1972, and died in Fremantle in early 2004. T erry Long, the department' s field officer on the Percival Lakes patrols, rose to become commissioner in the 1970s, after Gare retired.

He is now retired and lives in Mandurah, Western Australia. He, too, remembers the 1964 patrols clearly.

Terry Long and Frank Gare gave candid recollections of their work in the Department of Native Welfare. Long first reflected on his role in the 1964 patrols, with the wisdom of hindsight:

> Years later, when I did my own anthropological studies, I only wished that I had the knowledge and the foresight to have done something at the time I had met [the women], when it was fresh. We could have got something that was really unique from the women at that time. What had happened to those women was something really remarkable, really astounding, and deserved more attention than it got. Not from my point of view, but from theirs.
>
> I always thought it was wonderful that those women kept those youngsters in food all that time, without the assistance of their men, without knowing what had happened to the groups around them, being totally isolated like that. It was a wonderful story of courage and survival in those circumstances. They were in fact something quite unique in Aboriginal studies and human stories at that time. 1964 was not that long ago, and [it's remarkable] to think that people were living like that in a country as sophisticated as Australia as short a time ago as that.
>
> The point is, of course, that they couldn't talk for themselves and the chroniclers and myself — I was included — were lacking. And I'm sorry for that.[12]

Frank Gare similarly reflected on his career:

> I remember discussing this with my daughter once. She said, 'Why do you work in this Department?' She wasn't querying it, so much as trying to understand it. 'Do you feel sorry for these people, or did you join up because you have a soft heart?', or something like this. And I don't think I've got a very soft heart, and I explained that I joined because I wanted to see justice done — it was a matter of justice. Trying to make sure that Aborigines got a fair go, and I still believe that. It's the way to judge any action taken by Government: whether it's doing justice.[13]

The Martu

> I once asked an old man whether he was glad he had come in from the desert. 'Yes,' he replied, and pointed at his watch, 'otherwise I wouldn't know what time it is.'[14]

In the thirty years following the handover of Jigalong mission in 1969, the Martu instituted desert communities in Punmu, Parnngurr and Kunawarritji, and many people moved back to them. As private transport became more available it became easier for Martu to live their social nomadic existence, moving between Jigalong, these desert communities and others such as Strelley, Warralong, Yandeyarra, Bidyadanga, Wiluna and Fitzroy Crossing.

This period also saw massive growth in the white population of the region, with both Newman and Port Hedland growing significantly in response to the mineral boom in the Pilbara. That has brought its own problems, beyond the scope of this book.

In 2002, after nearly two decades of struggle, the Martu were granted native title over much of their country — geographically the largest claim in Australia to that time. It was a bittersweet victory, with Karlamilyi (the Rudall River National Park) excised from the native title area. One Martu speaker at the claim determination ceremony, Teddy Biljabu, eloquently expressed their outrage, saying that they had been given 'a body without its heart'.[15]

Yuwali's group

In 1964, after MacDougall and Long brought Yuwali's group to Jigalong, they left them in the care of the missionaries and left within two days, never to return. What happened to the members of Yuwali's group since that time can be glimpsed in the following brief summaries. The next forty years would demand of them constant adaptation to a rapidly changing world.

Although we cannot give detailed accounts of their lives, almost all made the huge transition from desert nomad to settled Martu. One interesting point to note from the summaries is that virtually all lived the remainder of their lives in Martu communities. Their lives demonstrate their individual and collective resilience. They persevered in the face of the many setbacks and tragedies wrought by forces and circumstances beyond the power of Martu ingenuity and flexibility to overcome and contain. (The information in the summary which follows is from interviews with Yuwali between 1987 and 2005.)

Until several of the members of the group were taken back to the Percival Lakes in the late 1990s, most of the group would not again see the lake country that had been their home.

Yuwali

PHOTO: SUE DAVENPORT, 2005

When Yuwali arrived at Jigalong she was about seventeen years old and unmarried.

On her arrival, Yuwali and the other adults were taken to The Camp, across the riverbed from the mission buildings.

Yuwali lived in a lean-to, built from branches, sticks and sheets of iron. Soon after her arrival, she was taken from The Camp to the senior girls' dormitory, to show her where the boys and girls stayed. The missionaries asked her to have a look in the dormitory but she was too frightened to go in, and went back to The Camp.

Yuwali says that she felt happy to be in Jigalong because there were many people and because people were so kind to her. The missionaries used to feed the Martu and gave them some money. At first, she didn't know about money and buried it in the riverbed; she and the other newcomers thought it was the same thing as paper, and worthless.

After about a year in Jigalong, she visited Wiluna, Meekatharra and Karalundi (a mission north of Meekatharra). Following her return to Jigalong she married. (Her brief marriage to Nyani at the Percival Lakes was not recognised by the Martu community.)

She stayed in Jigalong for a further three years and then went with her husband to work on a cattle station. She worked for wages as a domestic helper, washing dishes and clothes and working in the kitchen and dining room. She was happy working on the station, particularly as there were several other Martu girls also employed there. Later, she moved to Strelley Station[16], a cattle property west of Marble Bar, and lived there for four years.

Yuwali had three children. Her husband murdered his brother and after his imprisonment she left him and moved back to Jigalong, then to Camp 61 (an outstation of Strelley and a Martu settlement, now abandoned). There, she remarried and subsequently had one child.

In the early 1980s Yuwali moved to the newly established Martu outstation community of Punmu. When her second husband died in the early 1990s, she moved to Bidyadanga (the former La Grange Mission, near Broome) to be close to other members of her family who were living there.

Yuwali now lives at the Martu community of Parnngurr. A delightfully vibrant woman, with a gorgeous, infectious laugh, she has recently fought cancer. She remains an engaged and informed Martu woman.

Nyiwiljukurr

Nyiwiljukurr was Yuwali's father. He was also known as Parnpa, which means 'blind'. He had five wives — Kiparnu, Ngunyji, Jikartu, Nyipi and Kulata.

Nyiwiljukurr was living in the lake area before 1964, but at some stage took three of his wives and moved north. He was presumably still in contact with some of the women in Y uwali's group at least 18 months before September 1964, as Kulata had a nine-month-old baby when the group was picked up by the patrol. He had several important connections with Y uwali's group: he was married to Nyipi and Kulata, and was Junju's brother.

In 1967, Nyiwiljukurr was brought in by a patrol officer to La Grange Mission from Joanna Spring, north of Lake Percival. He was part of a large group that came in at that time, which included his other three wives. He died at Bidyadanga in the 1990s.

Yukurrpani

Yukurrpani was Y uwali's grandmother. Her husband died some time before 1962 and she did not remarry. After being brought in by the patrol she lived at Jigalong. She later moved to Strelley and then to the Aboriginal community of Y andeyarra. She died at Warralong community in the 1990s.

Nganja

Nganja was a woman of about thirty-eight at the time of the patrol. She had leprosy when the patrol found her . She had one daughter , Pakakalyi. Her husband had died from natural causes at Karilykarily. She and her small child were flown by medical staff directly from Swindells Field to Derby Leprosarium in October 1964. She died in 1965.

Pakakalyi

Pakakalyi had mild leprosy and at the time of the patrol was transferred to Derby Leprosarium with her mother. She remained in the Derby region and now lives at Balyu. She is married with one child.

Nyipi

Nyipi was Y uwali's mother. She identified with W irnpa country, around the lakes. Her husband, Nyiwiljukurr, was the blind man who was living in the Joanna Spring area when Nyipi was contacted by the patrol. After being brought in, she stayed in Jigalong while most of her children were at the mission school. In the 1970s, the family moved to La Grange to be with Nyiwiljukurr. Nyipi died in the 1980s.

Yaji

Yaji was Yuwali's brother, who was about ten at the time of this stor y. He attended Jigalong school then went to La Grange where he married and had two children. He died in his thirties.

Yiji

Yiji was also Yuwali's brother, and was about nine at the time of this story. He went to Jigalong school, then to Strelley , La Grange, Camp 61 and then to Punmu. He married at La Grange. His first wife died and he later remarried. He had two children from his first marriage and then one from his second. He died in the 1990s.

Mangayi

Mangayi is Yuwali's little sister, and was about six years old at the time of this story. She went to Jigalong school, then moved with her mother to Strelley and La Grange. She married a man from La Grange, has one child, and lives in Bidyadanga.

Kulata

Kulata was one of Nyiwiljukurr's wives. After living in Jigalong for some time she moved to Port Hedland. She remarried after Nyiwiljukurr died. She had two other children and died in Port Hedland in the 1990s.

Pilumpa

Pilumpa was Kulata's baby at the time of this story. After she grew up, she married and had one child. While she was still a young woman, she was picked up with another Martu woman by a white man near Newman. She was never seen again in the Newman area, and is thought now to be living outside Western Australia.

Pinkirri

Pinkirri was Kulata's son, and was about six years old at the time of this story. After coming in, he went to Jigalong school and then to Strelley. He later moved to La Grange and married his first wife, who died. Pinkirri spent some time in prison and then lived at 12 Mile camp (a small Martu community 20 kilometres from Port Hedland) with his second wife. He died in Port Hedland in 2004.

Karntipa

Karntipa was Kulata's mother, a widow at the time of the patrol. Her husband had died at Karilykarily, killed by a revenge expedition. She identified with Wirnpa country, the country around Lake Percival. After being brought in, Karntipa spent time living in Jigalong and Strelley, until she died at Jigalong in the 1980s.

Junju

Junju was a Manyjilyjarra woman, Nyiwiljukurr's sister. She was born around Well 35 on the Canning Stock Route. She was taken north to be married. Her husband was a Jiwaliny man who died at Mulyakirri (close to Swindells Field), allegedly killed because he and Junju had eloped (that is, he had stolen Junju from another man).

After coming in, Junju lived at Jigalong until the 1970s, when she moved to Carlindie Station, where she married a Strelley man. She then moved to Strelley and on to Camp 61, back to Jigalong and finally to Parnngurr, a Martu community west of the Canning Stock Route. Junju died at Parnngurr in 2003.

Kurtu

Kurtu is Junju's eldest son, aged around ten at the time of this story. He went to Jigalong school and then on to Strelley, where he went through the Law. He moved to Camp 61 and to Punmu in 1981. He lived for many years at Parnngurr. He married a daughter of Jikartu, the wife of Nyiwiljukurr, and had two children. They later separated and he remarried. He now moves between Martu communities.

Ngarrka

Ngarrka is Junju's daughter, and was about eight at the time of this story. She went to Jigalong school, and then went to work on Briar Station as a housemaid. She moved back to Jigalong then to Strelley, where she married. She went with her husband to Milli Milli Station where she worked as a housemaid. She later moved back to Strelley, then to Jigalong, to Camp 61 and finally to Parnngurr, where she and her family now live.

Marawurru

Marawurru was Junju's daughter, and was about four at the time of this story. She went to Jigalong school then on to Strelley and to La Grange. She married a man from Wiluna, and lived for many years at Bidyadanga. She died at Bidyadanga in 2004.

Tajaka

Tajaka is Junju's youngest child, a boy aged about two at the time of this story. He went to Jigalong school, then to Strelley and on to La Grange Mission. He married a woman from Balgo Mission and had two children. He later remarried. His main camp is now at Mulan community.

Japapa

Japapa was about fifty at the time of this story. Her other name was Parnpa, because she was blind in one eye. She was a Manyjilyjarra woman. Her husband, a Mangala man, had died at a site called Manupanja, to the north of Swindells Field. After being brought in, she went from Jigalong to Strelley. She died in the 1980s.

Yapaji

Yapaji is Japapa's daughter, and was fifteen at the time of this story. She married in Jigalong and had four children. She later moved to Strelley, where she still lives.

Ngarrpinyarninya

Ngarrpinyarninya was Japapa's son, aged about twelve at the time of this story. After being brought to Jigalong, he moved to Strelley and then onto La Grange. He ran away to Carnarvon with a married woman, later returning to La Grange, where he had a daughter. He died in his thirties after a motor accident.

Return to Wirnpa

> When the whitefellas take you away from your home, you feel no good in your heart, because your heart is in the desert, where you belong.[17]

In 1999, Yuwali, Junju, Ngarrka and Tajaka travelled back to the Wirnpa area with Sue Davenport. They revisited Kurtararra, Yulpu and Yimiri and other sites around the lakes.

The group, which included other traditional owners for this area, cleared out waterholes and burned country. They paid proper respects to the snake at Yimiri: lighting fires to let him know they were back, walking in single file across the lake, beating the ground with branches and then coating themselves in mud from the bulrush soak.

PHOTOS: TOP: SUE DAVENPORT, 1999; BOTTOM: PETER KENDRICK, 1999

Yuwali and Junju illustrated where the events in this story had occurred: where MacDougall and others had appeared, how Yuwali had hidden from the vehicles, where she had run, where all the women and children had run and where they hunted and camped.

Apart from needing to clean out the waterholes at Yimiri and Kurtararra, all was exactly as it had always been. At Yimiri, Yuwali walked over the large sandhill beside the lake, and picked up the grinding stones that she had last used in 1964. The 'mother and child' (i.e. the base stone and the grinding stone) sat where she had left them, thirty-five years before.

After returning from the trip to Wirnpa, Junju — an old woman by now — sat down for good.

When asked whether she was glad that she had come in from the desert, despite her fear and reluctance to come at the time, Yuwali simply answered:

> I'm glad to go back and see my country again. I am happy.[18]

References

Methods of citation vary slightly between the various state and Commonwealth archives. The citations below provide the details recommended by each archive for researchers wishing to access the relevant records. The following abbreviations are used:

DNA: Department of Native Affairs (Western Australia)

DNW: Department of Native Welfare (Western Australia)

NAA: National Archives of Australia

NAA(SA): National Archives of Australia (South Australia)

SROWA: State Records Office of Western Australia

WRE: Weapons Research Establishment

Many of the documents are grouped in files with an alpha-numeric prefix. The D174 prefix, for example, is used for LRWE and WRE correspondence files held in the NAA (SA). Commonwealth documents held in NAA collections created during the McLelland (Maralinga) Royal Commission have the following prefix:

A6455 Royal Commission into British Nuclear Tests in Australia, and Department of Prime Minister and Cabinet; 6455; 1 August 1984 to 30 November 1985.

A6456 Royal Commission into British Nuclear Tests in Australia; 6456, Original Agency Records Transferred to the Commission, R series, 1 August 1984 to 30 November 1985.

Introduction

1 R Tonkinson, *The Mardu Aborigines: living the dream in Australia's desert*, Holt, Rinehart & Winston, New York, 1991. Much of the material in this and the following chapters that describe Martu society has been drawn from that source.

2 J Marsh, *Martu Wangka to English dictionary*, Summer Institute of Linguistics Australian Aborigines and Islanders Branch, Darwin, 1992, translates *martu* as 'Aborigine; person; people; a man'.

3 Manyjilyjarra, Kartujarra, Putijarra, Warnman, Pijakarli (Southern Nyangumarta), Ngulipartu, Kurajarra and Kiyajarra. R Tonkinson, 'Local organisation and land tenure in the Karlamilyi (Rudall River) region', in G Wright (ed.), *The significance of the Karlamilyi region to the Martujarra of the Western Desert*, Department of Conservation and Land Management, Perth, 1989.

4 P Veth, 'The archaeological resource of the Karlamilyi (Rudall River) region', in G Wright (ed.), *The significance of the Karlamilyi region to the Martujarra of the Western Desert*, Department of Conservation and Land Management, Perth, 1989, states that 'Radio carbon dates from five stratified caves and rock shelters in the Karlamilyi (Rudall River) region illustrate continuous human occupation from at least 5,000 years ago', p. 116.

Part One

1 NAA: A6456; R087/020, (Department of Supply) Aborigines in joint project area — Welfare of. *The position regarding the setting up of a guided-missile range and a supporting developmental establishment in Australia – statement by the Minister for Defence in the House of Representatives*, 22 November 1946 (reproduced in a booklet with the Minister's public statement of 10 March 1947).

2 FEA Bateman, 1948, *Report on survey of Native Affairs*, Perth, WH Wyatt (Government Printer).

3 R Tonkinson, personal communication with S Davenport, Perth, 1999. This story was read to a range of appropriate Martu adults, all of whom agreed with the veracity of this account.

4 Yuwali, story, (oral translation by N Taylor), Punmu, Western Australia, 1999a.

5 Yuwali, interview, (oral translation by L Richards and D Taylor), Bidyadanga, Western Australia, 2000. Martu men could have multiple wives, a situation which could cause tensions in a group.

6 R Tonkinson, interview with P Johnson, Perth 2005.

7 Tonkinson, 1991, p. 21. Also see generally for discussion of the Martu spiritual perspective.

8 ibid.

9 ibid. See also See also R Tonkinson, 'Semen versus spirit child in a Western Desert culture', in M Charlesworth, H Morphy, D Bell & K Maddock (eds), *Religion in Aboriginal Australia: an anthology*, University of Queensland Press, St Lucia, 1984, pp. 106–23.

10 'The imperatives embodied in the Dreaming are the Law, which situates the origin and ultimate control of

power outside human society; that is, as emanating from the withdrawn but still watchful creative beings of the spiritual realm. From their human "descendants", these beings demand conformity to the Law and the proper performance of ritual. In return, they will ensure the reproduction of earthly society through a continuing release of life-giving power into the physical and human world.' Tonkinson 1991, p. 106.

11 Tonkinson 1991, pp. 133–42, discusses the dynamism within Martu religious life, in which change and innovation are accommodated within a sense of permanence.

12 Yuwali, interview (translation by N Taylor), Punmu, Western Australia, 1999b.

13 Yuwali, story (oral translation by D Oates, written translation by D Taylor), Punmu, Western Australia, 1987.

14 R Tonkinson, interview with P Johnson, Newman, 2004.

15 P Peterson, interview with S Davenport, Jigalong, 1999.

16 R Gould, 'Subsistence behaviour among the Western Desert Aborigines of Australia', *Oceania*, vol. 39, no. 4, 1969.

17 ibid., p. 265. Gould noted the scarcity of truly permanent water sources anywhere in the Western Desert. Most of the Western Desert has no coordinated drainage, and there are no permanent rivers or freshwater lakes.

18 Yuwali, 1999b.

19 Tonkinson, 1991, p. 30. In a dry time, a person out of their country is not easily able to find water sources from general principles, and can die without this detailed knowledge.

20 Yuwali, 2000. See also Tonkinson, 1991, p. 30.

21 Martu have been recorded as using at least 106 plant species as food sources, with an additional 42 species being used in other ways. See F Walsh, 'The use and management of animal and plant resources by the Martujarra', in G Wright (ed.), *The significance of the Karlamilyi region to the Martujarra of the Western Desert*, Department of Conservation and Land Management, Perth, 1989, p. 184, and F Walsh, 'An ecological study of traditional Aboriginal use of "country": Martu in the Great and Little Sandy deserts, Western Australia', *Proceedings of the Ecological Society of Australia*, vol. 16, 1990, p. 28. In relation to Martu diet and food types, see F Walsh, 1989, F Walsh, 1990, and F Walsh, *The influence of the spatial and temporal distribution of plant food resources on Martujarra subsistence strategies*, Department of Botany, The University of Western Australia, Perth, 1988. In relation to subsistence existence in the broader Western Desert, see Gould, 1969.

22 R Tonkinson, interview with S Davenport, Perth, 1999.

23 Tonkinson, 1991, p. 43, estimates that up to 80 per cent of the total food (by weight) was collected by women, citing the research of MJ Meggitt, *Desert people: a study of the Walbiri Aborigines of central Australia*, Angus & Robertson, Sydney, 1962, and R Gould 1969 in similar resource zones.

24 Yuwali, 1999b. Men would traditionally hunt larger game such as kangaroos, wallabies and emus, although they would also catch smaller game: various reptiles (goannas, snakes, frogs) and small marsupials.

25 P Veth & F Walsh, 'Camping places and plant use in Martujarra lands: a community resource document for Martu', unpublished document, Perth, 1986, pp. 18–19.

26 F Walsh, 1989 and 1990, identifies these three seasons, their determinants and their effect on movement and food gathering. The material on these seasons has been drawn from this work. Walsh first identified that these seasons are based on the position of the Pleiades constellation and certain climatic events.

27 P Veth, 'The archaeological resource of the Karlamilyi (Rudall River) region', in G Wright (ed.), *The significance of the Karlamilyi region to the Martujarra of the Western Desert*, Department of Conservation and Land Management, Perth, 1989, p. 130.

28 Yuwali, 1999b & N Chapman, interview with S Davenport & P Johnson, Punmu, 2004.

29 Yuwali, 1999b.

30 R Tonkinson, interview with P Johnson, Perth, 2005.

31 Walsh, 1988, p. 4.

32 R Tonkinson, interview with S Davenport, Perth, 1999.

33 Yuwali, 1999b. See also S Davenport (ed.), *Yintakaja-lampajuya: these are our waterholes*, Western Desert Puntukurnuparna and Pilbara Language Centre, South Hedland, 1988.

34 Yuwali, 1999b.

35 Tonkinson, 1991, p. 48.

36 Yuwali, 2000, and generally Tonkinson 1991, p. 51.

37 See Veth & Walsh, 1986, and Walsh, 1989, p. 208. See also P Latz, 'Fire in the desert: increasing biodiversity in the short term, decreasing it in the long term', in DB Rose (ed.), *Country in flames: proceedings of the 1994 symposium on biodiversity and fire in North Australia*, North Australia Research Unit, Darwin & The Australian National University, Canberra, 1995, especially chapter three.

38 Yuwali, 1999b.

39 ibid.

40 L Dousset, 'Politics and demography in a contact situation: the establishment of the Giles Meteorological Station in the Rawlinson Ranges, Western Australia', *Aboriginal History*, vol. 26, 2002. See also: Meggitt, 1962; R Berndt, 'The concept of the tribe in the Western Australian desert of Australia', *Oceania*, vol. 30, no. 2, 1959; and Gould, 1969.

41 It appears from evidence of late patrols that these areas were significantly greater than those likely to have been travelled when the desert was more populous; R Tonkinson, interview with P Johnson, Newman, 2004. For example, Nyarinyari, who was picked up at Well 35 on the same 1964 patrol as was Yuwali's group, had travelled several hundred kilometres up the stock route between April and October.

42 Yuwali, 2000.

43 SROWA: DNW, AN 1/25, Cons 1733, Broome Sub-District: Patrol reports (22.1.54–4.5.67). IN56/54, *Report by A Halton to Superintendent Northern Division*, 18 April 1967. La Grange mission is now Bidyadanga community, near Broome.

44 R Tonkinson, interview with P Johnson, Newman, 2004.

45 For the 'shocked' reaction of an experienced patrol officer in relation to this group, see W Edwards, letter written to his parents, 26 June 1964 (Edwards family letter collection, Ara Irititja Archive, Adelaide) and generally see N Peterson with J Long, 'Territorial organization: a band perspective', *Oceania Monographs*, vol. 30, University of Sydney, 1986, which records groups contacted by patrols between 1957 and 1971.

46 R Tonkinson, 'Field work notes. Swindells Field trip Oct 64 ex-desert Mardu', unpublished field notes held by the author, 1964.

47 R Tonkinson, interview with P Johnson, Newman, 2004. See also Tonkinson, 1991, p. 132.

48 F Myers, 'To have and to hold: a study of persistence and change in Pintupi social life', PhD thesis, Bryn Mawr College, 1976, pp. 60–1. The Pintupi people lived immediately to the east of the Manyjilyjarra and were culturally very similar to them. R Tonkinson, interview with P Johnson, Newman, 2004.

49 R Tonkinson, interview with P Johnson, Newman, 2004. Robert Macaulay was told that, in the past, revenge killers in the Rawlinson Ranges area usually killed the first person encountered, usually a woman because they were foraging. R Macaulay, interview with S Davenport, 2004.

50 Yuwali, 2000.

51 Tonkinson (interview with P Johnson, Newman, 2004) notes that none of his first contact stories ever mentioned personal mistreatment, which seems to have been more prevalent further north. But there had been killings along the stock route, including some killings at Kinyu, Well 35, in the twentieth century, of which people still speak; see Davenport, 1988.

52 For reactions to aeroplanes, see Davenport, 1988.

53 Nola Taylor, who, together with her mother, was with Nyipi at the time (N Taylor, interview with S Davenport, Parnngurr, 2000). This may have been either the Beadell crew, who bulldozed an east–west road south of Lake Percival to Callawa Station in 1963, or the WAPET crew in the lakes area, who had built a road in to Picture Hill over the previous two years.

54 NAA: A6456; R087/020, (Department of Supply) Aborigines in joint project area — Welfare of. *Report by Australian committee on guided projectiles on welfare of Aborigines located within the range area, tabled in the House of Representatives by the Minister for Defence on 6 March 1947*, 10 March 1947.

55 P Morton, *Fire across the desert: Woomera and the Anglo–Australian joint project 1946–80*, Australian Government Press, Canberra, 1989, p. 116.

56 NAA: A6456; R087/020, (Department of Supply) Aborigines in joint project area — Welfare of. *The position regarding the setting up of a guided-missile range and a supporting developmental establishment in Australia — statement by the Minister for Defence in the House of Representatives*, 22 November 1946 (reproduced in a booklet with the Minister's public statement of 10 March 1947).

57 ibid.

58 At this stage, the LRWO was an entirely British organisation.

59 Letter from JF Evetts to Chief Scientific Officer of the LRWO, AP Rowe, 22 January 1947, quoted in Morton 1989, p. 74.

60 NAA: A6456; R087/020, (Department of Supply) Aborigines in joint project area — Welfare of. *The position regarding the setting up of a guided-missile range and a supporting developmental establishment in Australia — statement by the Minister for Defence in the House of Representatives*, 22 November 1946 (reproduced in a booklet with the Minister's public statement of 10 March 1947).

61 D Thomson, *The Aborigines and the rocket range*, Rocket Range Protest Committee, Melbourne, 1947, p. 1.

62 ibid., p. 3.

63 ibid.

64 Mrs Blackburn is referred to in parliamentary papers by the name of her deceased husband, as Mrs Maurice Blackburn.

65 Australia, House of Representatives, 1947, *Debates*, vol. 190, p. 435 (6 March 1947).

66 NAA: A6456; R087/020, (Department of Supply) Aborigines in joint project area — Welfare of. *The long-range weapons project. Statement by the Minister for Defence*, 10 March 1947.

67 This key statement of the committee's assumption was not original. The phrase 'detribalisation is inevitable' was used as early as 1945 by the DNW. (See, for example, the annual report of the Department of Native Affairs, 1945, and SROWA, DNW, AN 1/25, Cons 1733, Native Policy in WA 1920–1960. Box 10 IN 803/45, *Policy*, 1945.
AO Neville, a co-opted member of the committee representing the Western Australian Government, had

until recently been the state's Commissioner of Native Affairs.)

68 NAA: A6456; R087/020, (Department of Supply) Aborigines in joint project area — Welfare of. *The long-range weapons project. Statement by the Minister for Defence*, 10 March 1947.

69 G Gray, 'Aborigines, Elkin and the guided projectiles project', *Aboriginal History*, vol. 15, no. 1–2, 1991, p. 154, fn11.

70 C Duguid, 'The rocket range, Aborigines and the war', address delivered to The Rocket Range Protest Committee at the Town Hall, Melbourne, 31 March 1947, p. 13.

71 Thomson 1947, p. 3.

72 AP Elkin, 'Guided projectiles and the welfare of the Aborigines', *Australian Journal of Science*, vol. 9, no. 6, 1947, p. 198.

73 C Duguid, *Doctor and the Aborigines*, Rigby, Adelaide, 1972, p. 152.

74 NAA: A6456; R136/005, Native Affairs: general. *Signal from Newman to Brown*, 21 February 1956.

75 NAA: A6456; R136/004, Native Affairs General. *Minute paper from W MacDougall to Range Superintendent*, 12 October 1951.

76 NAA: A6456; R136/004, Native Affairs: general. *Report by W MacDougall*, October 1950.

77 NAA: A6456; R22/008, Welfare of Aborigines. *Report by W MacDougall to the Secretary, SA Aborigines' Protection Board*, November 1954.

78 NAA: A6456; R136/004, Native Affairs: general. *Proposed survey of tribal Aborigines living near the south-eastern portion of the Central Reserve, WB MacDougall*, 3 March 1952.

79 NAA: A6456; R088/011, Giles Met. Station — construction: general. *Outward teletype message from O'Grady to Aitken*, 6 March 1956.

80 NAA: A6456; R136/005, Native Affairs: general. *Minute paper, reconnaissance surveys — Central Native Reserve; letter from WB MacDougall to Superintendent, Woomera*, 11 October 1955.

81 NAA: A6456; R029/270, WRE, Salisbury — Meteorology — Maralinga Project. *Teleprint from Range Controller, HJ Brown, to Secretary of the Board, E Cook*, 2 November 1955, quoting the intended article, which was prepared by Adelaide's *The Advertiser*.

82 ibid.

83 NAA: A6456; R022/008, Welfare of Aborigines. *Signal from Cook to Brown*, 4 November 1955. It appears from this exchange that Brown may have used a Defence power of embargo to compulsorily stop the article. If so, this would suggest the sensitivity of this issue, and the willingness of the government to use assertions of national security interests as a means of avoiding political embarrassment.

84 NAA: A6456; R022/008, Welfare of Aborigines. *Signal from Brown to Captain Jack Newman*, 4 November 1955.

85 NAA: A6456; R022/008, Welfare of Aborigines. *Minute paper, letter from WB MacDougall to Superintendent Range*, 17 December 1955.

86 ibid.

87 NAA: A6456; R 136/005, Native Affairs: general. *Report on patrol of Central Reserves April–July 1956 including appendices. WB MacDougall*, 6 August 1956.

88 NAA: A6456; R022/008, Welfare of Aborigines. *Report on patrol in conjunction with Mr Miller. From W MacDougall to Superintendent, Range*, 17 December 1955.

89 NAA: A6456; R136/005, Native Affairs: general. *Report by WB MacDougall to Superintendent WRE*, 16 January 1956.

90 ibid.

91 NAA: A6456; R136/005, Native Affairs: general. *Signal from Newman to Brown*, 21 February 1956.

92 Dedman made initial promises to the House to protect Indigenous interests in 1946, when news of the proposed range first came out. This was followed by his more complete public statement in 1947.

93 NAA: A6456; R029/022, (Department of Supply) Maralinga: acquisition by the Commonwealth of land tenure. *Memorandum from Woomera Controller, HJ Brown, to Chief Scientist, A Butement*, 5 December 1955.

94 NAA: A6456; R022/008, Welfare of Aborigines. *Welfare of Aborigines — Maralinga project — meteorological station etc. Letter from WA Butement, Chief Scientist, to HJ Brown, Controller WRE*, 16 March 1956.

95 NAA: A6456; R022/008, Welfare of Aborigines. *Letter from HJ Brown, Controller WRE, to Captain J Newman, Superintendent*, 20 March 1956.

96 DNW , *Annual report*, 1957, Appendix 6, p. 114; also R Berndt, 'The Warburton Range controversy', *The Australian Quarterly*, 1957, p. 37.

97 NAA: A6456, R22/008, Welfare of Aborigines. *Memorandum from HJ Brown, Controller WRE, to WA Butement, Chief Scientist, Department of Supply*, 7 March 1956.

98 Morton 1989, p. 94, citing a letter from Brown of 15 July 1983.

99 NAA: A6456; R022/008, Welfare of Aborigines. *Report by WB MacDougall to the Secretary, SA Aborigines' Protection Board*, November 1954.

100 NAA: A6455; RC100 Part 5, WRE, Salisbury. Native welfare and correspondence, general. Presented 25/11/1984 at Sydney. *Proposed new Aboriginal mission: central Australia. Memorandum from Woomera Controller, HJ Brown, to Chief Scientist, Alan Butement*, 25 November 1957.

101 NAA: A6455; RC100 Part 3, Welfare of Aborigines. Presented 15/10/1984 at Sydney. *Confidential signal from Woomera Controller, HJ Brown, to Chief Scientist, Alan Butement*, 25 January 1957.

102 SROW A: AAPA(WA), 60/58, *Letter from AW Fadden, Commonwealth Treasurer, to JJ Brady, WA Minister for Native Welfare*, 23 October 1957.

103 SROWA: DNW, AN 1/7, Cons 993, Militar y and Defence Guided Projectiles. IN 76/47, *Parliamentary speech by W Grayden, an independent member of the WA Legislative Assembly*, 15 August 1956. Grayden was to be a thorn in Middleton's side throughout the late 1950s.

104 DNA, *Annual report*, 1953.

105 DNA, *Annual report*, 1945, p. 8.

106 ibid.

107 DNA, *Annual report*, 1949, p. 6.

108 SROWA: DNW, AN 1/7, Cons 993, Militar y and Defence Guided Projectiles. IN 76/47, *Letter from WA Commissioner of Native Welfare to Superintendent WRE*, 12 May 1955.

109 SROWA: DNW, AN 1/7, Cons 993, Militar y and Defence Guided Projectiles. IN 76/47, *Letter from WB MacDougall to WA Commissioner of Native Welfare*, 14 October 1955.

110 SROWA: DNW, AN 1/7, Cons 993, Militar y and Defence Guided Projectiles. IN 76/47, *Letter from WA Commissioner of Native Welfare to WB MacDougall*, 27 October 1955.

111 NAA: A6456; R136/005, Native Affairs: general. *Letter from WB MacDougall to WA Commissioner of Native Welfare*, November 1955 (with hand-written marking 'Not Sent'). MacDougall's reference to his 'attempt to draw the attention of the public' presumably refers to his interview with newspapers, described earlier.

112 NAA: A6456; R029/222, (Department of Supply) Maralinga: acquisition by the Commonwealth of land tenure. *Memorandum from Woomera Controller, HJ Brown, to Chief Scientist, A Butement*, 5 December 1955.

113 ibid.

114 NAA: A6456; R022/008, Welfare of Aborigines. *Signal by MacDougall to Nossiter*, May 1956.

115 NAA: A6456; R136/005, Native Affairs: general, *Telegram from Superintendent, Range, Woomera to Commissioner for Native Welfare*, 27 April 1956.

116 NAA: A6456; R136/005, Native Affairs: general. *Telegram from Commissioner for Native Welfare to Superintendent, Woomera*, 27 April 1956.

117 J Long, telephone inter view with S Davenport, 2005.

118 SROWA: DNW, AN 1/8, Cons 1419, Reports: special 1968–1971, IN 30-5-2, 68–71. *Letter from WA Commissioner for Native Welfare to Robert Macaulay*, 7 August 1956.

119 NAA: A6455; RC100 Part 9. *General report no. 5 from Robert Macaulay to WA Commissioner for Native Welfare*, 8 March 1958.

120 C Duguid, *The Central Aborigines Reserve*, presidential address to the Aborigines Advancement League of South Australia, 21 October 1957.

121 SROWA: DNW, AN 1/7, Cons 993, Militar y and Defence Guided Projectiles. IN 76/47, *Parliamentary speech by W Grayden, an independent member of the WA Legislative Assemby*, 15 August 1956. Grayden cited 'critical extracts' from a report MacDougall had made to the WRE range superintendent barely a week earlier. Some months later Eric Cook, the secretar y of the WRE board, signalled controller Brown stating that the Commonwealth minister 'would like to know how a Commonwealth document came into Grayden's hands'. NAA: A6455; RC100 Part 3, Welfare of Aborigines. *Signal by Cook to Brown*, 25 January 1957.

122 NAA: A6456; R142/001, File Extracts. *Welfare of Aborigines: Maralinga, SA. Note from SG Middleton, WA Commissioner Native Welfare, to Minister for Native Welfare, WA, re speech by W Grayden in Legislative Assembly*, 23 August 1956.

123 NAA: A6456; R040/057. *Note from SG Middleton, WA Commissioner of Native Welfare, to Minister for Native Welfare, WA, re Warburton Ranges native matters; report of Parliamentary Committee*, 3 January 1957.

124 ibid.

125 SROWA: DNW, AN 1/7, Cons 993, native matters. Canning Stock Route. General correspondence. IN 330/57, *Report from Northern Office of DNW to the Commissioner of Native Welfare. Attached report from Ronald Berndt, notes on Canning Desert Basin natives and Grayden's comments*, 8 August 1957.

126 Berndt, 1957.

127 This pressure related to the Talgarno initiative, discussed in the next chapter.

128 SROWA: DNW, AN 1/7, Cons 993, Militar y and Defence. WRE. Reports and correspondence regarding natives and native reserves. IN 280/56, *Letter from Surveyor General, WV Fyfe, to SG Middleton*, 18 July 1958.

129 DNW , *Annual report*, 1959, p. 10.

130 NAA: A6455; RC100 Part 3, Welfare of Aborigines. *Confidential signal from Woomera Controller, HJ Brown, to Chief Scientist, Alan Butement*, 25 January, 1957.

131 C Duguid, press release by the Federal Council for Aboriginal Advancement, June 1958.

132 See Middleton's comments, supporting the WRE's expanded activities, in the previous chapter.

133 NAA: A6456; R029/222, (Department of Supply) Maralinga: acquisition by the Commonwealth of land tenure. *Memorandum from Woomera Controller, HJ Brown, to Chief Scientist, A Butement*, 5 December 1955.

134 Duguid, 1958.

135 NAA: A6456; R142/001, File extracts. *Letter from Secretary, Department of Supply, to R Doig, Under Secretary, WA Premier's Department*, 9 July 1958.

136 NAA: A6456; R087/068, (Department of Supply), replies by Toc H Minlaton regarding treatment of Aborigines in Commonwealth area resumed for rocket and bomb testing. *Letter from Athol Townley to Mr W Cook*, 10 July 1958.

137 SROWA: DNW, AN 1/7, Cons 993, Military and Defence, WRE. Reports and correspondence regarding natives and native reserves. IN 280/56, *Letter from SG Middleton, WA Commissioner Native Welfare, to Under Secretary, Premier's Department*, 22 July 1958.

138 The controversy surrounding the group of people said to be found in poor condition at Well 40 on the Canning Stock Route, discussed in the previous chapter.

139 NAA: A6455; RC100 Part 5, WRE, Salisbury. Native welfare and correspondence, general. Presented 25/11/1984 at Sydney. *A Survey of problems relating to Aborigines in the Talgarno area; report from R Macaulay to Superintendent, Woomera*, 15 September 1959.

140 Proclaimed in 1958, the Talgarno Prohibited Area (stretching from Broome to Port Hedland and well inland) was the area into which the inert warheads would fall (Morton 1989, p. 441). In the event, the appointment of the third NPO did not take place.

141 NAA: A6455; RC100 Part 5, WRE, Salisbury. Native welfare and correspondence, general. Presented 25/11/1984 at Sydney. *A survey of problems relating to Aborigines in the Talgarno area; report from R Macaulay to Superintendent, Woomera*, 15 September 1959.

142 Berndt, 1959.

143 NAA: A6455; RC100 Part 5, WRE, Salisbury, 15 September 1959.

144 NAA: A6456; RC100 Part 1, Atomic Weapons Tests: health effects. *Native reserves of south-western central Australia — their future, and Department of Supply interest.* Report by R Macaulay, 28 March 1960.

145 ibid.

146 ibid.

147 SROWA: DNW, AN 1/25, Cons 1733, Military and Defence, WRE. Reports and correspondence regarding natives and native reserves. IN 280/56, *Letter from WA Commissioner of Native Welfare to Director of Works*, 16 March 1960.

148 M Shephard, *A lifetime in the bush: the biography of Len Beadell*, Hyde Park Press, Richmond, 1998, p. 89.

149 ibid., p. 87.

150 DNW , *Annual report*, 1964, pp. 11–12.

151 NAA: A6456; R136/008, Native Affairs: reports by patrol officers. *Air reconnaissance. Report by R Macaulay to Superintendent, Woomera*, 4 November 1960.

152 Jeremy Long should not be confused with Terry Long of the DNW, who took part in the 1964 Percival Lakes patrols.

153 J Long, 'Report on first patrol west of Papunya, August 1963', manuscript held at Australian Institute of Aboriginal and Torres Strait Islander Studies.

154 ibid.

155 ibid.

156 SROWA: DNW, AN 1/7, Cons 993, Reserve for natives: central Australia No. 17614: inspection and reports. IN 226/63, *Search patrol — country north Rawlinna. Report from J Harman to the WA Commissioner of Native Welfare*, 17 October 1963.

157 Bruce McLarty of the DNW had undertaken a tour with MacDougall in 1957, but this concentrated on areas and groups which were already well known to the NPOs.

158 SROWA: DNW, AN 1/7, Cons 993, Reserve for natives: central Australia No. 17614: inspection and reports. IN 226/63, *Minutes of the fifth meeting of the Standing Committee on the Central Aboriginal Reserves held at Woomera, 3rd to 5th December 1963*, 3–5 December 1963.

159 ibid.

160 NAA: A6456; R145/034, Reconnaissance and patrol, range area: part 2. *Long-range patrol — Emu–WA Border, Neales Junction, 31st March to 7th April. Report by Senior Constable T Murray to Officer-in-Charge, Commonwealth Police Force, Maralinga*, 8 April 1964.

161 J Long, 'Report of patrol west of Papunya, April 1964', manuscript held at Australian Institute of Aboriginal and Torres Strait Islander Studies.

162 PE Playford, 'Report on native welfare expedition to the Gibson and Great Sandy deserts, April 1964', 1964.

163 NAA: A6455; RC100 Part 10, WRE, Salisbury. Reports and correspondence: Giles area. Presented 25/10/1984 at Sydney. *Report of patrol to Central Reserve; Canning Stock Route, Great Sandy Desert and Gibson Desert. Report from J Harman to WA Commissioner of Native Welfare*, 27 April 1964.

164 For more information on the European Launcher Development Organisation (ELDO), and on Woomera's history generally, see Morton, 1989.

Part Two

1 Y uwali, 2000.

2 Y uwali, 1999.

3 NAA: A6456, R088/019, Native Welfare: reports and correspondence, Talgarno Prohibited Area. *Report of Patrol 12th May to 23rd June 1964. Report by W MacDougall to Superintendent, WRE*, 29 June 1964.

4 NAA: A6456; R088/019, Native Welfare: reports and correspondence, Talgarno Prohibited Area. *Brief report on the ground–air search patrol of the designated impact area of Blue Streak F1, with notes and comments — May/June 1964*. Report by R Macaulay to Superintendent, WRE, 16 July 1964.

5 Y uwali, 2000.

Part Three

1 C Duguid, *Relentless assimilation in Western Australia and Northern Territory: end of the tribes*, 1964, p. 1.

2 *The Australian*, 2 September 1964, reporting a speech in federal parliament by Kim Beazley MHR.

3 Morton, 1989, pp. 462–3.

4 NAA: A6456; R088/019, Native Welfare: reports and correspondence, Talgarno Prohibited Area. *Brief report on the ground–air search patrol of the designated impact area of Blue Streak F1, with notes and comments — May/June 1964*. Report by R Macaulay to Superintendent, WRE, 16 July 1964.

5 T Long, 'Blue Streak Project: report by T Long, A/Superintendent (North West Division) to WA Commissioner of Native Welfare, 10 June 1964', personal papers of T Long.

6 ibid.

7 NAA: A6456; R088/019, Native Welfare: reports and correspondence, Talgarno Prohibited Area. *Report of patrol 12th May to 23rd June 1964, by W MacDougall to Superintendent, WRE*, 29 June 1964.

8 ibid.

9 NAA: A6456; R088/019, Native Welfare: reports and correspondence, Talgarno Prohibited Area. *Brief report on the ground–air search patrol of the designated impact area of Blue Streak F1, with notes and comments — May/June 1964*. Report by R Macaulay to Superintendent, WRE, 16 July 1964.

10 ibid.

11 ibid.

12 NAA: A6456; R088/019, Native Welfare: reports and correspondence, Talgarno Prohibited Area. *Letter from Kim Beazley, MHR, to CE Barnes, Commonwealth Minister for Territories*, 15 July 1964.

13 Duguid, 1964, p. 3.

14 NAA: A6456; R088/019, Native Welfare: reports and correspondence, Talgarno Prohibited Area. *Letter from WA Commissioner, Native Welfare, to Director, WRE*, 17 July 1964.

15 W Edwards, letters written to his parents, family collection, 26 June 1964.

16 W Edwards, telephone interview with P Johnson, 2005.

17 NAA (SA): D174, L558/24, Coordination of impact area (Talgarno) and vehicle flight safety requirements for north-westerly firings of the ELDO, SLV. *Signal from Boswell, WRE Controller, Salisbury, to Matthews, Department of Supply, Melbourne*, 24 July 1964.

18 NAA: A6456; R088/019, Native Welfare: reports and correspondence, Talgarno Prohibited Area. *Letter from WA Commissioner of Native Welfare to Director, WRE*, 15 June 1964.

19 ibid.

20 NAA (SA): Lieutenant Colonel Ernest George Foreshew. M1675/1 Diaries and Personal Papers. 1 January 1958 to 31 December 1985. *Diary of Ernest George Foreshew*. Entry headed 'Talgarno Search'.

21 Letter from Commissioner Frank Gare to the Minister for Native Welfare, 24 July 1964, from the personal collection of T Long.

22 ibid.

23 ibid.

24 NAA: A6456; R088/019, Native Welfare: reports and correspondence Talgarno Prohibited Area. *Letter from WA Commissioner of Native Welfare, FE Gare, to Director, WRE*, 3 August 1964.

25 NAA: A6456; R088/019, Native Welfare: reports and correspondence, Talgarno Prohibited Area. *Letter from Beazley to Barnes*, 15 July 1964.

26 Duguid 1964, pp. 1–2.

27 *The West Australian*, 2 September 1964.

28 Australia, House of Representatives 1964, *Debates*, vol. HR43, p. 788 (1 September 1964).

29 *The Australian*, 2 September 1964.

30 SROWA: DNW, AN 1/7, Cons 993, central Australian reserve for natives no. 17614. Inspections and reports and related matters. IN 293/64, *Signal from Kim Beazley to J Brady, Shadow Minister, Minister for Native Welfare*, 2 September 1964.

31 Western Australian Parliamentary Debates, vol. 167 (new series), p. 693 (2 September 1964).

32 NAA: A6456; R088/019 Native Welfare: reports and correspondence, Talgarno Prohibited Area. *Briefing note from WA Commissioner of Native Welfare, FE Gare, to Minister for Native Welfare*, 10 September 1964.

33 J Elphinstone, 'Health of natives in the Sandy Desert of Western Australia, 1964', report to the Commissioner of Public Health, 1964. Includes handwritten annotations initialled by Gare: 'Discussed. Dr Davidson not willing to delete all paras 6–8 but will alter "well-chosen" to "opportune" and "encourage" to "give the opportunity".'

34 ibid.

35 R Tonkinson, letter published in *The West Australian*, 5 September 1964.

36 ibid.

Part Four

1 NAA: A6456; R088/019, Native Welfare: reports and correspondence, Talgarno Prohibited Area. *Report of patrol 12th May to 23rd June 1964, by W MacDougall to Superintendent, WRE*, 29 June 1964.

2 NAA (SA): D174; L558/24, Coordination of impact area (Talgarno) and vehicle flight safety requirements for north-westerly firings of the ELDO, SLV. *Specification for the clearance of the Talgarno impact area for the F2 (SLV) firing*, 10 September 1964.

3 NAA: A6456; R088/019, Native Welfare: reports and correspondence, Talgarno Prohibited Area. *Report of patrol 12th May to 23rd June 1964, by W MacDougall to Superintendent, WRE*, 29 June 1964.

4 T Long, interview with Sue Davenport, Mandurah, Western Australia, 1988.

5 NAA (SA): WRE Woomera (SA); D250, Correspondence files, 1956–1968. Item, (Woomera) native patrol officer ground–air search F2, part 1, 1964. 56/2888 Part 1. *Signal from MacDougall to Superintendent, WRE*, 21 September 1964.

6 Y uwali, 1999.

Part Five

1 NAA: A6456; R088/019, Native Welfare: reports and correspondence, Talgarno Prohibited Area. *Brief report on the ground–air search patrol of the designated impact area of Blue Streak F1, with notes and comments — May/June 1964*. Report by R Macaulay to Superintendent, WRE, 16 July 1964.

2 NAA: A6456; R088/019, Native Welfare: reports and correspondence, Talgarno Prohibited Area. *Signal from MacDougall to Superintendent, WRE*, 24 September 1964.

3 NAA (SA): WRE, Woomera (SA); D250, correspondence files, 1956–1968. Item, (Woomera) native patrol officer ground–air search F2, part 1, 1964. 56/2888 Part 1. *Signal from WRE Director of Safety to WRE Superintendent*, 25 September 1964.

4 NAA (SA): WRE Woomera (SA); D250, correspondence files, 1956–1968. Item, (Woomera) native patrol officer ground–air search F2, Part 1, 1964. 56/2888 Part 1. *Signal from Macaulay to Foreshew, WRE Safety Officer*, October 1964.

5 T Long, interview, Mandurah, Western Australia, 2000.

6 T Long, 1988.

7 DNW , *Annual report*, 1964, pp. 11–12.

8 SROWA , DNW, AN 1/7, Cons 993, central Australian Reserve for Natives no. 17614. Inspections and reports and related matters. IN 293/64, *Briefing note from WA Commissioner of Native Welfare to Director of Works*, 1 September 1964.

9 NAA (SA): WRE, Woomera (SA); D250, correspondence files, 1956–1968. Item, (Woomera) native patrol officer ground-air search F2, part 1, 1964. 56/2888 Part 1. *Signal from MacDougall to Superintendent, Range*, 8 October 1964.

10 R Macaulay, interview with S Davenport, Canberra, 2004.

11 T Long, interview with Sue Davenport, Mandurah, Western Australia, 1999.

12 ibid. Frank Gare confirmed that the decision was devolved to the patrol officer's exercise of 'common sense'. (F Gare, interview, Fremantle, Western Australia, 1999).

13 *The West Australian*, 24 October 1964.

14 R Tonkinson, interview with S Davenport, Perth, 1999.

15 For a general discussion of first contact events, see M Gallagher, 'Contact in the Western Desert 1905–99', in *The significance of the Karlamilyi region to the Martujarra of the Western Desert*, Guy Wright (ed.), Department of Conservation and Land Management, Perth, 1989, pp. 140–74.

16 SROWA: DNW, AN 1/25, Cons 1733, Box 2. IN 35/34, *Chaining of natives 1921–1967*, which tracks the chaining of Indigenous people by Western Australian police and gaolers from 1921 to 1967. It includes discussion of the death of one witness who had been walked 300 miles [482 kilometres] to W yndham in chains.

17 Tonkinson, 1991, p. 161.

18 ibid., and citing personal communication with Ken Lance, a project officer from the Western Desert Puntukurnuparna.

19 Probably a classificatory, rather than biological, father.

20 R Nyaju, in Davenport, 1988.

21 J Judson, story of coming in to Jigalong in 1964 (oral translation by D Oates), Parnngurr, WA, 1999.

22 A Hamilton, 'Blacks and whites: the relationships of change', *Arena*, vol. 30, 1972, p. 41.

23 The retirement of ration depots and the growth of the missions is covered in the annual reports of the DNA between 1947 and 1955.

24 DNA, *Annual report*, 1947.

25 NAA: A6455; RC100 Part 8, WRE, Salisbury. Native welfare and correspondence, Maralinga area. Presented 25/10/1984 at Sydney. *Shell Lakes–Boundary Dam patrol, May to June 1959*. Report from R. Macaulay to WA Commissioner of Native Welfare, 12 January 1960.

26 SROWA, DNW, AN 1/7, Cons 993, Central Australian Reserve for Natives no. 17614. Inspections and reports and related matters. IN 280/56, *Report on tour by R Macaulay; Letter from SG Middleton WA Commissioner Native Welfare to WRE Controller, Salisbury*, 25 June 1959.

27 DNW , *Annual report*, 1955, p. 28.

28 NAA; A6455; RC 100 Part 1, Atomic weapons tests: health effects. Presented 25/10/1984 at Sydney. *The Aborigines of western central Australia: zone of transition, ANZAAS paper by R Macaulay*, 28 March 1960.

29 SROWA: DNW, AN 1/7, Cons 993, conference between native welfare officers of SA, WA, Department of Supply and Northern Territory (7.4.61 to 28.9.64). IN 451/61, *Proceedings of the first Standing Committee on Central Aboriginal Reserves. Aboriginal Affairs Planning Authority*, 14–16 August 1961.

30 Other groups coming in to missions between 1963 and 1967 were contrived amalgamations from the fragments of larger, once-distinct groups depleted over time by earlier migrations from the desert.

31 Peterson, 1986, p. 125.

32 For an account of the lives of Wari and his wife Yatungka, their solitary life in the desert for many years and the final search to bring them in to Wiluna, see W Peasley, *The last of the nomads*, Fremantle Arts Press, Fremantle, 1983.

33 The last group of Pintupi included members who had previously come in to settlements but had returned to the desert. The later history of this group was covered in an article by Paul Toohey in *The Bulletin* magazine, 28 April 2004.

34 Yuwali, interview with S Davenport (translated by D Oates), Newman, 2005.

35 ibid.

36 Y uwali, 1987.

37 Y uwali, 2005.

38 Duguid, 1964, after hearing that 42 people had been brought in to Papunya by the April 1964 joint NT, WRE and WA patrol.

39 R Tonkinson, 'Some suggestions regarding contact with desert Aborigines', short paper prepared for the WA Department of Native Welfare, Perth, 1965.

40 Y uwali, 1999a.

41 Pukina and Nyarinyari had many relatives at Warburton: the Carnegie, Ward and Morgan families.

42 In an article on a 1963 MacDougall patrol, John Allan described how MacDougall could not understand the language of a group of Martu they met at Jupiter Well, other than a few Pitjantjatjara words. Without guides, he operated 'by tedious question and sign language' to ascertain the range of the people. See 'Wongai Patrol' *Walkabout*, vol. 30, no. 9, September 1964.

43 Yuwali, 2005, confirmed this.

44 Y uwali, 1999b.

45 E Sailor, interview with S Davenport, Jigalong, 2000.

46 Peterson, 1986.

47 Y uwali, 2005.

48 Myers discusses at length the significance and power of social relations and obligations among the Pintupi *Pintupi country, Pintupi self: sentiment, place and politics among Western Desert Aborigines*, Australian Institute of Aboriginal Studies, Canberra, 1986. Most of the women in this group were Manyjilyjarra, neighbours of the Pintupi.

49 In relation to Martu marriage see Tonkinson, 1991, p. 98 and following.

50 Tonkinson, 1974, pp. 53–5.

51 Tonkinson, 1991, pp. 72–3.

52 See, generally, Tonkinson, 1991, pp. 57–78.

53 Dousset, 2002, p. 18.

54 R Tonkinson, interview with S Davenport, Canberra, 2002.

55 T Long, 1999.

56 T Long, 1988.

57 T onkinson, 2002.

58 T Long, 2000. According to Long, MacDougall was most uncomfortable about this.

59 The same word (from the verb *kanyila*, meaning 'hold') is used for the same concept of 'keeping, holding, nurturance, looking after' in Manyjilyjarra, one of the major Martu languages. (J Marsh, *Martu Wangka to English Dictionary*, Summer Institute of Linguistics, Australian Aborigines and Islanders Branch, Darwin, 1992.) In fact, eastern Manyjilyjarra and Pintupi are the same language. (Tonkinson, interview with P Johnson, Newman, 2004.)

60 Myers 1986, p. 282.

61 T Rowse, *White flour, white power: from rations to citizenship*, Cambridge University Press, Cambridge, 1998, pp. 43–4.

62 Long, 1988.

63 Yuwali, 2005.

64 DNA, *Annual report*, 1951, p. 21.

65 All discussion of missions in this book relates solely to missions in Western Australia, and policies concerning them.

66 Most missions to the west and north of the Western Desert were set up between the mid-1940s and the mid-1950s.

67 DNA, *Annual report*, 1952, p. 21.

68 ibid.

69 The annual reports of the DNA and DNW include appendices which list all agencies to whom payments were made by the department, and — in the case of settlements and missions — statistics relevant to each.

70 P Biskup, *Not slaves, not citizens*, University of Queensland Press, St Lucia, 1973, p. 282.

71 ibid., p. 253.

72 DNW, *Annual report*, 1957, pp. 89–92.

73 cf. A Haebich, *Broken circles: fragmenting Indigenous families 1800–2000*, Fremantle Arts Centre Press, Fremantle, 2000, pp. 348–54.

74 cf. Berndt, 1957.

75 SG Middleton, 'Policies and practices in Western Australia', *Proceedings of conference on welfare policies for Australian Aborigines*, Adult Education Department, University of New England, Armidale, 1960, pp. 35–6.

76 DNW, *Annual report*, 1953, p. 5.

77 Berndt, 1957, p. 41.

78 SG Middleton, Confidential briefing by Middleton to Minister for Native Welfare, *Warburton Ranges native matters: report of Parliamentary Committee*, 1957. DNW file 40/57: no further citation available.

79 SROWA: DNW, AN 1/7, Cons 993, Military and Defence, WRE. Reports and correspondence regarding natives and native reserves. IN 280/56, *Report from R Macaulay to S Middleton on visit to Warburton Mission, Nov 57*, 1 March 1958.

80 Gallagher, 1989, pp. 161–2.

81 The main missions Western Desert people moved into during the 1950s and 1960s were at Balgo and La Grange (both run by the Catholic Pallotine Order), Wiluna (Seventh Day Adventist), Warburton (United Aborigines Mission), Cosmo Newbery (United Aborigines Mission) and Jigalong (Apostolic Church of Australia).

82 The mission did not stay at the ration depot. A few years after it was founded, it moved about 10 kilometres to a better water source.

83 DNW, *Annual report*, 1957, p. 72.

84 T Long, 1999. For a detailed account of Jigalong and missionary–Martu relationships in the 1960s, see Tonkinson, 1974.

85 See, for example, DNW, *Annual report*, 1965, p. 19.

86 R Berndt & CM Berndt, *The University of Western Australia anthropological survey of the eastern goldfields, Warburton Range and Jigalong regions, 26th January to 2nd March 1957*, in Appendix 6 of the DNW's *Annual report*, 1957.

87 Despite the missions' common lack of a practical focus on the future, the enforced education that many children received from missionaries between 1950 and 1970 equipped them to become effective community leaders in the decades to come, particularly in negotiations with government authorities and mining companies.

88 SROWA: DNW, AN 1/7, Cons 993, Military and Defence guided projectiles. IN 76/47, *Letter from WA Commissioner of Native Welfare to WB MacDougall*, 27 October 1955.

89 For a detailed account of daily life at Jigalong, the preservation of the Law and the relationship between the missionaries and the Indigenous inhabitants in the 1960s, see Tonkinson 1974.

90 DNW, *Annual report*, 1955, p. 28.

91 Tonkinson, 1974.

92 M De Graaf, 'The Ngadadjara at Warburton Range', unpublished thesis held in the AIATSIS library, 1968, pp. 13–14.

93 Tonkinson, 1974, p. 33.

94 ibid., p. 37.

95 See R Tonkinson, 'Reflections on a failed crusade', in T Swain & D Bird Rose (eds), *Aboriginal Australians and Christian missions: ethnographic and historical studies*, The Australian Association for the Study of Religions, South Australia, 1988, p. 67 and Gallagher 1989, p. 164.

96 Berndt & Berndt, 1957, pp. 6–7.

97 Tonkinson, 1974, pp. 7–8.

98 Tonkinson, 1988, p. 69.

99 DNW, *Annual report*, 1964.

100 SROWA: DNW, AN 1/7, Cons 993, Military and Defence Guided Projectiles. IN 76/47, *Letter from WA Commissioner of Native Welfare to WB MacDougall*, 11 April 1956.

101 T Long, 1999.

102 Duguid, 1957.

103 NAA: A6456; R087/020, (Department of Supply) Aborigines in joint project area — Welfare of. *Report by Australian committee on guided projectiles on welfare of Aborigines located within the range area, tabled in the House of Representatives by the Minister for Defence on 6 March 1947*, 10 March 1947. The statement, 'Detribalisation is inevtiable' appears to have had its genesis in the Western Australian Government, used in annual reports and policy documents from 1945 onwards.

104 Duguid, 1958.

105 Berndt, 1959, p. 104 and generally Peterson 1986.

106 AP Elkin, 'Reaction and interaction: a food-gathering people and European settlement in Australia', *American Anthropologist*, vol. 53(2), 1951, pp. 164–86. See the discussion of these ideas in Rowse 1998, pp. 38–41.

107 NAA: A6456; R022/008, Welfare of Aborigines. *Report by WB MacDougall to the Secretary, SA Aborigines' Protection Board*, November 1954.

108 SROWA: DNW, AN 1/7, Cons 993, Militar y and Defence guided projectiles. IN 76/47, *Letter from WB MacDougall to WA Commissioner for Native Welfare*, 27 March 1956.

109 ibid.

110 NAA: A6456; R136/004, Native Affairs: general. *An appreciation of the native welfare problem affecting LRWO; report by WB MacDougall*, October 1950.

111 NAA: A6456; R136/005, Native Affairs: general. *Report by WB MacDougall to Superintendent, WRE*, 16 January 1956.

112 NAA: A6455; RC100 Part 9. *General report from Robert Macaulay to WA Commissioner of Native Welfare*, 8 March 1958.

113 Middleton, 1960.

114 Berndt & Berndt, 1957, pp. 115–16.

115 It is illuminating that exactly the same comments might be made about the attitudes of the Indigenous observers of European society. It is at least interesting to note how galling this may seem, if this were their attitude. 'They scoff at such things as the missionaries' claims that Jesus brings the rain in response to Christian prayer, because they believe only Aborigines have the power to bring rain. When they walked off the mission in 1962, the Aborigines angrily told the missionaries that no more rainmaking would take place on mission property. When they returned a few months later, they informed the missionaries that since Jesus had not brought the rain, they would perform the rain making ritual and end the drought Rain fell shortly after the rainmaking ritual ended. Nothing could convince a Jigalong Aborigine that whites can bring the rain.' Tonkinson, 1974, p. 145.

116 ibid., p. 139.

117 ibid. The reasons why the Martu chose to stay at Jigalong, rather than leaving to join wider Australian society, is a major theme of Tonkinson, 1974.

118 ibid., p. 140.

119 See generally, Tonkinson, 1974.

120 ibid.

121 Tonkinson, 1991, pp. 169–70. The incorporated Martu communities of Jigalong, Punmu, Parnngurr and Kunawarritji are 'dry' communities; that is, they prohibit the importation and consumption of liquor within their boundaries.

122 WEH Stanner, 'The Dreaming', in TAG Hungerford (ed.), *Australian signpost: an anthology*, Fellowship of Australian Writers, Canberra, 1956. Reprinted in *Traditional Aboriginal society: a reader*, WH Edwards (ed.), Macmillan, Melbourne, 1987, p.4.

123 Stanner, 1956, p. 63.

124 Tonkinson, 1991, p. 133.

125 ibid., p. 22, fn3.

126 See generally Tonkinson, 1991, Chapters 3–5 for discussion of the adaptability of Martu society, and particularly pp. 133–8 on the dynamism of Martu religious life. Tonkinson discusses the example of the Wirnpa myth, which was appropriated by the Martu at Jigalong from another group, and gradually modified and developed to address Martu territor y more directly.

127 Y uwali, 2005.

128 ibid.

129 This refers to Billy Gibbs's death in the mid-1990s. Gibbs was an important Martu leader and the husband of Dawn Oates (the speaker).

130 D Oates, conversation with Yuwali & S Davenport, Newman, 2005. Oates is a Manyjilyjarra woman, Yuwali's classificatory sister.

Epilogue

1 Generally, see the official histor y of the WRE in Morton, 1989.

2 ibid., p. 544.

3 ibid., p. 541.

4 NAA: A6456; R088/018, Policy matters associated with native matters. *Draft notes prepared as a basis for discussion on the future role of the native patrol officers at Woomera*, 26 February 1969.

5 NAA: A6456, R142/028, File extracts 31/12/65 to 22/5/70. *Letter from AS Cooley, Secretary of the Commonwealth Department of Supply, to the WA Commissioner for Native Welfare*, 6 May 1970.

6 NAA: A6456; R142/028, File extracts 31/12/65 to 22/5/70. *Letter from Frank Gare, WA Commissioner of Native Welfare, to Secretary of the Commonwealth Department of Supply*, 22 May 1970.

7 R Macaulay, interview with S Davenport, Canberra, 2001.

8 R Macaulay, foreword to 'Cleared Out', a resear ch report prepared by S Davenport, H Skeat & P Johnson

for the Australian Institute of Aboriginal & Torres Strait Islander Studies, 2001.

9 A five-minute section of film, which includes the women first walking in to MacDougall's camp at Kurtararra with Sailor and Nyani, is the only piece of his film collection that we, or archivists and historians we know, have been able to trace.

10 F Gare, interview with S Davenport, Fremantle, 2000.

11 J Ritchie (general editor), *Australian dictionary of biography*, Melbourne University Publishing, Melbourne, vol. 15, p. 202.

12 T Long, 1999.

13 F Gare, 2000.

14 M Gardiner, personal communication with S Davenport, Punmu, 1987.

15 R Lasker, personal communication with P Johnson, Parnngurr, 2003.

16 The Strelley Pastoral Station is owned by the Nomads group, a company formed by Don McLeod to develop pastoral and mining industries for Indigenous people in the Pilbara.

17 Y uwali, 2005.

18 Yuwali, interview with S Davenport, Punmu, 1999c.

Further reading

Duguid C 1972, *Doctor and the Aborigines*, Rigby, Adelaide.

Gray G 1991, 'Aborigines, Elkin and the guided projectiles project', *Aboriginal History,* vol. 15(1–2), pp. 153–62.

Folds R 2001, *Crossed purposes: the Pintupi and Australia's indigenous policy*, University of New South Wales Press, Sydney.

Haebich A 2000, *Broken circles: fragmenting indigenous families 1800–2000*, Fremantle Arts Centre Press, Fremantle.

Long J 1989, 'Leaving the desert: actors and sufferers in the Aboriginal exodus from the Western Desert', *Aboriginal History,* vol. 13(1), pp. 9–43.

Milliken R 1986, *No conceivable injury: the story of Britain and Australia's cover-up*, Penguin, Ringwood.

Morton P 1989, *Fire across the desert: Woomera and the Anglo-Australian joint project 1946–1980,* Australian Government Press, Canberra.

Myers F 1986, *Pintupi country, Pintupi self: sentiment, place and politics among Western Desert Aborigines*, Australian Institute of Aboriginal Studies, Canberra.

Rowse T 1998, *White flour, white power: from rations to citizenship*, Cambridge University Press, Cambridge, UK.

Stanner WEH 1956, 'The Dreaming', in TAG Hungerford (ed.), *Australian signpost,* anthology edited for the Canberra Fellowship of Australian Writers, Cheshire, Melbourne, pp. 51–65. Reprinted in WH Edwards (ed.) 1987, *Traditional Aboriginal society: a reader,* Macmillian Co, Melbourne.

Tonkinson R 1974, *The Jigalong mob: Aboriginal victors of the desert crusade,* Cummings, Menlo Park.

Tonkinson R 1991, *The Mardu Aborigines: living the dream in Australia's desert*, Holt, Rinehart & Winston, New York.

Wright G (ed.) 1989, *The significance of the Karlamilyi region to the Martujarra of the Western Desert,* Department of Conservation and Land Management, Perth.

Index

Note: Page references in italics indicate that the reference is only to a photo or map